VOLUME 489

JANUARY 1987

THE ANNALS

of The American Academy *of* Political
and Social Science

RICHARD D. LAMBERT, *Editor*
ALAN W. HESTON, *Associate Editor*

INTERNATIONAL AFFAIRS IN AFRICA

Special Editor of this Volume

GERALD J. BENDER

Director
School of International Relations
University of Southern California
Los Angeles

Ⓢ SAGE PUBLICATIONS *NEWBURY PARK BEVERLY HILLS LONDON NEW DELHI*

THE ANNALS

© 1987 *by* The American Academy *of* Political *and* Social Science

ERICA GINSBURG, *Assistant Editor*

Editorial Office: 3937 Chestnut Street, Philadelphia, Pennsylvania 19104.

For information about membership* (individuals only) and subscriptions (institutions), address:

SAGE PUBLICATIONS, INC.

2111 West Hillcrest Drive   275 South Beverly Drive
Newbury Park, CA 91320   Beverly Hills, CA 90212

From India and South Asia,   *From the UK, Europe, the Middle*
write to: *East and Africa, write to:*

SAGE PUBLICATIONS INDIA Pvt. Ltd.   SAGE PUBLICATIONS LTD
P.O. Box 4215   28 Banner Street
New Delhi 110 048   London EC1Y 8QE
INDIA   ENGLAND

SAGE Production Editor: JACQUELINE SYROP
* Please note that members of The Academy receive THE ANNALS with their membership.

Library of Congress Catalog Card Number 86-060308
International Standard Serial Number ISSN 0002-7162
International Standard Book Number ISBN 0-8039-2863-7 (Vol. 489, 1987 paper)
International Standard Book Number ISBN 0-8039-2862-9 (Vol. 489, 1987 cloth)
Manufactured in the United States of America. First printing, January 1987.

The articles appearing in THE ANNALS are indexed in *Book Review Index; Public Affairs Information Service Bulletin; Social Sciences Index; Monthly Periodical Index; Current Contents; Behavioral, Social Management Sciences;* and *Combined Retrospective Index Sets.* They are also abstracted and indexed in *ABC Pol Sci, Historical Abstracts, Human Resources Abstracts, Social Sciences Citation Index, United States Political Science Documents, Social Work Research & Abstracts, Peace Research Reviews, Sage Urban Studies Abstracts, International Political Science Abstracts, America: History and Life,* and/or *Family Resources Database.*

Information about membership rates, institutional subscriptions, and back issue prices may be found on the facing page.

Advertising. Current rates and specifications may be obtained by writing to THE ANNALS Advertising and Promotion Manager at the Beverly Hills office (address above).

Claims. Claims for undelivered copies must be made no later than three months following month of publication. The publisher will supply missing copies when losses have been sustained in transit and when the reserve stock will permit.

Change of Address. Six weeks' advance notice must be given when notifying of change of address to insure proper identification. Please specify name of journal. Send change of address to: THE ANNALS, c/o Sage Publications, Inc., 2111 West Hillcrest Drive, Newbury Park, CA 91320.

The American Academy of Political and Social Science

3937 Chestnut Street   Philadelphia, Pennsylvania 19104

Origin and Purpose. The Academy was organized December 14, 1889, to promote the progress of political and social science, especially through publications and meetings. The Academy does not take sides in controverted questions, but seeks to gather and present reliable information to assist the public in forming an intelligent and accurate judgment.

Meetings. The Academy holds an annual meeting in the spring extending over two days.

Publications. THE ANNALS is the bimonthly publication of The Academy. Each issue contains articles on some prominent social or political problem, written at the invitation of the editors. Also, monographs are published from time to time, numbers of which are distributed to pertinent professional organizations. These volumes constitute important reference works on the topics with which they deal, and they are extensively cited by authorities throughout the United States and abroad. The papers presented at the meetings of The Academy are included in THE ANNALS.

Membership. Each member of The Academy receives THE ANNALS and may attend the meetings of The Academy. Membership is open only to individuals. Annual dues: $26.00 for the regular paperbound edition (clothbound, $39.00). Add $9.00 per year for membership outside the U.S.A. Members may also purchase single issues of THE ANNALS for $6.95 each (clothbound, $10.00).

Subscriptions. THE ANNALS (ISSN 0002-7162) is published six times annually—in January, March, May, July, September, and November. Institutions may subscribe to THE ANNALS at the annual rate: $50.00 (clothbound, $66.00). Add $9.00 per year for subscriptions outside the U.S.A. Institutional rates for single issues: $10.00 each (clothbound, $15.00).

Second class postage paid at Philadelphia, Pennsylvania, and at additional mailing offices.

Single issues of THE ANNALS may be obtained by individuals who are not members of The Academy for $7.95 each (clothbound, $15.00). Single issues of THE ANNALS have proven to be excellent supplementary texts for classroom use. Direct inquiries regarding adoptions to THE ANNALS c/o Sage Publications (address below).

All correspondence concerning membership in The Academy, dues renewals, inquiries about membership status, and/or purchase of single issues of THE ANNALS should be sent to THE ANNALS c/o Sage Publications, Inc., 2111 West Hillcrest Drive, Newbury Park, CA 91320. *Please note that orders under $20 must be prepaid.* Sage affiliates in London and India will assist institutional subscribers abroad with regard to orders, claims, and inquiries for both subscriptions and single issues.

THE ANNALS

of The American Academy *of* Political
and Social Science

RICHARD D. LAMBERT, *Editor*
ALAN W. HESTON, *Associate Editor*

──────────── FORTHCOMING ────────────

FOREIGN LANGUAGE INSTRUCTION:
A NATIONAL AGENDA
Special Editor: Richard D. Lambert

Volume 490   March 1987

THE FULBRIGHT EXPERIENCE AND
ACADEMIC EXCHANGES
Special Editor: Nathan Glazer

Volume 491   May 1987

UNEMPLOYMENT: A GLOBAL CHALLENGE
Special Editors: Bertram Gross and Alfred Pfaller

Volume 492   July 1987

───────────────────────────────────────

See page 3 for information on Academy membership and
purchase of single volumes of **The Annals.**

CONTENTS

BOOK DEPARTMENT CONTENTS

PREFACE

The varied foreign policies of African states have received scant scholarly attention. In this respect, most observers have focused on the continent as a whole, viewing it as little more than a chessboard where East-West rivalries are played out. The collection of articles by eleven recognized experts that constitutes this volume of *The Annals* makes a significant contribution toward broadening our knowledge and understanding of international affairs in Africa.

African states are primarily concerned with the preservation of their sovereignty, independence, and prestige against perceived internal, regional, and global challenges. Frequently all three potential threats are salient factors when wars occur. For example, the wars in Ethiopia, Chad, Angola, Mozambique, the Sudan, Uganda, Namibia, and South Africa are all characterized by vigorous internal opposition groups, interference from neighboring countries, and intervention by great powers.

Ideology has been grossly exaggerated in past explanations of the international relations of African states. For example, in the Horn of Africa not only did the United States and the Soviet Union switch sides a decade ago, but regional alliances have persisted despite ideological changes in regimes, such as in the Sudan. Somalia's territorial claims and threats to neighboring countries have forged an enduring alliance between the two ideologically disparate regimes of Ethiopia and Kenya.

I. William Zartman, in "Foreign Relations of North Africa," examines relations between the North African states of Morocco, Algeria, Tunisia, and Libya, concluding that each state's foreign policy is characterized, above all, by a preoccupation with the other states in the region. Torn between dual pressures to work together as a community and to distinguish themselves from each other, they are caught up with the need to develop a sense of rank among themselves. Clement Henry Moore explores much of the same territory, but through a different optic, in "The Northeastern Triangle: Libya, Egypt, and the Sudan." He sees a tenuous balance between Cairo and Khartoum being threatened by Libya. Moreover, counterproductive American policies have actually strengthened Qaddafi's regime at home and, coupled with a deteriorating Egyptian economy, could precipitate a Nasserite, anti-American coup in Egypt, thereby altering regional alignments dramatically.

In "Nigeria Restrained: Foreign Policy under Changing Political and Petroleum Regimes," Timothy M. Shaw discusses a cyclical pattern in Nigeria's external relations, pursuant to the changes in its political constitution and petroleum production. Nigeria's aspiration to great-power status in the 1970s has yielded to austerity and modesty in the 1980s. Yet core concerns about internal development, regional and continental integration, and liberation in southern Africa continue despite the series of changes in governmental structure and oil profitability. If Nigeria can become more self-reliant and self-sustaining economically, its foreign policy will, accordingly, become far more influential.

The French role in Africa is examined in depth by Martin Staniland in "Francophone Africa: The Enduring French Connection." He notes that not only have relations remained close between France and its former African colonies after more than a quarter century of independence, but Paris has made a major effort to expand its sphere of influence beyond its ex-colonial core. Zaire is cited as an example where French interests and influence have grown considerably. Staniland also explores French economic and security interests on the African continent, as well as the varying influence of African states on French foreign policy.

Edouard Bustin, in "The Foreign Policy of the Republic of Zaire," views Zaire more as a pawn than an independent actor with respect to its foreign relations. He argues that whether in terms of Zaire's ability to insulate its domestic political processes from external interference, or to develop its capacity to opt between plausible alternatives, or to conceptualize its national interests in a broader perspective than that of the survival of a self-serving oligarchy, Zaire's foreign policy has been so notoriously deficient that its credibility is in doubt. He sees Zaire in the context of a fixed crisis area, a prize to be fought over or defended by a number of leading international actors—in other words, an object rather than a subject.

For more than a century the Ethiopian state has promoted the idea that it is a viable, multiethnic nation-state with clear, and sacrosanct, geographic boundaries. In "The Politics of State Survival: Continuity and Change in Ethiopian Foreign Policy," Edmond J. Keller notes that this basic factor in Ethiopia's internal and external policies has remained constant over time. Irrespective of the 1974 change from a modern imperial regime to a leftist-oriented mililtary government, Ethiopia's foreign policy priorities have been motivated by persistent claims for self-determination, expressed by politically subordinate ethnic communities questioning the legitimacy of Amhara hegemony. Keller posits that the state's weak and dependent character causes Ethiopian leaders to employ both international diplomacy and military force to advance their internal goals.

The East African countries of Kenya and Tanzania provide an interesting comparative context in which the evolution of their respective foreign policies is examined by David F. Gordon in "Anglophonic Variants: Kenya versus Tanzania." He states that over the past decade both countries have significantly broadened the range of issues on their foreign policy agendas in response to changes in both the regional and the international environments. Relations between the two countries deteriorated sharply in the late 1970s, then entered a new period of cooperation beginning in 1983. Both countries have been relatively successful in promoting national goals by means of their foreign policies.

The conflict in southern Africa is examined in two articles that focus on South Africa and Angola, respectively. In "Security versus Growth: The International Factor in South African Policy," Robert M. Price maintains that a key feature of South Africa's political dynamics is the linkage between its domestic affairs and its international relations. South Africa's access to international markets for vital capital and technology is threatened by the nature of its domestic socioeconomic and political systems. Threat becomes reality when the black majority's political opposition causes the nature of the South African system to become visible to the international community. In its efforts to maintain white rule, the South African government has, over the past 25 years, sought to meet this threat by uncoupling its domestic affairs from its foreign economic relations. Thus Pretoria has attempted to alter its domestic sociopolitical arrangements in ways that it hoped would make South Africa more acceptable to the international community. In addition, it has sought to reduce its vital dependence on the international economic system, viewing an increased autonomy in its economy as insulation against international threats to its regime. Recent economic sanctions applied by many countries will test how successful Pretoria has been in achieving economic independence.

For more than a quarter century, the United States and the Soviet Union have supported opposing sides in Angola. Gerald J. Bender, in "The Eagle and the Bear in Angola," avers that both superpowers have been stymied by their lack of control over their respective Angolan allies and frustrated by their lack of impact in determining events in that African state. Each of the superpowers has also proved to be unreliable as a patron to their Angolan clients. One important result is that most Angolans, no matter which side they are on, are extremely cynical about both the United States and the Soviet Union. While superpower intervention is usually justified in ideological terms, few Angolans are fighting for any particular ideology.

The final two articles focus on African states and international forums. In "The Organization of African Unity and Intra-African Functionalism," G. Aforka Nweke examines the role and record of the Organization of African Unity (OAU). He notes that the OAU was the product of a compromise between African government leaders who wanted a political union of all independent states and those who preferred functional cooperation as a building block toward the construction of an African sociopsychological community. Yet inherent contradictions in the ideas, behavior, and interests of OAU member states, in conjunction with the dynamics of international politics, have resulted in practically no functional cooperation. The Lagos Plan of Action, adopted in 1980 in order to achieve the goal of an African common market by the year 2000, is the most recent attempt—and hope—to achieve more intra-continental cooperation.

External economic relations of African states are analyzed by Thomas M. Callaghy in "Between Scylla and Charybdis: The Foreign Economic Relations of Sub-Saharan African States." During the last decade, economic foreign policies of sub-Saharan African states have focused increasingly on their severe debt and economic crises. Activities in this respect have included attempting to reduce debt service burdens and the rigors of rescheduling with the Paris and London Clubs; conducting difficult negotiations with bilateral and private creditors; bargaining over conditionality packages with the International Monetary Fund and the World Bank; distributing internally the painful costs of adjustment; coping with import strangulation; and devising new development policies and strategies. All of these actions have been critical, impinging as they do on the central issues of sovereignty, political order, development, and socioeconomic welfare.

James S. Coleman conceived the theme of this issue of The Annals in 1984 and made the initial contacts with most of the authors included herein. His sudden and unexpected death in April 1985, before this project could be completed, stunned not only the many individual African leaders and scholars who had known this unique human being, but the entire world of Africana as well. Jim Coleman's inspiration was invaluable and his influence on all of us has been immeasurable. Having benefited so much from working first for, then with, him, I feel both humbled and honored to have been associated with one of my great mentor's final intellectual endeavors, which I now dedicate to his lasting memory.

GERALD J. BENDER

ANNALS, *AAPSS*, **489**, January 1987

Foreign Relations of North Africa

By I. WILLIAM ZARTMAN

ABSTRACT: The North African states—Morocco, Algeria, Tunisia, Libya—occupy an island and are therefore preoccupied above all by relations among themselves. Torn between pressures to work together—community—and to distinguish themselves from each other—differentiation—they are caught up with the need to develop a sense of rank and relation among themselves and to carry their competition into the power vacuum of the poorer states that surround them. Although Tunisia and Libya may seek to achieve relations on the model of integration and Algeria may prefer a pattern of central-state dominance, the result is a checkerboard pattern of competition of limited rivalries, preferred by Morocco but played by all. Relations with the Arab and African worlds are determined by the North African states' bids for leadership, their need for support on security issues, and their extension of intra-Maghribi relations onto the two wider fields. The same intra-Maghribi purposes guide North African states' relations with Europe, especially France, and also with the two superpowers.

I. William Zartman, professor of international politics and director of African studies at the Johns Hopkins School of Advanced International Studies, received his M.A. from Johns Hopkins University and his Ph.D. from Yale. He is past president of the Middle East Studies Association and founding president of the American Institute for Maghribi Studies. He has authored six books and edited four on North African subjects, the most recent being, respectively, Ripe for Resolution: Conflict and Intervention in Africa *(1985) and* The Political Economy of Morocco *(1986).*

N ORTH Africa is an island.[1] It is surrounded by the Atlantic and Mediterranean on the west, north, and east, and by an even broader sea of sand, the Sahara, on the south. Both of these barriers are boundaries-in-depth, not fully isolating but requiring special efforts to cross, and separating the islanders from the people and countries on the other sides. This means that North Africans are thrown together and their foreign policies, above all, concern their relations with each other. It also means that differentiation and integration—a specially intimate type of conflict and cooperation—are the two major themes of their intra-island relations.

But for all their insular quality, the North African states are not a world apart. They are parts of other worlds and therefore live within circles of relations. Some circles, such as the central core of intra-Maghribi relations, involve their relations with each other, and demonstrate differentiation and integration within the various communities of identity of which the states are members.

Two of these circles are most important. One involves the cultural nation of which Maghribi states are a distant part, that is, the Arab world, with which they share a language, a religion, and a sense of history. The Maghrib ("The West" in Arabic) is a subregion of this region, with foreign relations both among its members individually and with the region as a whole. The other circle is the

geographic island continent of which North Africa is only the northwest corner. North African states are part of Africa, even though the continent is frequently thought of only as black or south of the Sahara, and the problem of both differentiation and integration is thereby posed again. In relation to both of these circles, the North African states are outposts, away from the core and closest to the Western, developed world. Membership in these circles seems to suggest that relations with other worlds are no longer relations with the Arab and African worlds, but with "The Other," as the North Africans referred to their colonizers before independence.

The next circle concerns relations with Europe, including the French metropole. Yet in a shrinking world, it is no longer possible to consider Europe as totally extraneous to North Africa. As the continent of the colonizer, Europe has made itself part of the Maghribi self, even if that part creates internal conflict and animosity. More materially, both Europe and North Africa are part of the Mediterranean world, another case of a boundary-in-depth that integrates as well as differentiates those that it divides.

Finally, North African states necessarily have relations with the great powers, which only impinge in a minor fashion on the identity of the region. Relations with the two superpowers can only be special, protecting and threatening at the same time. They are obviously imbalanced, too, since North Africa is in the nonaligned part of the free world. Although that means that its security relations do not fall under the Western North Atlantic alliance, it also means that North Africa shares the panoply of Western values and that its dominant economic relations are with the developed West.

1. For good reviews of North African society, see Clement Henry Moore, *Politics in North Africa* (Boston: Little, Brown, 1970); Elbaki Hermassi, *Leadership and Development in North Africa* (Berkeley: University of California Press, 1972); Halim Barakat, ed., *Contemporary North Africa* (London: Croom Helm, 1985); Richard Lawless and Allan Findlay, eds., *North Africa* (New York: St. Martin's, 1984); Richard Parker, *North Africa* (Boulder, CO: Westview Press, 1985).

North Africa and the Maghrib are two names for the same region, seen from different perspectives. The ambiguity carries over to the countries included. The Maghrib encompasses Morocco, Algeria, and Tunisia; the first and last were French protectorates and historic nations who recovered their independence in 1956, whereas the middle member was claimed as a direct part of France and became independent in 1962. North Africa can also be taken to include Libya. Libya was created as an independent kingdom in 1951, following the fall of colonizing Italy and the end of an Allied trusteeship, although it became active in foreign relations only after its imposed revolution of 1969. In some analysis, North Africa should also comprise Mauritania, which became independent from France in 1960 but left its West African associations in 1965 and joined the Arab League in 1973. Mauritania, however, will not be treated here as a member of the Maghrib, but merely of its periphery, like Mali, Niger, and Chad, the other states of the West African Sahel.

Much in the relations among the Maghribi states can be read from an examination of their vital statistics. (See Table 1.) Morocco and Algeria are equals in population, but oil has given Algeria a gross national product—and hence a per capita gross national product—more than twice that of Morocco. Tunisia and Libya are much smaller in terms of population, although Tunisia has made remarkable progress in economic development—and hence in gross national product in absolute and per capita terms—and, again, oil has given Libya economic means far out of range of the normal levels in the region. When the form of government is taken into account—Morocco's historic bourgeois

monarchy, Tunisia's liberal-party presidency, Algeria's institutionalized revolution, and Libya's revolutionary military junta—the basic dynamics of the region come into focus.[2] Morocco and Algeria are inherent rivals, neighboring states of the same size with differing histories, state systems, ideologies, and external allies. Libya is a newcomer to this structure, a rambunctious upstart that is both a challenge and an ally to its established radical Algerian neighbor. Tunisia is squeezed in between the two radical powers, a plum to be coveted and protected. Morocco, Algeria, and Tunisia all aspire to privileged relations with their former metropole, France, and hence are active rivals for its favors. Algeria and Libya have had good relations with the Soviet Union; Tunisia and Morocco, better relations with the United States. Because of their relatively advanced state of development and because of their autonomy within the larger regional Arab and African systems, all four states have played leadership roles in different ways from time to time within those two regions and have conflicted with each other in doing so. These then are the broad lines of their foreign relations.

INTRA-MAGHRIBI RELATIONS: MODELS AND CYCLES

North Africa is a region of brothers, perhaps similar in its relations between units to those of the Iberian peninsula some 500 years ago, although the world in which the African region exists is vastly different. Although Morocco and

2. For a thorough analysis of Maghribi domestic politics, see I. William Zartman et al., *Political Elites in Arab North Africa* (New York: Longman, 1982; Washington, DC: Johns Hopkins SAIS African Studies Program, 1986).

TABLE 1
NORTH AFRICA SOURCES OF POWER

	Area (thousands of square kilometers)	Population (millions)	Per Capita Gross National Product (dollars)	Per Capita Gross National Product (growth rate)	Armies (thousands of soldiers	Debt (billions of dollars)
Morocco	713*	22.0	760	2.2	149	13.6
Algeria	2,382	22.0	2,320	2.6	170	15.8
Tunisia	164	7.1	1,290	4.9	35	4.1
Libya	1,760	3.5	7,110	−2.0	73	10.0

SOURCES: World Bank, United Nations, and Arms Control and Disarmament Agency.
*Including Western Sahara.

Tunisia are historic entities, perhaps even historic states, the people are very similar across the region, as are their languages and customs; and the current boundaries are new creations, not historic divisions. The fact that the population is concentrated roughly along the coast means that nationals may well be more similar to their neighbors than to their fellow countrymen at the other end of the coast, that boundaries necessarily cut relatively heavily populated areas along the coast, and that south of the population concentration spreads a deep, less populated—or unpopulated— expanse of territory, some of which is within national boundaries and some of which comprises weaker, less populated neighboring states.

In this situation, the first basic characteristic of relations is the insular sense of community or integration—the notion of brotherhood and shared fate, wherein all states are inevitably tied together and none can fully opt out of the relationship, even though some might try to take limited leave from time to time. More so than the elusive Arab unity, North African unity is both a restraining fact and an asymptotic goal.

The second basic characteristic is the need for differentiation in an area where people could not tell themselves apart if they did not proclaim their differences. Separate national existence must be justified. This is easy enough to do given the structural elements of rivalry that have such an important impact on the region, but it makes that rivalry functional.[3]

The third characteristic is an inherent development dynamic in regional relations. Not only does a contained rivalry exist, but it is going somewhere: as new and growing states in a region, the Maghribi states feel a need to establish a sense of rank and relation among themselves as a basis of expectations. Such a sense can remain eternally fluid, but it is more likely to take the form of certain patterns and models, either agreed to by the parties or held in conflict by individual states. This sense of rank and relation is not limited to the region alone. It also has to do with the North African states' roles within their two larger identity regions of Arab and

3. See I. William Zartman, "Maghribi Politics and Mediterranean Implications," in *The Mediterranean Region,* ed. Giacomo Luciani (New York: St. Martin's, 1984).

African states, and with their relations with their former metropole and with the superpowers. The Arab world, Africa, and European and global relations become boards on which the game of regional rank and relations can also be played.

Finally, North African states have a special relationship toward the power vacuum that characterizes the peripheral area to their south. As a vacuum, the space must be occupied, and as the periphery to a region of power rivalries, it must become the subject of contest and preemption among the North African states themselves, lest either another Maghribi state or a third party dominate the peripheral region. These four characteristics—community, differentiation, rank, and vacuum—provide the dynamics of North African foreign relations.

Integration

There are three models of relations that the North African states could follow. The most idealistic is integration itself, whereby the states of the region give up some of their sovereignty or at least coordinate some of their decision making so that they are locked into common step on internal policies and/or external attitudes.[4] As in the case of most unity movements around the world—including Arab and African unity—it would be a mistake to think realistically about North African integration as the creation of one—or more—single states out of the present ones. But it is not unrealistic to consider integration as a model of coordination that

4. John Damis, "Prospects for Unity/Disunity in North Africa," *American-Arab Affairs,* 6(6):34-38 (Fall 1983). The issue, devoted to North Africa, contains other good articles on the region.

limits the ability of the sovereign units to strike out on their own.

There have been four different expressions of this model at various times. In 1958, the nationalist movements of the three countries of French North Africa met in Tangier to pledge common efforts toward the liberation of Algeria—the one of them that was not yet independent—and other coordinated policy goals. Nothing came of the meeting. In 1961, three of the four states were founding members of the radical African alliance that eventually led to the formation of the Organization of African Unity (OAU); at the founding meeting of the Casablanca Group were the host, Morocco, and Algeria, and Libya came by mistake. In 1964 and more particularly the following year, all four North African countries met to establish institutions of minimal functional cooperation. They lasted for a while at the price of not running very deep, but their slow movement was arrested in 1969 by the Libyan revolution. In 1984 and 1985, frightened by the intractable and precarious rivalry between Morocco and Algeria and by the dangers of being granted stifling protection by Algeria and Libya against each other's interference, Tunisia launched a call for a pan-Maghribi summit meeting to settle outstanding issues. But the issues were stronger than the reconciliation, and the time was not yet ripe for the meeting. Instead, two other forms of integration took place. During the 1980s, Algeria and Tunisia proceeded to erase their common border for many purposes, allowing for integration and coordination of populations on both sides of the border. At the same time, the two countries undertook a number of joint economic activities to strengthen functional cooperation beyond their borderlands. Then, in March

1983, Algeria and Tunisia signed a wide-ranging friendship treaty, to which Mauritania also adhered in December. While the treaty provided a framework for diplomatic cooperation between the three states, it also split the region and led directly to the signing of a counter-alliance, the Arab-African Union, between Morocco and Libya at Oujda in August 1984.

The lessons of the attempts to apply the integration model in its many forms are clear: attempts to unite divide. Yet, at the same time, efforts at functional cooperation spread quietly underneath official attitudes of conflict and do leave their effects. Unfortunately, integration is not a dominant mode of relations. For integration can always be interrupted and destroyed, easily and at a stroke, whereas cooperation cannot be instituted as rapidly and conflict cannot be interrupted and dispelled with the same decisiveness. The difficulty in instituting integration is evident in the one set of extra-regional relations that has tried to treat the Maghrib as a single area: those with the European Communities. The communities have maintained association agreements with the three states of the region since 1969, but they have never been able to negotiate a common region-to-region agreement. Despite common products exported from the Maghribi nations, state differences prevail. Nonetheless, the spirit of integration lives on. As seen, it surfaces at times of tension to restrain conflict, and even at times of military conflict, awareness of a linked destiny in the region imposes limits on behavior. North African states have only fought each other once, in 1963, when Morocco and Algeria clashed over their undefined border. But most striking is the way the current conflict over the Sahara has been carried out

with careful avoidance of direct contact between the two countries' armies.

Integration is the model preferred by two neighbors, Tunisia and Libya, but their versions of the model differ so much as to be incompatible and to prevent their own implementation of their preferences, even bilaterally. Tunisia is a small country squeezed between two "heavies;" it therefore looks to integration as a form of cooperation between neighbors that replaces the danger of conflict and lowers security threats. The states themselves are not to disappear; only their borders will become more cooperatively permeable through functional integration.

Libya's integration is different.[5] Libya feels that boundaries between any Arab states only serve the narrow interests of the ruling elites and the imperialist dividers and conquerors. All such states should therefore unite, to follow the progressive revolutionary path as Libya sees it. Libya's Qaddafi is a man with a vision, blessed with a country of vast resources—particularly during the oil-boom years of the 1970s—but with too little population and no central strategic location in the Arab world. Therefore Libya under Qaddafi is impelled to unite, both to seek the mass and location that it lacks and to provide correct leadership to the Arab people. Libya indeed united with Egypt, Sudan, and Syria in the early 1970s, with Tunisia in 1974, with Syria again in 1980, with Chad in 1981, with Algeria less explicitly in 1975, and with Morocco in 1984. None of these unions lasted, but the drive to integrate remains and, in the

5. See I. William Zartman and A. G. Kluge, "Heroic Politics: The Foreign Policy of Libya," in *The Foreign Policies of Arab States,* ed. Bahgat Korany and Ali Dessouki (Boulder, CO: Westview Press, 1985).

process, creates hostile relations with Libya's neighbors.

Pluralism

The second model of relations, therefore, is the pluralist model, in which the states of the region interact on the basis of sovereign equality. This is the model preferred by Morocco, but it is practiced by all the states of the region. It is the underlying pattern of the classical balance of power, as practiced in Europe and other areas where there have been a number of roughly equal states. Its dynamics allow for alliances between weaker states to bring a threatening state back into place, but alliances are only as long-lasting as the danger. Such a model of relations has a basic configuration, referred to as Kautilyan, after the ancient Indian statesman who spelled out its underlying principles: "My neighbor is my enemy; my neighbor's neighbor, my friend." The dynamics are well expressed in the North African proverb, "My cousins and I against the others, my brother and I against my cousins, myself against my brother." The result is a checkerboard set of relations, with boundary matters playing an important part.

A neighbor is a most likely enemy because, as the country next door, it is the most likely source of trouble, subversion, and even territorial claims. When Morocco and Algeria became independent, there was not even a disputed boundary between them; after the first 500 kilometers from the Mediterranean there was no boundary at all until the western end of Algeria. After the 1963 war, which ended in a draw, a committee of the OAU studied the problem to let it cool down, and in 1972 the two parties signed an agreement delimiting and providing for demarcation of the boundary. Algeria ratified the treaty and King Hassan has declared that it stands, even though Morocco has not yet ratified it. Tunisia's war over Algerian territory came in 1961 with the French, before Algerian independence. The issue remained, and it worsened when oil was discovered under the border in 1964. Only in 1970 was a border agreement and a treaty of friendship drawn up, to be reinforced, after some intervening disputes, by the border and friendship treaty of 1983. The Algerian-Libyan border was delimited at the time of independence, but it was also the subject of a conflicting, nonratified treaty of 1934, which Colonel Qaddafi siezed upon when he came to power. There has never been an actual border war between the two countries, but their armies do meet periodically on each other's territory and escort each other back home. The unsettled boundary has remained a major issue between the two neighbors. Between Libya and Tunisia, the boundary was demarcated before independence and therefore did not contribute to the wary and frequently hostile relations since Qaddafi's revolution. The only area of boundary dispute was in the offshore oilfields, which was finally resolved by the International Court of Justice in 1982.

Once the dividing lines between the neighbors were established, conflict moved on to rivalries in the power vacuums to the south. Each Maghribi state practices a different strategy to ensure its security and interests. Algeria and Libya have large parts of the Sahara within their own frontiers, which allow them to occupy the vacuum directly and to pose their outposts closer to the Sahara's southern edge. A basic element of President Boumedienne's foreign policy was the need for agreed-upon and demarcated borders, and so Algeria has long worked in cooperation with the governments of Mauritania, Mali, and Niger and has sought firm border agreements. The latter were not completed until 1985, 1984, and 1983, respectively, when demarcation was accomplished. Good relations between Algeria and the latter two states have posed no problem, and Algeria has met annually with them since the late 1970s to coordinate their views on Saharan problems.

Algerian interest in Mauritania was more direct, since a dominant position in Mauritania would help Algeria pursue its rivalry with Morocco and would also extend Algerian protection to a Mauritania threatened by Moroccan claims. From 1967 to 1974 Algeria was the dominant neighbor of Mauritania, often exceeding the influence of France, which had long served as Mauritania's distant protector. Algeria, for example, helped Mauritania establish its own currency independent of the franc zone. After the Mauritanian military coup of 1978, Algeria returned in strength to reestablish its position of dominance, only to find active competition from both Morocco and Libya. Rivalries among the three would-be protectors contributed to the instability of the weak Mauritanian government until at least 1984, when a more nationalistic military leader sought to replace protection with simply good relations with all his neighbors.

Qaddafi's Libya sees itself as a revolutionary movement rather than simply as a territorial state. It has therefore sought to fill any neighboring vacuum that it could find, particularly where Qaddafi saw socioethnic affinities as well. Thus, encouraged by the same unratified border treaty that gave it problems with Algeria, Libya has claimed and occupied

the Aouzou strip of northern Chad since 1973, and it extended its protection over most of the rest of the country in 1980 and 1981, when it signed a unification agreement with the Chad it occupied. Since 1983, Libya has returned to occupy the northern half of the country under the cover of the former Chadian government, now an opposition movement, and it governs the territory as part of its own. (Algeria supports another Chadian opposition movement, and Morocco has shifted sides according to the Kautilyan alliance of the moment.) Similarly, Libya has infiltrated subversive groups into Niger, Mali, and Sudan on occasion, since its role as a protector is preempted by Algeria in the first two and by Egypt in the third. Whenever those established protectors are shaken in their roles—as, for example, when the protected government is overthrown, as in Sudan in 1985—Libya presses its candidacy.

It is in regard to Morocco's activities in the Saharan vacuum that the greatest conflict has arisen.[6] Colonization deprived Morocco of its traditional holdings to its south and then consecrated the situation by creating independent states in the former Moroccan territory. Morocco contested the existence of Mauritania until 1969, when it came to terms with reality, and it gave up its claims on western Algeria in the treaties of 1970 and 1972. It has, however, maintained its claim over the Spanish Sahara, and after 1974 it reversed the alliances in the region to attain its goal. Morocco and Mauritania split the terri-

6. On the Saharan issues, see John Damis, *Conflict in Northwest Africa* (Stanford, CA: Hoover Institute, 1983); I. William Zartman, *Ripe for Resolution: Conflict and Intervention in Africa* (New York: Oxford University Press, 1985), chap. 2.

tory among themselves as part of the Spanish withdrawal in 1975, and Morocco became the protector of Mauritania. In the process, the Morocco-Algeria rivalry was escalated several notches, and Algeria found a ready agent, the Popular Front for the Liberation of Saqiet el-Hamra and Rio de Oro (Polisario) to conduct a proxy war against Morocco. In 1978, the Polisario caused the overthrow of the Mauritanian government, Morocco took over the entire Western—formerly Spanish—Sahara, and the Kautilyan checkerboard pattern was restored. The Polisario has been pushed back to its Algerian camps, but Algeria's powerful diplomatic support has won its government in exile recognition from a majority of the African states, membership in the OAU, and recognition from 65 states in the Non-Aligned Movement. The conflict has kept Morocco and Algeria balanced on the edge of war with each other since 1975, and it has imposed a heavy burden on the Moroccan treasury and a lesser one on the Algerian and Libyan budgets in the pursuit of the war between Morocco and the Polisario.

Rivalry in the region, competition for the surrounding vacuum, the checkerboard pattern of relations, and the resulting efforts of rivalry to appropriate integration have led to the institutionalized stalemate of the mid-1980s in North African relations. The Algerian-Tunisian Friendship Treaty of March 1983 that was extended to include Mauritania at the end of the year excluded Morocco and Libya on the pretext that they had not settled their border problems with Algeria. Not surprisingly, the two excluded states, being neighbors of their common neighbor, formed their own alliance, the Arab-African Union, in August 1984. In the process they also exchanged Moroccan support of Libyan claims over its peripheral vacuum in Chad for Libyan agreement not to support the Polisario against Moroccan claims on its peripheral vacuum. Efforts since then, essentially led by Tunisia, have been to return relations to the integration mode, which was, ironically, embodied in both the competing alliances. But the summit that will soften the checkerboard pattern of rivalries can only take place once the contest over the Western Sahara has finally been decided in favor of either Morocco or Algeria's proxy, the Polisario. The OAU has decreed a referendum to settle the issue, but it has not been willing to enforce its decisions, made in early 1982, about the details of holding the referendum. Proximity talks under U.N. auspices were held in mid-1986 to discuss the issue, but no progress can be made until Algeria makes the decision to sponsor an accommodation.

Hegemony

The third model of relations stands between the other two. It is a model of hegemony, in which all states retain their sovereign distinction, but relate, not as autonomous and competitive equals, but as subordinate members of a regional group dominated by one of their number. It is the model favored by Algeria and suggested by its keystone position in the region, its geographic size and resource richness, and its revolutionary origins.[7] Algeria does not seek either regional integration or indepen-

7. See Nicole Grimaud, *La politique étrangère de l'Algérie* (Paris: Karthala, 1985); Bahgat Korany, "Third Worldism and Pragmatic Realism: The Foreign Policy of Algeria," in *Foreign Policies of Arab States,* ed. Korany and Dassouki; John Entelis, *Algeria: The Revolution Institutionalized* (Boulder, CO: Westview Press, 1986).

dent interaction on equal terms, but rather claims a position of leadership and dominance, in a pattern of relations that Boumedienne termed "the natural equilibrium of the region." None of the other Maghribi states share the same aspirations, above all because they cannot. They have neither the position nor the resources to dominate the others. Tunisia struggles against dominance by its neighbors, Morocco's Atlantic position gives it an outward outlook that none of the others share, and Libya under Qaddafi looks for leadership, but far beyond the confines of the Maghrib. Algeria, however, to the extent that its leadership is rejected, is condemned to act within the second pattern of checkerboard rivalries, as flanking states react against its pretensions at dominance.

The interaction of these models of relations between the North African states—the basic checkerboard rivalries and the attempts to overcome them either through single-state dominance or through egalitarian integration—has led to the ups and downs that have characterized intra-Maghribi relations since independence. The period from Moroccan and Tunisian independence in 1956 until 1961 or 1962 was characterized by cooperation between the newly independent states and the Algerian independence movement. As independence neared, however, harmony broke down. In 1961, Algeria and Tunisia opened up disputes over boundary and other issues, whereas Morocco and Algeria tightened their cooperation, as Morocco tried to handle its Algerian border problems with diplomacy. The split was transferred to the rest of the African continent in the competing pre-OAU alliances, Morocco and Algeria in the Casablanca Group and Tunisia in the Brazzaville Group. The Moroccan-

Algerian war of 1963 broke this cooperation and threw the region into bitter bilateral hostility; the reaction was to pose the integration option, and a period of institutionalized cooperation between all four countries began in 1964 and lasted until 1969. Bilateral relations took longer to catch up, however. Both Morocco and Tunisia gradually moved to resolution of specific disputes with Algeria, including border problems, from the late 1960s until about 1974.

But in the mid-1970s, a new cycle of mutual hostility began with a longer and deeper intensity than ever before, lasting over a decade to present times. Morocco and Algeria fell out in 1974 over the Saharan question and began their proxy war the following year. Tunisia and Libya began an extended period of fluctuating conflict in 1974 with the collapse of the Jerba Agreement that was to unite them. The following year, Algeria and Libya signed an agreement at Hassi Messaoud to share the burden of supporting the Polisario and to pledge cooperation in other radical causes. The expected call for integration in order to dull the conflict was slow in coming for many reasons: Tunisia, the usual caller, was threatened by its neighbors and feared that each might take integration as an excuse for dominance, while on the other side, hostilities between Morocco and Algeria were too deep and personalized during Boumedienne's reign to be susceptible to reconciliation. Only after 1983 have attempts been made to overturn the cycle.

EXTRA-MAGHRIBI RELATIONS—
OUTER CIRCLES AND SOURCES

The relations of North African states with their two major identity circles—the Arab and African worlds—are above all a function of their intra-Maghribi relations and rivalries and of their perceived ideological positions. Since their geographic positions relative to the rest of these two worlds are roughly common, and since their commercial position is competitive—except for oil—and therefore common, too, the only, but crucial, differentiation is on the basis of ideological orientation. As relatively well-developed states with a sense of mission behind them, Morocco, Algeria, and Libya have sought to lead factions within the Arab League and the OAU. When one of them is preoccupied with a policy issue that concerns a vital interest, however, ideological positions and group leadership become subservient to that goal. Thus Morocco's policy among Arab and African states has, more than anything else, been dedicated to gaining support on the Saharan issue, and, to a somewhat lesser extent, Libya's policy has often been dominated by its concern for support on the Chadian issue.

Beyond those specific concerns, Morocco's policy among Arab states has been focused on moderate leadership. Although Morocco had troops in position in the Golan Heights when the October 1973 Arab-Israeli war broke out, Morocco has above all worked to support Egypt in the peace process and was host to the initial Egyptian-Israeli meetings that led to Sadat's visit to Jerusalem in 1977. Since the war, Fez and Rabat have been the sites of Arab summits, and King Hassan has sought to play the conciliatory role of a good host. Within a wider circle based on the Arab world, King Hassan is chairman of the al-Qods (Jerusalem) Committee of the Islamic Conference Organization, and he uses the position both to buttress and to deploy his prestige in the cause of the recovery of Jerusalem. The Arab

League has long been behind Morocco on the Saharan issue and so Morocco has a freer hand in Arab politics, although it did temper its support for the Camp David agreements to avoid a vulnerability that could be turned against it by Algeria.

On the African front, Morocco's position is different. When the Polisario's government in exile was admitted to the OAU in 1983, Morocco left, making good a threat it had made for a long time. Morocco continues to have good relations with many African countries and has long been leader of a moderate group particularly concerned with Communist activities on the continent. Morocco sent troops to Zaire as part of the U.N. operations in the early 1960s and again against dissident invasions from Angola in 1977 and 1978. Morocco has not served on an OAU mediation committee since 1975—and only on one committee then, seeking to restore unity to the warring Angolan parties—and it has been among the moderate states on most major issues except dialogue with South Africa. Morocco in the OAU, however, has been on the defensive since the mid-1970s, on account of the Saharan issue.

Algeria has been a member of the Rejectionist Front among the Arab states, only moderating its position around 1983 as the front began to fall apart. But it has always maintained enough flexibility in that position to pursue another of its foreign policy themes, that of mediation and reconciliation. Boumedienne mediated an agreement between Iran and Iraq in 1975, and after the shah's overthrow Algeria spent much effort in trying to mediate the Iran-Iraq war, this time without success. Algeria also sought to reconcile the various factions of the Palestine Liberation Organization. In its wider circle based on the Arab world, Algeria has been an active member of the Organization of Petroleum Exporting Countries and a leader of the hard-line position on pricing, along with Libya, in opposition to the free-market leadership of Saudi Arabia. In its foreign policy expression of its Arab identity, Algeria remains the institutionalized revolutionary.

In Africa, Algeria's position has been similar. Ever since Ben Bella, Algeria has found the continent a primary terrain of activity. Algeria's more developed position, its sense of proper directions in Third World strategy, its history of revolutionary liberation, and the presence of some willing allies who are not competitors all give it a good opportunity for leadership in OAU circles. This sense of proper directions has been sharpened since the mid-1970s by a personally felt task, that of beating Morocco on the Polisario issue, which Algeria finally accomplished politically in 1983. Beyond strictly African issues, Algeria has also been the leader of the New International Economic Order campaign of the mid-1970s, forcing the U.N. special sessions of 1976 and 1977, cajoling the poorer African states into a more enlightened pursuit of their interests. This campaign lost steam with the death of Boumedienne and the change in world economic conditions, as has the OAU itself, but Algeria still cultivates a broad position of leadership in Africa.

Tunisia joined the Arab League in 1958 just long enough to walk out of it for three years in protest against meddling Egyptian domination of Arab affairs, and it has been an idiosyncratic player in Arab politics ever since. When Egypt was expelled from the league after the Washington treaty with Israel, however, Tunis suddenly became the

seat and secretary-general of the league, in 1980, and when the Palestine Liberation Organization was expelled from Beirut by the Israeli invasion of 1982, Tunisia became the site of its camps and headquarters. Tunisia has been a moderate among the Arabs, as it has in all things, but not to the point of exposing itself with an endorsement of the peace process. The Arab League and its politics among Arab states are above all a means of protection for Tunisia to overcome its small-state vulnerability.

Africa is a less important arena to Tunisia. The country is not involved in African leadership struggles nor does it find as strong a security support from African states. Tunisia is generally among the moderates on African issues, but it has never been the site of an OAU meeting, rarely served on a mediation committee, and never played a major role in broader Third World forums.

Libya is at the opposite extreme. It sees itself as the leader of the progressive revolutionary forces in the Arab, Muslim, and broader African and Third World communities and therefore has a strong leadership calling in both Arab and African circles. In Arab circles, this means a strong role leading the Rejectionist Front, although Libya's positions are often so radical that they even offend other Rejectionist members such as the PLO, with whom Qaddafi has broken on a number of occasions, and Syria. Qaddafi is a bitter foe of post-Nasserite Egypt and of Sudan during much of Numeiry's rule, since both countries rejected his radical options and leadership. The moderate turn of Arab foreign policies in the mid-1980s is considered a betrayal of the cause by Qaddafi, whose natural—in the Kautilyan sense—and ideological allies are Syria and, beyond the Arab world, Iran. But no one has followed his leadership, and his radical Islamic revisionism has often offended other Muslims. Qaddafi is a lone rider.

In Africa, he rides less alone. His expansionist, even aggressive, policies in Chad have earned him disapproval in African circles and his over-eager attentions and even subversion in other states have increased his rejection. Yet to the African radicals, he is a valuable ally, and poorer states find Libyan aid tempting, especially when they are radical, too. Libyan relations are nurtured with Ghana, Benin, Burkina Fasso, and Ethiopia, but also with the Central African Republic and the radicals of southern Africa—Mozambique, Zimbabwe, and Angola. Africa is divided into clear zones for Qaddafi: the Muslim area of the Sahel and the Sudan, where he seeks to increase his influence to the point of bringing all the people of the area under his leadership if possible, and the rest of the continent, where he works with individual states as potential allies on whose people and territory he has no designs.

Thus Maghribi states play out their rivalries and extend their leadership on the Arab and African scenes. Where they aspire to lead the same ideological clientele, as do Algeria and Libya, they sometimes work together on common causes, but at other times rival each other for the same followers. But the first priorities go to use of the Arab and African spheres for the defense of national security or security issues such as Chad or the Sahara.

The third circle—the Mediterranean or European world—is also an identity area to the extent that the Maghribi states have been marked by their colonial past during their passage into the modern world. Again, the ensuing relationships involve more than simply a defense of markets or a liquidation of the last colonial ties. Intra-Maghribi rivalries and relations are projected into their dealings with Europe, especially with the former metropole, and are reciprocated in turn. France has long adopted the checkerboard pattern as its own image of North African relations; the different colonial statuses enjoyed by the three territories institutionalized the checkerboard, and the independence of the two protectorates of Morocco and Tunisia in 1956 in order to consolidate France's hold over the direct colony in Algeria did the same. After Algerian independence six years later, all three states—but particularly Morocco and Algeria—aspired to a special relationship—and hence a preferred relation over the others—with the metropole. Instead, Tunisian relations with France soured after the Bizerte battle in 1961, Moroccan relations were broken after the assassination of opposition leader Mehdi ben Barka by Moroccan security forces in France in 1965, and Algerian relations, never really recovered from the bitter decolonization and the rapid outdating of the plans for balanced relations negotiated in the independence agreements of 1962, completely soured over the final destruction of that balance in the Algerian nationalization of the French-owned oil industry in 1971.[8] The post-Gaullist president Valéry Giscard d'Estaing was the first French head of state to visit the three Maghribi countries, in mid-1975, but his predilections were with Morocco. French refusal to give Algeria the special position it demanded or to back Algeria on the Saharan question maintained the imbal-

8. See Nicole Grimaud, "Algeria and Socialist France," *Middle East Journal,* 40(2):252-66 (Spring 1986); Paul Balta, "Foreign Policy in North Africa," ibid., pp. 238-51.

ance. When the Socialists won the 1981 elections, however, a new view of trans-Mediterranean relations came to Paris, one that adopted the third model and looked to preferential ties with Algeria as the basis of a Franco-Algerian axis that would improve the French position in the Third World. The honeymoon did not last. A Moroccan lobby within the Mitterrand government, an unchanged position on the Saharan issue, and an inability to deliver on the basic ongoing grievances, such as labor, aid, invest-ment, and simple political sympathies, all restored the French position to one of balancing among the rivalries of intra-Maghribi politics.

The final circle of relations is with the great powers and it, too, repeats the basic checkerboard pattern of North Africa. Morocco and Tunisia have good and close relations with the United States; Algeria and Libya rely similarly on the Soviet Union. Morocco and Tunisia depend on the United States for a large part of their armaments, although France is the first arms supplier of both. Morocco has been associated with the United States since 1982 in a military facilities contingency use agreement in connection with the Rapid Deployment Force for the Middle East. Tunisia has no such agreement, but the United States has extended a security guarantee to the country, most notably in 1980 when Tunisia was infiltrated by subversive groups from Libya. Morocco and Tuni-sia have little trade with the United States; France and the rest of the Euro-pean Community are their major commer-cial partners. Their attachment to the United States is political and ideological. Tunisia's President Habib Bourguiba has long supported American policies, including some far afield, such as those concerning the Vietnam war. Morocco's

King Hassan is perhaps the only Arab leader who refers to his country as part of the West. This year, 1987, marks the celebrated bicentennial of the Moroccan-American treaty, the first friendship and cooperation treaty entered into by the young United States with the first foreign country to grant it recognition and a treaty whose spirit at least continues today. Foreign support from the leading Western power is important to the secu-rity of Morocco and Tunisia and is consistent with their general political views as open, liberal, free-enterprise countries.

The relation of Algeria to the Soviet Union is not the same as that of Lybia to the Soviet Union, and both are different from Morocco's or Tunisia's relation to the United States. Neither Algeria nor Libya is a Communist country, neither enjoys any security guarantee from the Soviet Union, and neither has any his-toric relationship with Russia. Both, however, are armed primarily by the Soviet Union, both have Eastern bloc technicians and advisers, and both have some affinity for Soviet foreign policy positions.

Of the two, Algeria has a much more nonaligned position on world issues and stands in no characteristic hostility to the West, particularly since the advent of President Chadli Benjedid in 1979. Algeria's counterbalancing relations with the United States have improved grad-ually and sporadically since it served as an effective mediator in the Iranian hostage crisis that same year, despite ideological differences and gas price disputes; the United States is a major commercial partner of Algeria.

Libya, too, is no Soviet satellite, a point often missed by observers, but its relations with the Soviet Union are much closer than Algeria's and it often runs on a parallel course with the Soviets, the two countries serving each other's purposes while pursuing their own. Libya has frequently pressed for a friendship treaty with the Soviet Union as a protection for its own security, but Moscow has consistently refused, regarding Colonel Qaddafi as too erratic to be a reliable treaty ally. Qaddafi's policies make him avowedly hostile to the West, an attitude that the United States reciprocates overenthusiastically. Libya has significant trade with the Soviet Union, if only to pay its heavy armaments debt, but its prime trading partners are in Western Europe. Once again, Libya's cold-war friendships are, above all, determined by its regional politics, the effects of which send neighbors to seek power and protection from outside powers and the great powers, impelling Libya in turn to seek counter-alliances for its own security on the great-power level. The reverse—that great powers dictate local political relations—is not true.

In sum, the foreign relations of North Africa are determined above all by the positions and interests of the North African states. Although they have been independent members of the community of nations for only 25 to 30 years, the states of the Maghrib have a good sense of their national interests and a growing tradition of historic bases for their positions. Although their policies are often made by a limited number of individuals, among whom the head of state plays a dominant role, these policies are not merely personal or idiosyncratic but have a firm grounding in national needs and public attitudes. That does not prevent public opinion from being volatile on specific points, in North Africa as elsewhere, or leaders from misunderstanding the needs of their nation. But it does mean that outside observers and practitioners alike need to see the world from within the North African states outward to understand the sources and directions of their foreign policies.

ANNALS, *AAPSS,* **489,** January 1987

The Northeastern Triangle:
Libya, Egypt, and the Sudan

By CLEMENT HENRY MOORE

ABSTRACT: The Triangle may be viewed as a regional subsystem articulating power relationships between core and periphery. The core can be seen as an unevenly weighted dumbbell consisting of Cairo and Khartoum connected by the Nile. The periphery consists of Libya and the upper reaches of the Nile that escape the control of the Egyptian and Sudanese governments. The challenge to this regional subsystem is that Libya, with help from the other peripherals, might grab the dumbbell. Under modern conditions, established states usually dominate their peripheries, although energetic peripheries can budge inert centers. Two attempted coups against Qaddafi in March 1985 reflected serious dissension within his military establishment. Since then overt U.S. actions against Libya have strengthened Qaddafi's regime at home and in the region. Dysfunctional U.S. policies, coupled with a deteriorating Egyptian economy, could precipitate a Nasserite, anti-American coup in Egypt and dramatic regional realignments.

Clement Henry Moore is Elie Halévy Visiting Professor at the Institut d'études politiques de Paris. He served until 1984 as director of the Business School at the American University of Beirut and has taught at the University of California, Los Angeles, the University of Michigan, and the American University in Cairo. He has written extensively on North Africa and is a former board member of the Middle East Studies Association.

COLONIAL regimes appear to have irrevocably altered power relationships between urban centers and rural peripheries in the Third World. Successor regimes of Western-educated elites almost invariably broke any lingering restraints on urban-based state power. In the semiarid zones of the Middle East and North Africa in particular, the Western impact ruptured the cyclical rise and fall of tribal dynasties described by Ibn Khaldun in the fourteenth century.[1] Tribal peripheries are no longer supposed to capture urban centers.

Anomalies like Lebanon and Yemen only appear to corroborate the tendency of urban centers to achieve dominion over their unruly peripheries. In Lebanon the new financial and commercial elites achieved a shared interest in limiting state building. A sectarian distribution of power was useful for keeping government weak and preserving the free-enterprise system—until the marginalized populations of Beirut and its suburbs exploded. In Yemen, Western impact remained too limited to coastal enclaves to restructure power relationships. Yet even in the midst of tribal warfare, an urban power base seemed essential. After losing the civil war in Aden in January 1986, ex-President Hassani was not favored to stage a comeback. An odds maker explained, "It is difficult to carry out an insurgency in one's own tribal area once one has lost the capital."[2]

The Northeastern Triangle, however, suggests a slight variation on the theme.

The Triangle may be viewed as a regional subsystem articulating power relationships between core and periphery. The core can be seen as an unevenly weighted dumbbell, consisting of Cairo and Khartoum connected by the Nile. The periphery consists of Libya and the upper reaches of the Nile that escape the control of the Egyptian and Sudanese governments. The challenge to this regional subsystem is that Libyans, with help from the other peripherals, might grab the dumbbell.

Field Marshal Abu Ghazala, Egypt's minister of defense, implied as much in September 1981, that is, even before Anwar el-Sadat's assassination and Jafar al-Numeiry's demise: "Egypt is now in a very critical situation because of the threat surrounding it from the West and from the South." The Sudan also feared a Libyan invasion.[3] If Egypt is the gift of the Nile, then whoever controls the Nile controls Egypt. The dumbbell has become more vulnerable, its southern weight at least temporarily diminished, if not uncoupled, by the April 1985 coup that toppled Numeiry's pro-Egyptian regime. As for Egypt, can its polity not be likened to those cities besieged by tribes in Ibn Khaldun's day—those flesh-pots whose conquerers go soft after two or three generations, their solidarity attenuated by civilized virtues and vices?

THE LIBYAN CONNECTION

The metaphor of a Libyan periphery defined by the Nile Valley rather than some other center deserves closer scrutiny. Before World War II, Libya was a

1. Ibn Khaldun, *Muqaddimah*, trans. F. Rosenthal (New York: Pantheon Books, 1958), brilliantly interpreted in Ernest Gellner, *Muslim Society* (Cambridge: Cambridge University Press, 1981), pp. 16-35.

2. John Kifner, "Massacre with Tea: Southern Yemen at War," *New York Times*, national ed., 9 Feb. 1986.

3. Bahgat Korani and Ali E.H. Desouki, *The Foreign Policies of Arab States* (Boulder, CO: Westview Press, 1984), p. 130; John O. Voll and Sarah P. Voll, *The Sudan* (Boulder, CO: Westview Press, 1985, pp. 128-32.

geographical expression of Italian colonial grandeur; its indigenous societies were a wasteland. Its deserts bordering on the Mediterranean then became sites of some of the greatest tank battles in history, pitting the British against the Third Reich. The wasteland became independent in 1951 only because the great powers could not agree how to divide up its constituent parts of Tripolitania, Cyrenaica, and the Fezzan. Nasser's Egypt and Bourguiba's Tunisia, regional powers emancipated in the late 1950s, settled for a buffer in which adjacent foes checked each other: a Nasserite Tripolitania contained by a pro-Tunisian Cyrenaican monarchy.

In December 1969, just after Muammar al-Qaddafi seized power, Libya became committed to a Federation of Arab Republics with Egypt and the Sudan. Harmony within the Triangle, however, did not long survive the death of Nasser, Qaddafi's revolutionary father figure. Numeiry withdrew to repair relations with the Sudan's non-Arab south, and Qaddafi subsequently broke with Sadat. Since Egypt stopped his "people's invasion" in 1973, he has sought union with Tunisia, Syria, Algeria, Morocco, and any other interested Arab country. He has, in fact, sported paper unions with Syria since 1978 and Morocco since 1984. He also invaded Chad, supported Rawlings's regime in Ghana, and most recently became an honorary citizen of Burkina Fasso, formerly Upper Volta.

On paper, then, the Northeastern Triangle seems no more than one *union manquée* among others. Its most permanent expression may have been an article by Professor Boutros Boutros-Ghali, written before he became Egypt's secretary of state for foreign affairs

under Sadat and Mubarak.[4] In this academic publication, Boutros-Ghali anticipated Egyptian disenchantment with pan-Arabism; the Arab League should encourage four functional subregional units: the Fertile Crescent, the Arab Gulf, the Maghrib, and the Triangle. He implied that Egypt, which dominated the Arab League, had overextended its pan-Arab leadership and should settle for the Sudan and Libya. But why should Qaddafi gravitate to the dumbell in preference to his sub-Saharan neighbors, the Maghrib, or other Arab states?

One answer is that Algeria would block any westward moves even if post-Bourguibian Tunisia were not too resilient to be bought. A weakening dumbbell may be a riper picking. Beyond the present conjuncture, however, Qaddafi seems fixated on Egypt, land of Nasser and center of the Arab world, for geopolitical as well as sentimental reasons. In his words:

the revolutionary sees tomorrow and dreams of the future as if it were real because he is sure it can be realized. It is a vision that those who are not revolutionaries cannot see or do not believe can be realized. I, for example, believe that the Arab nation could be a paradise, that it could be a single, strong state. I can imagine the possibility of linking the Nile with the great artificial river, so that the desert between Egypt and Libya can be watered and planted with crops, so that the Western Desert can be filled with fruit and be a lush garden.[5]

Qaddafi is as much a social architect as Mohammed Ali, who ruled Egypt

4. Boutros Boutros-Ghali, "Joint Arab Action in the Framework of the Arab League," *Maqallat as-siyassat al-duwaliya* (Cairo), in Arabic, no. 20 (Apr. 1970).

5. *Al-Ray* (Tunis), 23 Aug. 1985.

from 1805 to 1849, and Gamal Abdel Nasser, who ruled from 1952 to 1970. He, too, understands the requirements for stable dominion; water, not oil, drives political construction beyond the confines of Ibn Khaldun's kind of society. By 1986 virtually all development projects in Libya had ground to a halt for lack of oil revenues, but Qaddafi pushed work ahead of schedule on his great artificial river, to pipe fossil water 1900 kilometers from southeastern Libya to the Mediterranean. Just as Mohammed Ali improved irrigation from the Nile to create an agrarian base for an empire, a process culminating, for a time, in Nasser's High Dam at Aswan, so Qaddafi replicates the Egyptian experience and intends to transform uprooted Libyans, and perhaps other Arabs, into productive and manageable farmhands. No matter that the project may fail to reproduce a mini-Egypt, much less a market return on investment. It taps Qaddafi's peripheral *jamahiriyya* ("peopledom") into ancient waters that are sufficiently Nilotic for political purposes to make Libya part of the Triangle.

LIBYA AS PERIPHERY

Yet Libya remains a periphery, a kind of antistate within the Triangle as well as within the international system of states. To be sure, the country no longer resembles Ibn Khaldun's tribal society, but Qaddafi expresses a special sort of tribal ethos. He may appear to be an "anachronism,"[6] not for his pan-Arabism but for his puritanism. His religious fundamentalism reenacts a scenario familiar to the fourteenth-century observer of Islamic society. The call to piety can vastly enhance the vigor and solidarity of tribal rebels and enable them to seize power and expand it.

Qaddafi makes this call in modern, radical idiom, reflecting the agonies of a society butchered by Italian fascism and subsequent oil wealth. His Islam, of course, is not that of the turbaned establishment. It is instead God's message as revealed by the Prophet Muhammad and recorded in the Koran, stripped bare of all scholarly interpretation and accessible to all men and women. Since divine revelation is so central, Qaddafi propagated a new Muslim calendar, counting not from the Prophet's departure from Mecca to create a new community, but from his death, which sealed all revelation.

Qaddafi's Third Universal Theory calls for direct democracy as the alternative to multi- or single-party dictatorship. *The Green Book,* in which he spells out his political, economic, and social theories, may be unique among official charters and ideologies in that it neither legitimates an existing regime nor defines the national identity of its potential audience. *The Green Book* is indeed official, written by a head of state and propagated through government channels, including the Libyan school system.[7] But rather than favoring a specified elite or regime, it repudiates all elites and regimes. One apparent result was that Qaddafi resigned from all his public offices. Unlike other official ideologies, his Universal Theory makes no

6. Fouad Ajami, *The Arab Predicament* (Cambridge: Cambridge University Press, 1981), p. 126.

7. Muammar Al Qathafi, *The Green Book,* 3 vols. (Tripoli: Public Establishment for Publishing, n.d.). On schools, see John P. Mason, *Island of the Blest: Islam in a Libyan Oasis Community* (Athens: Ohio University Center for International Studies, 1977), p. 145.

nationalist appeals nor does it express the virtues of Libyan nationhood, because the audience is intended to be universal, not exclusively Libyan, Arab, or even Islamic.

The Universal Theory does, however, serve as a cognitive map, spelling out a distinctive political culture for Libya. As Qaddafi put it, "This formulation is absolutely necessary, first of all for ourselves, so that we may not feel that we are working in void, and then for the intellectuals, who are so prone to succumb to the influence of ready-made theories."[8] The contents come straight from Rousseau, although Qaddafi claims never to have read *The Social Contract.* Their common starting point is that the only legitimate sovereign is the people, therefore popular sovereignty cannot be delegated without ceasing to express legitimate sovereign acts. Thus an elected parliament or other ostensibly representative body cannot act as sovereign. The only legitimate sovereign is all the people actually deliberating—and not simply voting by plebiscite—in a general assembly.

The two radical democrats also share similar views on law and civil religion. Each is a political moralist, intending not in Rousseau's misunderstood words to "force men to be free," but instead to encourage a community of public-spirited individuals without which no general will is possible. Only a tightly knit community based on simple laws derived from religion and tradition can keep public opinion under control, relatively uncorrupted, and consisting of individual opinions free of excessive dependence upon the opinions of others. Qaddafi, too, shares Rousseau's distrust of independent religious establishments.

In fact Qaddafi parts company with Rousseau only in presenting the Libyan system of popular congresses as the solution to the problem of democracy. For Rousseau, no solution can be definitive, and "in the strict sense of the term, there never has been, and never will be, a real democracy . . . it is impossible to imagine a people remaining constantly assembled to attend to public business."[9] There are uncanny resemblances, however, between the Libyan system of popular congresses and the system Rousseau once proposed for Corsica, the one country left in the Europe of his day that seemed "capable of legislation," that is, of institutional arrangements wherein the general will might be expressed.[10]

The Libyan system has not, of course, provided responsible government. *The Green Book* does not specify the modes of selection of various executive bodies and their relationships with the popular congresses. Eventually so-called revolutionary committees displaced the popular congresses and people's committees. *The Green Book* has, however, promoted a distinctively Libyan antibureaucratic political culture. As Lisa Anderson humorously contends, Libya may be the sole illustration of Qaddafi's contention that the political structure of the state "is affected by its social structure in the form of tribes, clans and families . . . and adopts its characteristics." She concludes:

The continued role of the "hinterland culture" in Libyan political ideology constituted symbolic rejection of a world dominated by the bureaucratic, hierarchical organization

8. Mirella Bianco, *Gadafi: Voice from the Desert* (London: Longman, 1975), p. 111.

9. Jean-Jacques Rousseau, *The Social Contract and Discourses,* trans. G.D.H. Cole (New York: Dutton, 1950), p. 65.

10. Ibid., p. 49; F. M. Watkins, ed. *Rousseau: Political Writings* (New York: Nelson, 1953), pp. 286, 304-6; cf. Qathafi, *Green Book,* 2:35.

of the modern state, a form of organization the Libyans had known only briefly, partially, and for the vast majority, to their unalloyed detriment.[11]

Protected by foreign hierarchies, including East German security services, Qaddafi has redefined Libya as periphery. Enough people probably still listen to his radical, antielitist message. The Italians and then oil wealth obliterated most of the social distinctions that support elites in other, more normal, state-centered societies.

THE NILE VALLEY

The core of the Triangle is the Nile Valley. Egypt never did fit Ibn Khaldun's model of tribal dominion because hydraulic civilization supported strong central government, keeping the peripheries at bay. In terms of the contemporary realities of state power, the Triangle is almost reducible to the much smaller triangle of the Nile Delta, which encloses most of Egypt's population. Yet just as Cairo, at the southern apex of the delta, dominates Egypt, so the peripheral sources of the Nile, much further south, potentially dominate the valley.

Egypt outstrips the rest of the Triangle on all dimensions of state power. Its population, approaching 50 million, is more than double the Sudan's and 15 times that of Libya. Its manufactures in 1982 outdid the Sudan's more than tenfold and Libya's almost eightfold.[12] Despite excessive Soviet purchases since 1972, the Libyan armed forces are hardly

a match for Egypt's, however much the latter may be in disarray while making a transition from Soviet to U.S. and other Western armaments.[13] And on their home ground, at least, Egypt's wily intelligence services have consistently shamed Qaddafi by outwitting Libyan plots to assassinate exiled politicians.

Further south, however, Cairo's position has eroded. The Sudan has been its Achilles' heel ever since modern technology rendered possible the control and allocation of the Nile's water supply. In 1924, in an Egypt by then nominally independent of British rule, the murder of Sir Lee Stack, the British governor-general of the Sudan, triggered a British ultimatum to the Egyptian government. Egyptian garrisons were expelled from the Sudan, and the British threatened an indefinite expansion of irrigation in the Sudan at Egypt's expense. The issue of Sudanese governance was the thorniest one in Anglo-Egyptian relations until 1954, when each partner of the Anglo-Egyptian Condominium established in 1899 finally agreed to Sudanese independence, rather than a Unity of the Nile Valley under Egyptian rule.

Nasser broke the deadlock in 1953 in part because his High Dam project promised direct Egyptian control over the water supply. Alternative schemes for Nile control had more waterworks in the Sudan, Uganda, and Ethiopia. Agreement was reached with the Sudan in 1959 for allocating their respective shares of the water on terms considered favorable to Egypt.[14] No agreements were

11. Lisa Anderson, *The State and Social Transformation in Tunisia and Libya, 1830-1980* (Princeton, NJ: Princeton University Press, 1986), pp. 267-69, citing Qathafi, *Green Book,* 3:23.

12. World Bank, *World Development Report 1985* (New York: Oxford University Press, 1985), pp. 186-87.

13. Anthony H. Cordesman, "The Middle East and the Cost of the Politics of Force," *Middle East Journal,* 40(1):11 (Winter 1986).

14. Hans-Heino Kopietz and Pamela Ann Smith, "Egypt, Libya and the Sudan," in *The Cambridge History of Africa,* ed. Michael Crowder (Cambridge: Cambridge University Press, 1984), 8:527.

ever reached, however, with the other upstream riparian states. Only by default has the river continued to flow freely to the core Nile states of the Sudan and Egypt.

Best available estimates indicate, moreover, that both governments will soon face serious water shortages if their ambitious plans for reclaiming and irrigating new lands are even partially implemented. So evident is the impending shortage, yet so ignored in official discourse, that John Waterbury asks; "Could it be that Egypt and the Sudan are rushing ahead with projects that will use unavailable water in unspoken anticipation of future bargaining once the crisis is at hand?"[15]

The 1959 Agreement for the Full Utilization of the Nile Waters set up a Permanent Joint Technical Commission to implement and supervise the agreement. Despite variable political relations between the two countries, the Permanent Joint Technical Commission has faithfully implemented functional cooperation in this policy sector so vital to both regimes. Efforts to increase the flow of the Nile, however, have met political and military obstacles.

THE DUMBBELL UNCOUPLED?

The regime of Jafar al-Numeiry, which governed the Sudan from May 1969 to April 1985, introduced a golden age of political cooperation with Egypt. Though the Unity of the Nile Valley was not achieved, Egypt finally gained the next best outcome, a closely allied and subservient regime in Khartoum. On at least

two occasions Sadat's military assistance saved Numeiry from military coups. In return, Numeiry went out on a political limb for Sadat. He was the only Arab leader apart from the sultan of Oman publicly to endorse Egypt's concessions at Camp David leading to a separate Egyptian peace with Israel.

Numeiry terminated the civil war with the non-Arab, non-Islamic southern Sudan in 1972. That most bloody of wars, "which over 17 years took the lives of possibly 500,000 to 1.5 million people,"[16] had blocked Nile projects of benefit to Egypt as well as the Sudan. In the mid-1970s the two governments reached a series of agreements to carry out Nile projects located for the most part in the southern Sudan. The first step was to clear the Sudd swamps, where precious Nile waters were lost, by cutting a diversionary canal extending some 200 miles north of Jonglei. Excavation began in late 1977, but the Jonglei Canal was only two-thirds completed when all work ceased in 1984. The Sudan's southern periphery had by then exploded again into armed rebellion, anticipating the end of Numeiry's regime. But it was not the periphery that did him in.

The general was formally dismissed by his fellow officers, not guerrilla rebels, after urban-based professional associations, not rural parties, had triggered massive demonstrations in Khartoum and Omdurman, not the provinces. In Khartoum the main targets of the mob were not only Numeiry's official party headquarters and a luxury hotel but also the Faisal Islamic Bank.[17] Numeiry's

15. John Waterbury, *Hydropolitics of the Nile Valley* (Syracuse, NY: Syracuse University Press, 1979), p. 240; for estimates of supply and demand, which included benefits from the Jonglei, see pp. 226, 236.

16. Alasdair Drysdale and Gerald H. Blake, *The Middle East and North Africa* (New York: Oxford University Press, 1985), p. 214.

17. Abbas Abdelkarim, Abdallah el-Hassan, and David Seddon, "The Generals Step In," *Merip Reports,* 135:20 (Sept. 1985).

imposition of traditional Islamic norms and sanctions—including the amputation of limbs for theft—and food and fuel prices were at issue. In 1983 he had tried to preempt Islamic opposition by adopting fundamentalist legal reforms. He thereby alienated much of his urban support while also provoking the southern insurrection.

The Transitional Military Council (TMC) that succeeded Numeiry conducted new elections in April 1986 except in the southern provinces. It has meanwhile attempted to keep up cordial relations with Egypt, Saudi Arabia, the United States, the International Monetary Fund, and the World Bank, while developing new ties with Libya, Ethiopia, and the Soviet Union. If placating everyone is like squaring the circle, the Sudan's international relations only reflect its internal dilemmas. The Sudan's geographic expanse and demographic heterogeneity make it one of the least governable countries in Africa. If the Sudan is Egypt's most vulnerable link in Nile control, its southern and western peripheries are the Sudan's Sudan.

THE SUDAN'S PERIPHERIES

Since the time of the British, economic development favored the northeast of the Sudan, where the Blue and White Niles converge. Colonial policy after 1930 was to detach the southern Sudan from the Arab-Islamic north and eventually integrate it into British East Africa. Only in 1946 did the British change their policy, but there was not time to redress economic and cultural disparities before Sudanese independence. Despite some political, administrative, and cultural autonomy accorded to the south by the agreement in 1972 to end the civil war, capitalist development continued to favor the northeast. Fatima Mahmoud offers some evidence that capital accumulation involved substantial transfers of resources from the western and, to a lesser extent, southern parts of the country to the northeast.[18] Numeiry's open-door policy of attracting Saudi capital for agribusiness reinforced this tendency.

Drought in the Saharan Sahel has further marginalized the Sudan's western populations of Darfur and Kordofan. Their ancestors had constituted the backbone of the Mahdist uprising against the Egyptians and British in 1881. Perceived as underrepresented during Numeiry's regime, officers from the western provinces attempted at least two coups against him. Sadiq al-Mahdi's Umma Party derives much of its strength from this area, where Qaddafi's Islamic appeals have also met positive responses.

Just as the west, however peripheral, is welded to Khartoum by historical legacies of struggle, so the south is also being integrated under the banner of Colonel John Garang's Sudanese People's Liberation Army (SPLA). Unlike earlier secessionist movements,[19] the SPLA is committed to liberating the Sudan, not just the south. It has continued, however, to combat the TMC, which it views as a mere continuation of the Numeiry regime. It has interdicted continued work on the Jonglei Canal and also on Chevron's project to pipe oil from newly discovered fields in the south to Port Sudan. Both projects symbolize continued exploitation of southern riches for the sake of the northeast. Meanwhile, defending against

18. Fatima Babiker Mahmoud, *The Sudanese Bourgeoisie* (London: Zed Books, 1984), pp. 122-26.

19. Dunstan M. Wai, *The Afro-Arab Conflict in the Sudan* (New York: Africana, 1981), p. 111.

the insurrection is costing the virtually bankrupt government $400,000 per day.

After the April 1986 elections, the TMC is supposed to give way to a new government that may have a stronger hand for negotiating with the SPLA. But any Sudanese government faces a number of constraints. While satisfying southern economic, cultural, and political aspirations, it must also cope with the Islamic sentiments of the Muslim Brotherhood and the Umma Party and contain potential fundamentalist upsurges from the western region. It will also have to heed Egypt's vital interest in resuming the Nile projects. Sadat was speaking for Egypt when he declared in May 1978, "We depend upon the Nile 100 percent in our life, so if anyone, at any moment, thinks to deprive us of our life we shall never hesitate [to go to war] because it is a matter of life or death."[20]

THE DEAD WEIGHT OF EGYPT

With the exception of one counterproductive military sally over the Sudanese border in 1958, the Egyptian armed forces have not acted without British or Sudanese cooperation in the Sudan since the Mahdi expelled them in 1881. Unilateral military moves are virtually unthinkable unless the Sudan somehow develops the capacity to cut Egypt's water supply. Expanding the supply, by Jonglei and other projects, presupposes continued cooperation.

Egypt did use military force effectively, however, to sustain Numeiry in power. After the Egyptians aborted the 1976 coup against him, 12,000 of their troops were reported to be stationed in the Sudan. But if any had remained by 1985, they were powerless to act. In September violent demonstrations against John

20. Waterbury, *Hydropolitics*, p. 78.

Garang's SPLA provoked a minor mutiny of enlisted men in Omdurman. The government portrayed the mutiny as an SPLA and foreign—Ethiopian—plot. Mubarak then declared publicly that Egypt would stand by the Sudan's side "to confront any foreign interference or aggression." Anxiously he telephoned the head of the TMC, only to be told that all was well. Sudanese sources denied Egyptian reports that the Sudan's foreign minister had requested President Mubarak to intervene to break the deadlock in negotiations between Garang and the TMC. In Sadat's heyday, no public excuses would have been needed to rush to Numeiry's rescue. Secret understandings to the same effect had initially been spelled out by the defunct Federation of Arab Republics.

The Egyptians were more tempted to exercise military force against their other periphery, Libya. The vendetta between Sadat and Qaddafi had degenerated into a border war in 1977, but teaching the Libyans a lesson turned out to be more expensive than the Egyptians had anticipated. When an Egyptair flight was hijacked to Malta in November 1985, Mubarak saw backstage Libyan prompting of the Palestinian actors. Though humiliated that his elite commando units killed so many passengers while liberating so few, Mubarak sensibly did not lash out at the alleged source of his embarrassment, greater though the provocation seemed than the perceptions that had led to battle in 1977.

The principal reason for Mubarak's restraint has been domestic public opinion. Egyptian society has no internal peripheries, but its politics are nonetheless stalemated. Neither the Nasserite Left nor the Islamic Right accepts Egypt's alliance with the United States and implementation of the Camp David accord. Mubarak's centrist forces and his relatively loyal opposition face diminishing support. Symptomatic are the positive responses among students as well as fellow villagers to the Egyptian soldier who killed five Israeli tourists in a contested border zone. More ominous for Mubarak, even as a political allegory, was the widely believed report that the soldier was in turn "murdered on the orders of the army high command, to prevent him from revealing what he knew of Israeli espionage within the Egyptian army, and to sabotge a promise of clemency Mubarak had given him."[21] Widespread riots of the Egyptian security forces in February 1986 further jeopardized Mubarak's presidency.

Collapsing oil prices mean less private as well as public investment from the Gulf states as well as decreased remittances from the million-odd Egyptians working in the Gulf. Indeed, the specter of their return, for the same economic reasons that Qaddafi expelled some 800 Egyptians in 1985, already paralyzes economic decision making. Mubarak has appeared to be politically weak because he walks a tightrope. He aroused controversy by rehabilitating the Nasserite journalist Mohammed Hassanain Heikal. A barrage of letters from the Egyptian business community opposed a presidential decision to let Heikal resume publication of his column "In All Sincerity."[22] To keep the support of the United States and international financial institutions, Mubarak must sustain Sadat's open-door economic policies and acceptable relations with Israel. Any prolonged fight against fellow Arabs, however, would consequently be perceived as doing Israel's and America's bidding, thereby risking a military or popular backlash.

REGIONAL STALEMATE

Just as Egypt seems stalemated, so the Triangle appears to be frozen in its mutual oppositions. The Sudan cannot recover Numeiry's close relationship with Egypt without antagonizing its peripheries. Yet no new Sudanese government can switch allegiances to the Libyan suitor without provoking the combined wrath of Egypt and Saudi Arabia and a possible military intervention.

On the other hand, Libya cannot directly lift the Egyptian end of the dumbbell. Though stalemated, Egyptian political forces are virtually unanimous in their opposition to Qaddafi. The huge majority of the Egyptian middle classes remains unimpressed by the man who once told their women that they should stay at home because, unlike men, pregnant women cannot jump out of a plane in a parachute. Some of the fundamentalist minority may accept Libyan support, but it is unlikely that Nasserism and fundamentalism will converge under a Qaddafi banner. To that extent it is correct to argue that tribal peripheries can no longer capture urban centers, at least not Egypt's megalopolis.

CHANGING INTERNATIONAL ALIGNMENTS

Indirectly, however, energetic peripheries might still budge inert centers. Superpower policies in the region could contribute either to Qaddafi's fall, to his regaining modest influence within the Triangle, or, conceivably, to a regional realignment with radical regimes in Cairo and Khartoum, as well as Addis Ababa.

21. Claudia Wright, "Mubarak Fears US-Backed Coup," *New Statesman,* 11 Mar. 1986.
22. Simon Ingram, "Caution Is the Word," *Middle East International,* 266:8 (10 Jan. 1986).

The radical scenario probably requires unintentional assistance from the United States.

Unable to negotiate with Garang's guerrillas, the Sudanese TMC has requested Soviet assistance in persuading Ethiopia to cut off support for the SPLA. Ethiopia probably holds the key to any agreements between Garang's forces and the Khartoum government.[23] The Sudan's response to Ethiopian mediation would be to cease its support for the Eritrean and Tigrayen rebels. Along with Saudi Arabia, however, the United States supports these groups and funnels food and possibly other supplies through Port Sudan. Without some understanding among the superpowers, a trade-off of more autonomy for the south in return for that of Eritrea seems unlikely.

The United States could unintentionally provoke the radical scenario by pursuing its present policies of supporting hard-liners within the TMC, continuing the pressure on Mubarak to adhere to Israeli interpretations of Camp David, and sustaining an ineffectual offensive against Libya. Though two attempted coups against Qaddafi in March 1985 reflected serious dissension within his military establishment, overt U.S. actions against Libya have strengthened Qaddafi's regime at home and in the region. Continued U.S. acquiescence to Israeli occupation of the West Bank and Gaza, coupled with a deteriorating Egyptian economy, could yet trigger a Nasserite, anti-American coup in Egypt. Egypt's natural allies would then be Libya, Ethiopia, and a Sudanese government that could accommodate its western

and southern peripheries. Anachronistic U.S. postures would then have made Qaddafi's less so.

Free elections in the Sudan probably enhanced the political influence of the western provinces in Khartoum. Erstwhile alliances between Sadiq al-Mahdi, Qaddafi, and Ethiopia's Mengistu could support a new regional alignment.

To prevent such an outcome, Mubarak or moderate military successors might continue to readjust Sadat's foreign policies toward more genuine nonalignment, rather than directly confront a realigned Sudan. Flexible U.S. responses could encourage the needed deal between Khartoum and Addis Ababa. Such an accommodation might enhance Qaddafi's influence in Khartoum if he in turn refused to support intransigent Arab-Islamic elements in the Sudan's western provinces. Imitations of desert warriors no longer capture cities, but they can work the corridors of regional relationships and effect changes. In time, too, arbitrarily commanded economies usually open up to regional and international markets. Libya's economy could eventually follow its neighbors'—offering further opportunities for functional cooperation within the Triangle. Qaddafi, however, rejects such evolution: "We have become certain that the theory that advocates the realization of Arab unity gradually and through economic integration . . . has been proved wrong."[24]

If he remains intransigent, and scuttles a Sudanese reconciliation that flexible superpower policies could otherwise facilitate, he is likely again to become very isolated. Picadors might then do

23. Quarterly Economic Report, *The Sudan,* no. 4, *1985* (London: Economist Intelligence Unit, 1985), p. 11.

24. Quarterly Economic Report, *Libya,* no. 4, *1985* (London: Economist Intelligence Unit, 1985).

him in unless the United States rages too much about international terrorism and raises more red flags to energize the peripheral bull.

POSTSCRIPT

Shortly after these lines were written, the air strikes conducted on 15 April 1986 by the United States Navy and Air Force against what were believed to be Libyan terrorist targets in Tripoli and Benghazi turned Qaddafi into a regional hero. The radical scenario has become more plausible, not that tribal peripheries actually conquer urban centers as in Ibn Khaldun's day.

ANNALS, *AAPSS,* **489,** January 1987

Nigeria Restrained: Foreign Policy under Changing Political and Petroleum Regimes

By TIMOTHY M. SHAW

ABSTRACT: The cyclical pattern of Nigeria's external relations has followed that of its political constitution and petroleum production. Aspirations to great-power status in the 1970s have yielded to austerity and modesty in the 1980s. Yet core concerns about development, integration, and liberation continue despite a series of changes in governmental structure and oil profitability. Throughout, there have been lively debates about preferred policy directions and alternative analytic explanations, symptomatic of the openness of Nigeria's political culture. If its political economy can become more self-reliant and self-sustaining, then its foreign policy can yet be influential. But leadership in Africa requires the redefinition of established linkages with other, mainly Western, economic partners. If Nigeria can use the present period of economic difficulty to reduce its oil dependence, then its ambitions in and for Africa may yet be realized in the coming decade.

Timothy M. Shaw is professor of political science and director of the Centre for African Studies at Dalhousie University in Nova Scotia, Canada. Dr. Shaw holds a Ph.D. from Princeton University and has lectured, researched, and traveled extensively in Africa over the last twenty years. He has been president of the Canadian Association of African Studies and is author of Towards a Political Economy for Africa: The Dialectics of Dependence *(1985).*

The entire dynamic foreign policy concept, as Nigeria has employed it to date, reflects a certain unreality, not only about the Nigerian ability to force changes in Africa but also about the desired changes.[1]

Nigeria did seem to win a special place in the US firmament and the American popular consciousness. On a continent so full of violence and radicalism, Nigeria came to seem from afar like a calm, trustworthy, even conservative nation. For all its domestic turmoil, it did not have a significant movement that advocated Marxist or even a mainstream socialist solution to the country's problems.[2]

The nature of the crisis which the Nigerian state was undergoing when the military overthrew the Shagari government was such that it could be categorised as *organic* . . . the December 1983 coup was not just a military intervention in the usual conventional sense, but rather a decisive political intervention by an armed fraction of the Nigerian dominant classes aimed at saving the state (in this case, a "stunted" one, ie. of the neo-colonial genre) from imminent collapse.[3]

The foreign policy of the Federation of Nigeria is in certain respects atypical, in others fairly representative of . . . African states . . . . On many African and international issues, its policy has been surprisingly modest and restrained. This is a quite remarkable position, considering the fact that . . . several Nigerian leaders pioneered in the African nationalist awakening.[4]

In just 25 years since independence, Nigeria has experienced a meteoric rise and fall in its foreign policy status and success;[5] the continuing decline in the price of petroleum highlights the precipitousness of this fall from grace. In its wake, national regimes have been removed, civilian and military alike, and foreign policy analyses have been revised. The fanciful notion, apparently held by scholars as well as statesmen, that Nigeria was Africa's great power and was prepared to follow declarations with actions has been discarded almost as quickly as it was discovered. The last decade has thus witnessed a rapid sequence of political and intellectual assertiveness followed by a new mood of reevaluation, redefinition, and retreat.

POLITICAL ECONOMY AND
FOREIGN POLICY: FROM
RENTIER TO DEBTOR STATE

There was and remains an element of truth in claims for Nigeria's distinctiveness. It is still *primus inter pares* in West Africa and an influential actor in continental and global affairs. But it did exaggerate its potential and overextend its capacity in the late 1970s and early 1980s.[6] Thus the current period of revisionism should not overlook the continuing as well as changeable bases of Nigeria's political economy and foreign policy. Unlike so much of the continent in crisis, Nigeria has both ebullience and resilience: Nigerian capitalism remains

1. R. O. Ogunbambi, "The Dilemma of Nigeria's African Policy," *Journal of African Studies*, 12(1):12 (Spring 1985).

2. Sanford J. Ungar, *Africa: The People and Politics of an Emerging Continent* (New York: Simon & Schuster, 1985), p. 155.

3. Herbert Ekwe-Ekwe, "The Nigerian Plight: Shagari to Buhari," *Third World Quarterly,* 7(3):617, 618 (July 1985).

4. James S. Coleman, "The Foreign Policy of Nigeria," in *Foreign Policies in a World of Change,* ed. Joseph E. Black and Kenneth W. Thompson (New York: Harper & Row, 1963), p. 379.

5. See Timothy M. Shaw and Olajide Aluko, eds., *Nigerian Foreign Policy: Alternative Perceptions and Projections* (London: Macmillan, 1983), esp. pp. 1-34 and 164-90.

6. See Pauline H. Baker, "A Giant Staggers: Nigeria as an Emerging Regional Power," in *African Security Issues: Sovereignty, Stability and Solidarity,* ed. Bruce E. Arlinghaus (Boulder, CO: Westview Press, 1984), pp. 76-97.

resourceful and potentially resurgent. The new modesty in Nigeria's stance may be welcome by neighbors and supporters alike, but it should not lead to an underestimation or misperception of Nigeria's not inconsiderable power and potential, both now and in the future.

The seemingly dramatic sequence in Nigeria's foreign policy fortunes and economic frustrations since the start of the 1980s is essentially a function of changing internal—political—and external—financial—regimes: the return of the generals and the demise of petro-naira. Underlying apparent constraints and cycles, however, is a large and active political economy. Nigeria's agricultural base has been overshadowed and undermined by the preoccupation with petroleum, but it has not been altogether ruined. Although the inherited colonial commodity structure of cocoa, palm oil, and groundnuts has shrunk, food production and distribution remain fundamental bases of the national economy. Likewise, under the imperative of foreign exchange restrictions, local manufacturing may yet come to rely on internal rather than imported inputs. In short, Nigeria's massive market of almost 100 million still offers potential opportunities and profits not found elsewhere on the continent. The ubiquitous informal economy, without its smuggling and black-marketeering elements, could be recognized as one vehicle of exchange and survival, particularly if its female bases were appreciated.

Windfall results from the petro-naira bubble generated fanciful notions of instant industrialization and continental dominance at the level of the state. But these were always elusive because at the level of individuals, private enrichment took precedence over collective goods. Traditional forms of inducement esca-

lated into unprecedented plunder: "dash" became rape. The leadership aspirations of the country were undermined by the consumption habits of its citizens. For only a decade—1971-81—Nigeria attracted an unending stream of merchant venturers, and a few Nigerians exported the proceeds of the loot. Meanwhile, indigenous capacities were diminished and international involvements were short-lived. With the inevitable bursting of the bubble in the early 1980s the rentier state became a debtor state and the soldiers returned to abort the second Shagari presidency.[7]

The Second Republic, from 1979 to 1983, marked the zenith and decline of Nigeria's aspirations to become, overnight, both a newly industrializing and a newly influential country (NIC). The erstwhile Brazil of Africa had not properly laid the foundations for its elevation into a NIC despite the relative subordination of its surrounding territories. Nigerian capitalism was too rapacious and impatient: the technocratic fraction of the indigenous bourgeoisie that sought to invest in infrastructure, technology, and basic needs never had a chance against bureaucratic, comprador, military, and political fractions.[8] Even the petite bourgeoisie was mesmerized by dreams of petro-naira contracts and affluence. The future would obviously take care of itself, so the fourth five-year plan announced, if the price of oil just remained around $40 a barrel. The 1985-86 15-month economic emergency

7. See Toyin Falola and Julius O. Ihonvbere, *The Rise and Fall of Nigeria's Second Republic, 1979-84* (London: Zed, 1985), pp. 206-34.

8. See Timothy M. Shaw and Orobola Fasehun, "Nigeria in the World System: Alternative Approaches, Explanations and Projections," *Journal of Modern African Studies,* 18(4):551-73 (Dec. 1980).

indicates just how inappropriate that assumption was.

Even sweet Bonny Light never reached this apex, so Nigeria's grandiose schemes were never feasible, regardless of whether significant percentages of each contract had or had not gone into European bank accounts or exhorbitant local costs. The obverse of Nigeria's massive market is the demand for basic services, which the state was never able to satisfy. Despite partisan and ethnic claims to the contrary, social services have never been free or extensive in Nigeria in pre- or post-independence eras. Bourgeois inclinations have moderated redistributive measures and reinforced competitive, acquisitive urges: private rather than public good has always been the game in Nigeria. The most visible indicators of such individualistic values were the dramatic arson fires set along the marina in the old External Affairs and new international telecommunications buildings, intended to destroy incriminating evidence of embourgeoisement. In general, personal aggrandizement took precedence over collective advancement.

The corruption of Nigerian society, reinforced by the trauma of civil war, was intensified by the petroleum boom and partisan tension. The Gowon and Obasanjo periods were hardly pristine, yet the scope and scale of private plunder then was minuscule compared to the sacking of the public purse under the hapless Shagari regime, an era of personal jets and fortunes. The size of the acquisitiveness and aggrandizement became apparent with the revelations of the Irikife Commission on oil revenues and the Johnson Matthey banking inquiry. The precipitous decline in oil prices undermined the logic of corruption and accumulation; networks and coali- tions based on the trickle-down of cash quickly disintegrated, to be replaced in the second set of national elections in mid-1983 by widespread rigging. Buhari inherited a disillusioned populace and an exhausted exchequer on New Year's Eve 1984. But his reformism was not enough; even Shagari had attempted to deflate expectations of further growth before his ignominious removal. It took a second palace putsch to bring king- maker Babangida to power in mid- 1985—a man in Murtala's mold—to take a grip on the constraints and chal- lenges of debt.

DEBATES AND DIRECTIONS

Nigeria's distinctive political eco- nomy, from boom to bust, has been placed on center stage by recent radical analysis.[9] Prior to the oil era there was little such critical discussion or organ- ization, notwithstanding the searing experience of a civil war. But in the decade of the 1970s, as the economy appeared poised for takeoff, as tertiary education mushroomed, and as national pride expanded, a few skeptical voices began to be raised: Did Nigeria really have the resources and the resilience to become a NIC? Was Nigerian capitalism capable of transcending its colonial, comprador origins? Was oil power a feasible foreign policy stance in the new international division of labor? And could capitalist black Nigeria confront capitalist white South Africa given that both were central to multinational cor- porations' African activities? In short, could an extroverted economy sustain an activist diplomacy?[10] As the 1980s

9. See Falola and Ihonvbere, *Rise and Fall of Nigeria's Second Republic,* pp. 1-17; Ekwe- Ekwe, "Nigerian Plight."

10. See, inter alia, Olajide A. Bamisaye and Julius O. Ihonvbere, "Policy Priorities and the

dawned, the nationalists were still assertive, the realists skeptical, and the materialists critical. The balance in this debate was already moving away from the nationalists and toward the realists and materialists as the period of austerity and instability began.[11]

Studies of Nigerian foreign policy and political economy reflect the state's international salience and internal divisiveness: they are important and intense. They are also largely indigenous, reflective of the multiplication and expansion of Nigeria's universities and research institutes in the last 10 to 15 years. Like the national political economy and culture, most have been orthodox in their mode of analysis; diplomatic history, international relations, strategic studies, and decision making still dominate the field of Nigerian foreign policy.[12] However, as the limits of power—as concept and currency—became apparent, as more radical inquiries into political eco-

nomy were popularized, and as the national economy went into decline, alternative approaches were recognized.[13] This revisionist mood has drawn strength from the international trend toward political economy, whether materialist or not, as well as from the national tendency toward reevaluation.

The continued resilience of the dominant, nationalist genre is symbolized by the elevation of one of its major advocates, Bolaji Akinyemi, to the post of foreign minister under Babangida. One of Nigeria's leading scholars and advisers,[14] who as director of the prestigous Nigerian Institute of International Affairs for eight crucial years, 1975-83, advised and criticized leaders and diplomats from Murtala to Buhari, Akinyemi now has the opportunity to reorient foreign policy in very different circumstances. He has often advocated more assertiveness in external relations, being particularly insistent that Nigeria should put Africa first and challenge the West more.[15] It was not that he pre-

Crisis of Development in Contemporary Nigeria," *Journal of General Studies,* 4(1):74-85 (Dec. 1983); Emeka Nwokedi, "Sub-regional Security and Nigerian Foreign Policy," *African Affairs,* 84(235):195-209 (Apr. 1985); Oye Ogunbadejo, "Nuclear Capacity and Nigeria's Foreign Policy," in *Africa Contemporary Record,* vol. 16, *1983-1984,* ed. Colin Legum (New York: Africana, 1985), pp. A136-A151.

11. Timothy M. Shaw, "Introduction: Nigeria as Africa's Major Power," in *Nigerian Foreign Policy,* ed. Shaw and Aluko, pp. 1-20; cf. Tunde Adeniran et al., "Papers on International Relations," in *Proceedings of National Conference on Nigeria since Independence,* vol. 1, *Political Development,* ed. J. A. Atanda and A. Y. Aliyu (Zaria: Gaskiya, 1985), pp. 188-303.

12. Ibid. For confirmation that traditional scholarship remains dominant even in the mid-1980s, see Olajide Aluko, "The Study of Nigerian Foreign Policy" (Paper delivered at the International Studies Association Conference, Anaheim, CA, Mar. 1986); Alaba Ogunsanwo, *Our Friends, Their Friends: Nigeria's External Relations, 1960-85* (Yaba: Alfa Communications, 1986).

13. See Falola and Ihonvbere, *Rise and Fall of Nigeria's Second Republic,* pp. 235-65.

14. See, inter alia, A. Bolaji Akinyemi, ed., *Nigeria and the World: Readings in Nigerian Foreign Policy* (Ibadan: Oxford University Press for Nigerian Institute of International Affairs, 1978); idem, *Foreign Policy and Federalism: The Nigerian Experience* (Ibadan: Ibadan University Press, 1974), passim; idem, "Mohammed/Obasanjo Foreign Policy," in *Nigerian Government and Politics under Military Rule, 1966-79,* ed. Oyeleye Oyediran (London: Macmillan, 1979), pp. 150-68.

15. A. Bolaji Akinyemi, "Nigerian Foreign Policy in 1975: National Interest Redefined," in *Survey of Nigerian Affairs, 1975,* ed. Oyeleye Oyediran (Ibadan: Oxford University Press for Nigerian Institute of International Affairs, 1978), pp. 106-14; idem, "Nigerian-American Relations Reexamined," in *Survey of Nigerian Affairs, 1976-77,* ed. Oyeleye Oyediran (Lagos: Macmillan for Nigerian Institute of International Affairs, 1981), pp. 105-14.

ferred more radical economics or non-aligned politics, just greater visibility and influence.

It may be difficult to repeat the diplomatic victories associated with Angola[16] and Zimbabwe since the global context has changed and the liberation of either Namibia or South Africa is more problematic. Further, in regional affairs, Nigeria has sustained a series of bloodly noses, from Chad to the Cameroons, as well as administered arbitrary expulsion notices to aliens in 1983 and 1985. Thus Akinyemi may have to revise his optimistic estimations about the salience of the oil weapon as well as refrain his personal outspokenness given the disciplined hierarchy of military government. His initial forays into West African, Commonwealth, and European relations have hardly been triumphal: bureaucratic clout lies under post-civilian and post-petroleum regimes with supreme headquarters and financial ministries.[17]

Akinyemi's elevation and redesignation remain symbolic, however, of the acceptability and respectability of the realist paradigm in Nigerian foreign policy. His predecessor as foreign minister, Ibrahim Gambari, was also drawn from and has returned to orthodox academe, incidentally succeeding Akinyemi, albeit briefly, as director of the Nigerian Institute of International Affairs in

1983.[18] And the Murtala-Obasanja foreign minister, Joe Garba, is back at the United Nations. In short, despite differences in emphasis and style, Nigeria does have a foreign policy elite that moves in and out of universities, institutes like the Nigerian Institute of International Affairs in Lagos and National Institute (for Policy and Strategic Studies) at Kuru, and governments. Characteristic of such an informed, attentive public was the April 1986 National Conference on Foreign Policy Options to the Year 2000, held at Kuru. At this conference, a successor to the earlier Adedeji review panel, Akinyemi's essential nationalism was criticized for being unradical and unrealistic.

Symptomatic of the continued acceptability of orthodox social science is the high proportion of establishment scholars in the 17-person Political Bureau set up in early 1986 to organize a further national debate, following that on finance, on the return to civilian rule by 1990. Unlike the large Constitutional Drafting Committee of the mid-1970s, the mid-1980s' group is less broadly based; there is little danger of a critical Osoba-Usman minority report this time. Likewise, notwithstanding the widespread availability of more radical analysis, it has yet to achieve a degree of acceptance, especially perhaps in a renewed military era.[19]

16. Cyril Kofie Daddieh and Timothy M. Shaw, "The Political Economy of Decision-making in Africa Foreign Policy: The Cases of Recognition of Biafra and the MPLA," *International Political Science Review,* 5(1):21-46 (Jan. 1984), reprinted in *How Foreign Policy Decisions Are Made: A Comparative Analysis,* ed. Baghat Korany (Boulder, CO: Westview Press, 1986), pp. 61-85.

17. Fidel Odum, "Foreign Policy under Military: Akinyemi's Blues," *African Concord,* 70:12 (12 Dec. 1985); idem, "Akinyemi Interviewed: Wanted—Union of Regional Powers," ibid., pp. 8-11.

18. Ibrahim Gambari, "Nigeria and the World," *Journal of International Affairs,* 29(2):155-69 (Fall 1975); idem, *Party Politics and Foreign Policy: Nigeria under the First Republic* (Zaria: Amadu Bello University Press, 1980), passim.

19. On the earlier military period, to late 1979, see the informed critical analyses by John F.E. Ohiorhenuan, "The Political Economy of Military Rule in Nigeria," *Review of Radical Political Economics,* 16(2-3):1-27 (Summer and Fall 1984); A. T. Gana, "Dependent Industrialization, Foreign

Thus, despite the intense International Monetary Fund (IMF) debate, the trend in Nigeria is toward revived capitalism rather than innovative socialism. The climate of austerity has led to renewed emphasis on agriculture and local inputs and on production rather than consumption or defense; it has yet to recognize women's work and the informal sector. The mood favors privatization and retrenchment rather than parastatals and mega-projects. In the process of reorientation, the poor as well as the rich will suffer as deregulation and desubsidization lead to higher costs, smaller incomes, and fewer services. Yet support for Babangida's reformism is more resilient than that for Buhari as the latter was seen to be too beneficent toward Shagari's entourage and too disrespectful of human rights.

The August 1985 coup was a reaction against repression as well as against recession; Nigerians are as laissez-faire in politics and debate as they are in economics and exchange.[20] Their democratic—as well as anarchistic!—inclinations cannot be contained for long by either soldiers or politicians. This poses problems for orderly process, but it also ensures opposition to intrusive praetorians. Renewed liberalization in economics thus balances continued liberalism in politics: the so-called Kaduna mafia constitutes both checks and balances on political and economic pressures.[21]

FROM OIL POWER TO NAIRA DEVALUATION

Although Babangida's reformism may limit some of the excesses of previous regimes—mega-projects, state proliferation, capital city, and massive corruption—it cannot quickly escape the legacy of misgovernment and misjudgment.[22] Deflationary pressure has moderated popular expectations arising from the petro-naira dream, but it cannot eliminate them entirely. Moreover, the mix of aristocracy and meritocracy, let alone influence and corruption, is too immediate to control bourgeois urges. Nigeria is a class, as well as ethnic, society, a correlate of capitalism as well as regionalism. Class inequalities may become more intense as deflation and population increase. While the illusion of expansion continued, antagonisms could be moderated by promises and handouts. Now that contraction is all too apparent—oil doom rather than boom—such social controls may be less effective.[23] The several Maitaitsine riots in the northern half of the country may thus constitute

Policy and the Dynamics of Class Struggle in Nigeria, 1960-1980," *Nigerian Journal of International Studies,* 5-7:62-80 (1981-83).

20. Timothy M. Shaw, "Nigerian Coups and Foreign Policy," *International Perspectives,* pp. 17-19 (Nov.-Dec. 1985).

21. Ekwe-Ekwe claims that this northern "mafia," a faction in the country's dominant power bloc, has been "largely responsible for planning and executing all military coups in

Nigeria in the past twenty years. "Nigerian Plight," p. 619. See also Adebayo Olukoshi and Tajudeen Abdulraheem, "Nigeria: Crisis Management under the Buhari Administration," *Review of African Political Economy,* 34:95, 96-101 (Dec. 1985).

22. For an orthodox perspective, see Akinola A. Owosekun, "A Case Study of Stabilisation Measures in Nigeria," *Africa Development,* 10(1-2).208-16 (1985); J. O. Aderibigbe "The Current Austerity Measures and Their Impact on the Nigerian Economy," ibid., pp. 217-35. Cf. C. I. Igweonwu, "The Economic Component of the Nation's Foreign Policy Formulation: A Neglected Issue," *Nigerian Forum,* 5(5 and 6):106-15 (May and June 1985); Femi Aribisala, "The Management of Austerity in Contemporary Nigeria," ibid., pp. 147-56.

23. For a more radical perspective, see Yusufu Bala Usman, "Understanding and Resolving the Current Economic Crisis in Nigeria," *Africa Development,* 10(1-2):169-207 (1985).

not so much Muslim fanaticism as popular reaction.[24] Nigeria's substantial but disorganized military and police resources may thus be called upon increasingly to contain proletarian and peasant alienation. Conversely, the unreliability of state services combined with difficulties of urban life may combine to deproletarianize and de-urbanize some marginal social elements. A return to the land for personal survival may also advance national self-reliance and social order, reducing pressure on and by the state: a distinctive variety of Third World deregulation.[25]

Meanwhile, although Nigeria has steadfastly declined unacceptable IMF conditions, it has never abandoned capitalist principles and predilections. The balances between state and private sectors and between bureaucratic, national, and comprador factions may shift,[26] but the mixed economy has greater longevity than any national constitution. The early 1986 budget revealed determination to balance accounts as well as interests: IMF terms without the loans. Yet if Nigeria can administer and absorb its own medicine, it may yet become less extroverted: not so dependent on either oil exports or imports of food, manufactures, and inputs. Moreover, a less over-heated economy may direct more attention to repair and rehabilitation than to inappropriate and grandiose projects while needing less labor migration and capturing more local multiplier effects. Any deemphasizing of the import-export sector will reduce the prospects for corruption, particularly smuggling and black marketeering.

In short, de facto devaluation and desubsidization may give the political economy a necessary breathing space to moderate expectations, repair much damage, and restructure social and economic relations. In turn, these changes may yet provide a more realistic and sustainable basis for foreign policy interests into the next century.[27]

RESILIENCE
WITHOUT ARROGANCE

The new realism in political economy apparent in Babangida's first months may spill over into foreign policy aspirations and analyses. If Nigeria can take its own medicine—economic and political, social and psychological—then it may yet be able to lay the foundation for a successful post-petroleum period.[28] In this eventuality, its external as well as internal goals may become more modest, but also more attainable. The petronaira era generated inflation in both economy and diplomacy: Africa's great power was to lead the continent toward liberation and integration. Instead, Ni-

24. See Paul M. Lubeck, "Crisis, Authoritarianism and Labour: The Popular Classes under the Buhari Regime"(Paper delivered at the African Studies Association Conference, New Orleans, LA, Nov. 1985).

25. See Naomi Chazan and Timothy M. Shaw, eds., *Coping with Africa's Food Crisis: A Comparative Study of Popular Responses* (Boulder, CO: Lynne Rienner, forthcoming).

26. For an informed analysis of national and international capital in Nigeria, see Bjorn Beckman, "Neo-colonialism, Capitalism and the State in Nigeria,"in *Contradictions of Accumulation in Africa: Studies in Economy and State,* ed. Henry Bernstein and Bonnie K. Campbell (Beverly Hills, CA: Sage, 1985), pp. 71-145.

27. See Olajide Aluko, "Nigerian Foreign Policy in the Year 2000," in *Nigerian Foreign Policy,* ed. Shaw and Aluko, pp. 191-204; idem, "Nigerian Foreign Policy under the Second Republic"(Paper delivered at the Canadian Association of African Studies Conference, Montreal, May 1985).

28. See Olusegun Obasanjo, "Nigeria: Which Way Forward?" *West Africa,* 3547:1694-95 (19 Aug. 1985); Larry Diamond, "Nigeria Update," *Foreign Affairs,* 64(2):326-36 (Winter 1985-86).

geria has witnessed the slowing down, even reversal, of change in southern Africa along with ambiguous progress toward regionalism in West Africa. These tendencies were always present, masked momentarily by the oil boom. The bursting of the bubble has led to renewed recognition of the essential characteristics of Nigeria's political economy: a distinctive mixed economy along with an irrepressible openness of politics, media, and expression. Wars against indiscipline can never work for long in Nigeria's ebullient social culture; austerity can only briefly dampen the national spirit.

Yet sustained revival of the economy and diplomacy can only be effected if the dynamism of Nigeria's political economy is directed away from corruption and toward production.[29] Such a basic reorientation would require a transformation in national policies and alliances, for underlying the outward orientation is the continuing dominance of comprador elements—the ubiquitous import-export traders and agents. If the military, along with more nationalistic and technocratic elements in the local elite, can contain this group and encourage national, rather than international, capital and accumulation,[30] the economy may be able to sustain itself, achieving eventually that elusive takeoff point promised many years ago by Walt Rostow and other modernization theorists: the NIC dream. If, however, the Babangida regime controls the economy only long enough for another period of spendthriftness, the unending cycle of importation, corruption, and accumulation abroad will remain unbroken: the foreign exchange nightmare.

The Mohammed-Obasanjo interregnum pointed the way that Babangida seems determined, in different circumstances, to take. But any premature return to either civilian or comprador rule will lead to the evaporation of gains and a return to cynicism and confrontation. Radical forces may yet be embryonic in laissez-faire Nigeria, but the mixture of austerity for most and affluence for the minority will help generate the oft-predicted revolutionary pressures.[31] The real choice for Nigeria, then, despite the rhetoric of the political, IMF, and foreign policy debates, is not between civilian and military rule or between socialism and barbarism, but rather between different capitalisms: more or less successful and more or less indigenous.

NIGERIA TOWARD THE TWENTY-FIRST CENTURY

Nigeria's longer-term future has suffered from inflation of both aspiration and situation. Even before the oil decade, Nigeria was one of Africa's few major actors; even without the petro-naira period it would have wielded a certain influence if it had been judicious in balancing capabilities with targets.[32] But just as the economy had to go into a real tailspin before austerity and emergency

29. See Douglas Rimmer, "The Overvalued Currency and Over-administered Economy of Nigeria," *African Affairs,* 84(336):435-46 (July 1986); "Nigeria: Striking a Delicate Balance," *Time,* 17 Feb. 1986, pp. 44-45.

30. See Ohiorhenuan, "Political Economy of Military Rule," pp. 10-23; Beckman, "Neo-colonialism, Capitalism and the State," pp. 92-110.

31. See Claude Ake, *Revolutionary Pressures in Africa* (London: Zed, 1978), pp. 95-107.

32. See Olajide Aluko, "Necessity and Freedom in Nigerian Foreign Policy," *Nigerian Journal of International Studies,* 4(182):1-15 (Jan. and June 1980).

were declared, so diplomacy had to be discredited before the dawning of any new realism. If Nigeria's current modesty of style and goal is maintained, it may once again achieve acceptability and visibility.[33] If personal or national aggrandizement is rekindled prematurely, however, Nigeria's credibility may be undermined for many years to come. The more realistic elements in the military, industry, universities, parties, and other sectors need to take the more chauvinistic groups in hand, a not inconsiderable task.

The internal bases of foreign policy as well as external ambitions and conditions will determine Nigeria's success rate. In this century's remaining decade and a half, domestic capabilities will depend in part on external terms of trade. The salience of the latter can be minimized if more autonomous development directions are adopted along the lines of the International Labor Organization's *First Things First:* more rural, agricultural, basic-needs-oriented development that also produces more inputs for the presently stymied manufacturing sector.[34]

The internalization of Nigeria's inherited extroverted economy—a slow but sure path to development—affords greater prospects for sustained expansion and influence than any short-lived windfall from the Organization of Petroleum Exporting Countries. Of course, another Middle East war might revive the price and demand for oil, but, until the year 2000, projected structural changes in the world economy—yielding a postindustrial, post-petroleum period—will likely keep both down. The conjuncture of internal inflation and instability with external contraction and devaluation has been difficult, yet ultimately therapeutic. It may constitute a new basis for a set of innovative external as well as domestic relations, notably those with the European Economic Community and the United States, on the one hand, and with Africa, on the other.[35]

The real issue remains, however, whether Babangida can succeed where Mohammed was prevented: the transformation of Nigeria's political economy from oil dependence to national independence. Will Nigeria be self-reliant or will it continue to be vulnerable to international forces, fancies, and futures? Will Africa's ambitious newly industrializing and newly influential country of the 1970s become a newly insignificant country in the 1990s?[36] The new realism about both national economy and foreign policy satisfies at least one prerequisite:

On its 25th anniversary, Africa's most populous nation—and potential superstate—has precious little to celebrate. Like most of the continent, Nigeria is economically broke,

33. See "Gambari Interviewed: Nigeria's Foreign Policy under the Military—a New Direction?" *New Nigerian,* pp. 8-9 (19 Feb. 1984); "Tête-à-Tête: Dr. Ibrahim A. Gambari," *Spectrum,* 1(3-4):11-23 (Mar.-June 1984).

34. See International Labor Organization, *First Things First: Meeting the Basic Needs of the People of Nigeria* (Addis Ababa: JASPA, 1981). See also Adebayo Adedeji, "Some Reflections on Nigeria's Economic Performance since Independence and Thoughts on Future Prospects" (Pamphlet, Economic Commission for Africa, Sept. 1985).

35. Sanford Ungar points to this central contradiction in his *Africa,* p. 150: "Nigeria's political and economic evolution has focused new attention on its role within Africa and in the Third World generally. The main trend in Nigerian foreign policy in recent years has been to forge close political, economic, and even philosophical ties with the United States, all the while reasserting Nigeria's adherence to the principles of nonalignment and African unity."

36. See Shaw, "Nigerian Coups and Foreign Policy," p. 19.

politically unstable and tribally divided. But unlike much of Africa, its leaders are at least prepared to concede this reality.[37]

As the late James Coleman noted in his pioneering study of Nigeria's foreign policy, Nigeria's "comparative 'moderation'" was always a source of disappointment to nationalist "patriots who had hoped that their country would assume a more 'dynamic' role of leadership in African and world affairs, a role they believed it was destined by size and population to play."[38] On the other hand, external forces constrained this activism and external interests encouraged the conservatism, merely reinforcing dominant political and intellectual forces.[39] Jim Coleman's caution,

expressed in the early 1960s, is still relevant 25 years later. That is, although new elites in the Third World have enjoyed "considerable autonomy and freedom of action in their conduct of foreign relations," choice is limited: "Nigeria's foreign policy is affected by such basic factors as Nigeria's geography, the character of the Nigerian population, as well as the relevant aspects of Nigeria's history, early as well as recent, her economy, and her political system."[40]

The salience and ranking of such factors remain issues in contemporary Nigerian foreign policy analysis and practice: *plus ça change. . . !*

---

37. "Editorial: Nigeria under Gen. Babangida," *Globe and Mail,* 10 Oct. 1985.

38. Coleman, "Foreign Policy of Nigeria," p. 379.

39. On resistance to radical or theoretical analyses of Nigerian foreign policy as well as on

current financial and organizational constraints— "the future prospects for the study of Nigerian foreign policy are not bright"—see Aluko, "Study of Nigerian Foreign Policy," p. 13.

40. Coleman, "Foreign Policy of Nigeria," p. 380.

ANNALS, *AAPSS*, **489**, January 1987

Francophone Africa: The
Enduring French Connection

By MARTIN STANILAND

ABSTRACT: France's relations with its former colonies remain close after 26 years of independence, and France has tried hard in the last decade to expand its sphere of influence beyond the ex-colonial core. This article examines French economic and security interests in Africa, as well as the role of Africa in France's foreign policy. It also considers some of the contradictions in French policy, the problems encountered by the Socialist government between May 1981 and March 1986, and the longer-term trend toward greater discretion and discrimination in dealing with African states. Finally, it discusses the analytic problems raised by the peculiar postcolonial relationship between France and French-speaking Africa.

Martin Staniland is an associate professor in the Graduate School of Public and International Affairs at the University of Pittsburgh. He has written books on politics in northern Ghana and on theories of political economy, as well as articles on politics in Ghana, Benin, and the Ivory Coast. He is currently working on a book about American responses to African nationalism.

NOTE: This article was made possible by a grant from the Howard Heinz Endowment of Pittsburgh.

A French scholar recently noted that ministers of French-speaking African states make some 2000 visits to Paris in an average year. Between 1960 and 1978, another scholar has calculated, French and African presidents held 280 meetings, and Presidents de Gaulle, Pompidou, and Giscard d'Estaing made 32 state visits to Africa.[1]

What sustains this close relationship between France and the French-speaking countries? Why does it survive in such apparent vigor when relations between ex-imperial countries and ex-colonies are so often clouded by suspicion and hostility? And what kind of relationship is it?

FRANCE AND THE
FRANCOPHONE FAMILY

While France and its African partners have a number of institutions, historical experiences, and cultural conceptions in common, it is misleading to speak of one relationship. Of the 20 so-called Francophone states, 15—Mauritania, Senegal, Mali, Guinea, Burkina Fasso (previously Upper Volta), the Ivory Coast, Niger, Benin, Chad, the Central African Republic, Gabon, the Congo, Madagascar, Djibouti, and the Comoros—were previously direct dependencies of France; 2—Togo and Cameroon—were French-administered U.N. trust territories; and 3 were ruled by Belgium—Zaire as a colonial territory, Rwanda and Burundi as trust territories.

During the 26 years since independence, France has developed an indi-vidual relationship with each state. From France's point of view, its trustiest allies are to be found in the heartland of the defunct French West African and French Equatorial African federations.[2] The Ivory Coast and Senegal stand out as two countries that have had leaders whose political careers were intimately involved with French political history throughout the Fourth and Fifth Republics.[3] Roughly 50,000 French citizens now reside in the Ivory Coast and 20,000 in Senegal. Both countries house French bases and still have defense agreements providing for French intervention in case of internal or external threat; both continue to receive high levels of aid and investment.

The closeness of the governments of Gabon, Togo, and Zaire to France is less sentimental, more recent, and more conditional in character. In states such as Mali, Niger, Cameroon, and Mauritania, France is now dealing with leaders who have come to power since independence, in many cases following several

---

1. Alfred Grosser, *Affaires extérieures: La politique de la France 1944-1984* (Paris: Flammarion, 1984), p. 176; Brigitte Nouaille-Degorce, *La politique française de coopération avec les états africains et malgache au sud du Sahara* (Bordeaux: Centre d'étude d'Afrique noire, 1982), pp. 463-65.

2. French West Africa consisted of Mauritania, Senegal, Mali (then Soudan), Guinea, the Ivory Coast, Niger, Benin (then Dahomey), and Burkina Fasso, with Togo attached for administrative purposes; French Equatorial Africa consisted of Chad, the Central African Republic (then Ubangi-Shari), Gabon, and the Congo, with Cameroon attached. Both federations were dissolved in 1960 and the individual territories became independent on their own, despite various attempts to reestablish regional entities.

3. Félix Houphouët-Boigny, president of the Ivory Coast, represented the territory in the French National Assembly from 1946 until 1959 and was a minister in four French governments between 1956 and 1959. Leopold Sedar Senghor, president of Senegal until 1981, also served in the French National Assembly for 14 years, and was a junior minister from 1955 to 1956. Other Francophone leaders who held senior political offices in France in the fifties included Modibo Keita, first president of Mali, and Sékou Touré, president of Guinea from 1958 until 1984.

others. Such leaders, while clearly oriented toward France, lack the sense of involvement with French politics—and the personal relations with French politicians—characteristic of the older generation. With these states—and with others such as Benin, the Congo, Burkina Fasso, and Madagascar that have adopted rhetorically anti-imperialist positions—France's relations fluctuate according to policies adopted and interests advanced, somewhat as with any foreign country.

Yet the latter comparison may be misleading. For better or worse, French relations with the Francophone states are not simply on a "state-to-state" basis, with all the individual self-sufficiency such a phrase implies. Some critics, in both Africa and France, argue that it would be better for all concerned if relations were more formalized: the loss of family feeling would be more than compensated for by the increased mutual respect and self-respect created by a normal international relationship. Indeed, radical critics suggest, such a demystification would expose just how depressingly normal the actual ingredients of French-African relations are—that is, just how much inequality, dependence, and exploitation are hidden under the republican rhetoric of liberty, equality, and fraternity.[4]

FRENCH-AFRICAN ECONOMIC RELATIONS

France is a major supplier of goods and services to the Francophone states

and a major purchaser of their exports, albeit on a much reduced scale compared with the early sixties. The significance of Africa as a trading partner for France has weakened, however. By 1979 only 3.1 percent of France's exports went to Africa, as against 6.3 percent in 1960, and only 2.1 percent of France's imports came from Africa, as against 6.7 percent in 1960. Between 1960 and 1975 France's share in the external trade of the Francophone countries declined from 80 percent to approximately 45 percent. But Francophone states, in the mid-eighties, were still depending on France for between 40 and 60 percent of imported goods and services.[5]

Within this general decline, some more specific trends have appeared. Following the more explicitly mercantilist direction in French policy, trade—as well as aid and investment—has become concentrated on three or four countries that are sufficiently developed to offer attractive markets and investment opportunities or that contain valuable energy and mineral reserves. Thus, in 1978, the Ivory Coast, Gabon, and Cameroon alone provided over two-thirds of French imports from former French dependencies in Africa and the same three took 68 percent of the French exports to the Francophone group.[6]

Pursuit of the same objective of securing markets and sources of fuels and strategic minerals has changed the composition of French imports. It has

4. For typical radical critiques of French African policy, see Guy Martin, "The Historical, Economic, and Political Bases of France's African Policy," *Journal of Modern African Studies,* 23:189-208 (June 1985); Rajen Harshe, "French Neo-Colonialism in Sub-Saharan Africa," *India Quarterly*, 36:159-78 (Apr.-June 1980).

5. John Chipman, *French Military Policy and African Security,* Adelphi Paper no. 201, (London: International Institute for Strategic Studies, 1985), p. 2; Philippe Hugon, "L'Afrique noire franocophone: L'enjeu économique pour la France," *Politique africaine*, 5:76, 77, 79 (Feb. 1982).

6. Hugon, "L'Afrique noire francophone," p. 81.

also led France to expand or repair its relations with countries that are not former French colonies. In 1983, energy and fuel products constituted over 62 percent of France's imports from Africa, with agricultural and food products comprising no more than 14 percent, a reversal of the balance obtaining in the colonial and early post-independence periods.

When Mitterrand came to power in 1981, French trade with all African countries represented only 7 percent of its external trade; between 1981 and 1984 no French trade minister visited sub-Saharan Africa.[7] French capital, traditionally wary of venturing abroad, has been particularly shy of African countries, because of poor investment conditions and the preference of African governments for state-controlled enterprises.

In 1979, only 20 percent of French public and private investments in less developed countries went to France's African ex-colonies, known collectively as the African and Malgache states. French investors have shown little interest in industrial development in Africa, preferring to promote extractive enterprises and very large and arguably wasteful prestige projects. Two notorious projects were the 22-story international commerce center in Kinshasa, Zaire—abandoned when the air-conditioning plant failed and it was found that none of the windows in the building

would open—and the Burundi color television scheme.[8]

Yet France's economic relations with Africa have been consistently useful to France in at least four respects. First, France has maintained a substantial trade surplus with Africa, compensating significantly for the deficit it suffers in its trade with other parts of the world. Although this surplus has diminished in the last four years, in 1981 it was equivalent to 10 percent of France's global deficit.[9]

Second, France's domination of Franc Zone institutions assured, at least until 1983, substantial liquidity for the French treasury. Twelve Francophone states have a common currency, the Communauté financière africaine (CFA) franc, which is tied to the French franc at a fixed rate of 50 CFA francs to 1 French franc and is issued by two central banks, for western and equatorial Africa, respectively. While the French treasury guarantees the convertibility of the CFA franc and provides "practically unlimited overdrafts" to the central banks, member states "are required to transfer at least 65 *per cent* of their foreign exchange earnings to the Bank of France."[10]

This system has been helpful to African countries in that it enables those with balance-of-payments problems to draw on foreign exchange reserves created by those in surplus. On the other hand, it involves a surrender of national autonomy in determining monetary pol-

7. Daniel C. Bach, "La France en Afrique subsaharienne: Contraintes historiques et nouveaux éspaces économiques," in *La politique extérieure de Valéry Giscard d'Estaing,* ed. Samy Cohen and Mari-Claude Smouts (Paris: Fondation nationale des sciences politiques, 1985), p. 305; Jean-François Bayart, *La politique africaine de François Mitterrand* (Paris: Karthala, 1984), p. 89.

8. See Benoît Verhaegen, "Les safaris technologiques au Zaïre," *Politique africaine,* 18:76-81 (June 1985); Bayart, *La politique africaine,* p. 44.

9. Bach, "La France en Afrique," p. 305. For more recent figures, see Martin, "France's African Policy," p. 199.

10. Antonio-Gabriel M. Cunha, "The Other Side of the Coin," *Africa Report,* 29:59 (Sept.-Oct. 1984).

icy and interest rates. Further, it makes the African currency hostage to the fortunes of the French franc and the French economy.

The third benefit is the dominance enjoyed by French companies providing services to commerce such as transportation and insurance. Finally, Africa is an important source of strategic raw materials for France, which in some cases has been granted preferential access to them.

FRENCH-AFRICAN SECURITY RELATIONS

In 1985, approximately 6800 French troops were stationed in Africa, mainly in Djibouti, Senegal, and the Central African Republic, with smaller contingents in Cameroon, Gabon, and the Ivory Coast. Such troops and the bases they occupy are not engaged in active conflicts, as are the forces dispatched at various times from France to Chad, Zaire, Mauritania, and a number of other Francophone states. Their role is that of a trip wire in case of internal or external threats to the security of the states in which they are located and in case of similar threats to others with which France has defense agreements.[11] These agreements date back to independence—that is, for most countries to 1960.

The number and content of the defense agreements have changed significantly, however, especially following an

11. On French strategic planning for Africa, see Pierre Lellouche and Dominique Moisi, "French Policy in Africa: A Lonely Battle against Destabilization," *International Security*, 3:108-33 (Spring 1979); Chipman, *French Military Policy and African Security*; Pascal Chaigneau, *La politique militaire de la France en Afrique* (Paris: Centre de hautes études sur l'Afrique et l'Asie modernes, 1984).

outburst of abrogations and revisions initiated by the African states in 1972. Only Senegal, the Ivory Coast, Togo, and Gabon publicly renewed the original defense treaties that provided for French intervention in the event of domestic or foreign challenges to the governments concerned and at their request. Similar defense arrangements have been made more recently, more secretly, or with more restricted provisions with Cameroon, Djibouti, the Comoros, and Zaire.

Such agreements, it should be noted, do not impose an obligation on France to intervene automatically on request. Indeed, French intervention has not been limited to countries that have signed defense accords. For instance, Chad, in particular, has no formal defense agreement with France. Moreover, the forces available for use in Africa are much greater than the 6800 currently based there.

Since the mid-sixties, French strategy has involved the maintenance in France of a sizable reserve earmarked for rapid deployment in Africa. This reserve was created as a way of ensuring that France would be able to support its treaty commitments in Africa. It was also meant to deter African and non-African countries from attacking Francophone states. Its establishment was, however, inspired as much by political as by military considerations, specifically by the desirability of shedding the neocolonial image created by a permanent stationing of large French garrisons in Africa. This image was confirmed in African eyes by several interventions, especially that in Gabon in 1964 when French forces flew in to reinstate President Léon Mba after the Gabonese army had overthrown him. Conceived as the third layer of a military structure comprising also the forces based abroad and the armies of the Francophone states, the intervention forces were reorganized under Giscard d'Estaing and again, in 1983, by Mitterrand. They now constitute a rapid deployment force, numbering up to 47,000 men, which is better equipped and has a broader mission than its predecessor.[12]

French-African military relations go well beyond provisions for intervention. Sixteen countries have military technical assistance agreements with France that allow France substantial influence over the training and weaponry of African and Malgache states. In 1985, over 1900 African officers were being trained in France, and arrangements for military aid give France a large say in determining the firepower of African forces, which has been kept modest. Indeed, through its role of supplier, France is able to shape the balance of power in the western and equatorial African regions. As John Chipman points out, "Careful not to overendow African armies, the French are able to ensure that it is difficult for one country to launch an attack on another."[13] Countries on the edge of aggression or conflict might hesitate, Chipman suggests, because of uncertainty about whom France, as a principal arms supplier, would favor.

AFRICA IN FRENCH FOREIGN POLICY

France—as the foregoing sections suggest—has some important, if limited, economic interests in Africa, as well as a military capacity with which to defend these and other interests. It remains to be asked, first, how France's diplomacy protects—and is shaped by—French interests, and, second, how France's diplomacy uses—and is limited by—French strategic resources.

Where, first, does Africa fit into French foreign policy? Its significance, as French policymakers frequently say, is to ensure major-power status for France. Africa provides a sphere of influence in which France is largely unchallenged by the superpowers. The possession of such an exclusive sphere provides, in turn, a right of entry to the club of world powers. Africa is a continent within France's means, which are now somewhat reduced. As one of Giscard's foreign ministers, Louis de Guiringaud, put it, "Africa is the only continent where France has the capacity to make a difference . . . the only one where she can still change the course of history with 500 men."[14]

This claim to global status and regional leadership is symbolized by the annual conferences, alternately in France and in Africa, of the French and Francophone African presidents held since 1973.[15] Attendance at these conferences has increased to include leaders from ex-Portuguese, ex-Spanish, and even ex-British territories, in accordance with the wish of all French presidents since de Gaulle to expand French influence beyond the inherited core of ex-French colonies. Such expansion involves risks.

12. Chipman, *French Military Policy and African Security*, pp. 15-16.
   13. Ibid., p. 22.

14. *L'express* (Paris), 22 Dec. 1979, p. 38, cited in Bach, "La France en Afrique," p. 285. In a later article, de Guiringaud remarked that "neither the size of [Africa's] population nor the scale of its economic problems are out of proportion to what France can devote to a long-term commitment abroad." Louis de Guiringaud, "La politique africaine de la France," *Politique étrangère*, 47:443 (June 1982).
   15. See Jean-Luc Dagut, "Les sommets franco-africains: Un instrument de la présence française en Afrique," in *Annee africaine 1980* (Bordeaux: Centre d'étude d'Afrique noire, 1981), pp. 304-25.

One is to seem to be challenging the Organization of African Unity; another is to antagonize would-be African powers, particularly Nigeria, whose leaders and intellectuals sometimes seem to regard their own country as the Prussia of Africa.

France's efforts to maintain influence in Africa pay off, in fact, in two superficially contradictory ways. First, they enable France to present itself, in old-fashioned geopolitical terms, as a power to be reckoned with. Second, they enable France, in a much more contemporary idiom, to pose as a champion of Third World countries. France's activities in Africa thus add to its credibility in two roles that it has sought to play more generally in international politics—that of alternative world leader to the United States and the Soviet Union, and that of intermediary between North and South.

Whether French diplomacy can actually realize such a combination, whatever its logical and aesthetic appeal, has been a challenge for policymakers and a common point of attack for critics. The combination of roles involves specific imperatives that can easily conflict with each other or lead to problems for a country of France's limited means.

One imperative is a need to maintain exclusivity in a sphere of influence. Since neither the United States nor the Soviet Union has shown any sustained interest in supplanting France in the African and Malgache states—although the French suspect otherwise—this need has created few difficulties. Under Giscard, French policymakers were, admittedly, alarmed by Soviet and Cuban actions in Angola and the Horn of Africa, while under Pompidou, Giscard, and Mitterrand, fear of an American incursion into France's sphere has been perennial—and deftly exploited by some Francophone leaders, notably Mobutu of Zaire and Bongo of Gabon.[16]

The real challenge to French influence arises when a Francophone state becomes an arena for confrontation between the superpowers, as seemed possible in Zaire in 1977 and 1978 and in Chad in 1983. Such situations could in theory enhance French influence, but in the cases cited they created outside pressures as well as the danger of France being seen as an agent of a superpower. Indeed, Giscard's critics, both Gaullist and Socialist, identified such a role when they said that France should not be "the gendarme of Africa," that is, a tool of American and other, non-French Western interests.

NETWORKS AND PERSONALISM

Maintaining a sphere of influence also involves cultivating relations with governments in the relevant area. Foreign policy in both France and the Francophone African countries tends to be a personal prerogative of presidents. Most African regimes, moreover, are highly personal in their constitutions, a fact invoked by French Africa hands—as well as interested African leaders—in support of their belief that in Africa political culture values the quality of individual relations over the formalities of bureaucratic—including diplomatic—procedure.[17] Critics claim that this culturalist view is essentially specious—

16. On Bongo's flirtation with the United States after Mitterrand's election, see Pierre Péan, *Affaires africaines* (Paris: Fayard, 1983), pp. 249-51. The French have recently shown some concern about Cameroon's drifting into the American orbit; see Celestin Monga, "Cameroun: La percée américaine inquiète la France," *Jeune Afrique* (Paris), 4 Dec. 1985, p. 63.

17. For an excellent discussion of the connection between images of African society and posi-

a rationalization for dictatorship and forms of nepotism and corruption associated with it.

The fact remains that Franco-African relations have been conducted within a tight, informal network. Central roles have been played in this network by French presidential aides, such as the famous Jacques Foccart, whose web of old Gaullist friends and African contacts gave him a fearsome reputation for omniscience and manipulation during his reign as secretary for African and Malagasy affairs between 1960 and 1974. In April 1986, to the astonishment of many in France and Africa, Foccart was appointed by the new prime minister, Jacques Chirac, as his adviser on African affairs.[18] The Foccart network included such secret service figures as Maurice Robert, whose African experience stretched back to the 1940s when, as principal of a school for soldiers' children, he became acquainted with two students, Seyni Kountché and Mathieu Kérékou, now presidents of Niger and Benin, respectively.[19] It also involved mercenaries like Robert Denard. Foccart himself described his job in

quite mundane terms as being concerned with "*copinage des présidents et la fin du mois*" ("keeping presidents happy and getting civil servants paid").[20]

Under Giscard and Mitterrand, similar go-betweens have been used, although none has acquired Foccart's aura of skulduggery. Since 1982, President Mitterrand's own son, Jean-Christophe, has been an assistant to Guy Penne, the president's adviser on African and Malagasy affairs. This appointment was naturally seen as confirming Mitterrand's fidelity to the tradition of informal diplomacy in Franco-African relations.

The problem with a diplomacy dependent upon personal acquaintance is obviously that of blurring the line between personal and official obligations. Loyalty to friends can take precedence over, or become confused with, the impersonal imperatives of foreign policy making. Interestingly, the French president most damaged by yielding to this temptation in conducting relations with African regimes was Giscard d'Estaing. Giscard, in a French diplomat's words, was "a man who was by character and temperament very remote from Africa, but who yielded to its charms and found there . . . a kind of counterweight to the intellectualism and analytic spirit which were extraordinarily dominant in his personality."[21] His political career was undoubtedly damaged by the personal friendships he formed with two notoriously brutal and corrupt African leaders, the Emperor Bokassa I of the Central African Republic and President Mobutu of Zaire.[22]

---

tions regarding French policy, see Bayart, *La politique africaine,* pp. 119-25.

18. As the *Economist* noted, "In bringing back this secretive Gaullist figure as his official adviser, Mr. Chirac could not have demonstrated more plainly that he sees Africa as his domain as much as Mr. Mitterrand's." "Foccart is Back," *Economist,* 5 Apr. 1986, p. 50.

19. Roger Raligot and Pascal Krop, *La Piscine: Les services secrets francais 1944-1984* (Paris: Editions de seuil, 1985), p. 228. Robert was appointed French ambassador to Gabon in 1979 at the instigation of President Bongo. In 1964, he had flown into Gabon with the French paratroops who reinstated Bongo's predecessor, Léon Mba. Péan, *Affaires africaines,* p. 139. On Foccart's role, see Samy Cohen, *Les conseilleurs du président* (Paris: Presses universitaires de France, 1980), pp. 146-69.

20. Quoted in Kaye Whiteman, "President Mitterrand and Africa," *African Affairs,* 82:336 (1983).

21. Pierre Hunt, "Témoignages et interventions," in Bach, "La France en Afrique," p. 319.

22. In October 1979 the French satirical

REALPOLITIK VERSUS
HUMAN RIGHTS

A similar, albeit less individualized, problem has dogged French African policy since 1981. Mitterrand was initially committed, as a Socialist and an advocate of human rights, to distancing himself from the more repressive and unsavory African leaders—"the scoundrels," as they were known among French foreign affairs experts. Typically, but not exclusively, this description referred to Mobutu, Bongo of Gabon, Dacko of the Central African Republic, and Touré of Guinea.[23] At the same time, he set out to mend relations with the more progressive Francophone regimes, such as those in Benin, the Congo, and, more recently, Burkina Fasso, as well as with socialist governments elsewhere in Africa, notably those in Tanzania, Angola, and Mozambique.

Quickly, however, the earlier pattern of domination by the old guard of conservative African autocrats reemerged. Previously criticized leaders such as

Mobutu, Bongo, and Touré were admitted to favor again or, indeed, courted. At least two major speeches on human rights to be delivered during Mitterrand's African tour in May 1982 were dropped, the president, in Daniel Bach's words, "not wishing to embarrass certain Francophone heads of state." Also, the non-Francophone government of Ethiopia was assured that, despite the French Socialist Party's commitment to self-determination for the rebellious province of Eritrea, the new French government recognized and supported Ethiopian sovereignty.[24]

Such realpolitik has naturally disappointed human rights advocates as well as the exiled opponenets of particular regimes. It reveals the costs and limitations of maintaining a post-imperial sphere of influence. It also, by implication, raises questions about French claims to speak for and intercede with the South in North-South matters. Is the Third World with which Giscard especially and Mitterrand have claimed a special affinity any other than the world of sometimes despotic and usually unelected leaders that, in its Francophone chapter, gathers annually to celebrate a unity, the actual political meaning of which remains obscure? And is it coincidental that those leaders whose "African genius for human relations" has given them specially privileged access in Paris happen also to control countries with valuable mineral resources or to be faithful diplomatic allies of France in such arenas as the United Nations?

---

weekly, *Le canard enchaîné*, revealed that Giscard had received presents of diamonds from Bokassa, both when Giscard was minister of finance and when he visited the Central African Republic as president. Giscard did not deny receiving such gifts, questioning only their alleged value. *Le canard enchaîné* later revealed that two cousins of the president had also accepted such gifts.

23. Bayart, *La politique africaine,* p. 23. The case of Guinea is particularly interesting. Having broken away from the proposed French community in 1958, it followed a completely different course from that taken by the other Francophone states until the mid-seventies. Ironically—considering Sékou Touré's socialism—the rapprochement was effected by the conservative Giscard, who, indeed, considered it one of the main achievements of his presidency. The Left was alienated from Touré because of his bad human rights record; this was a dislike Touré reciprocated, describing Mitterrand, when leader of the Socialist Party, as a "Nazi."

24. Daniel C. Bach, "La politique française en Afrique après le 10 mai 1981," *Année africaine 1981* (Paris: Pedone, 1983), p. 245. Bayart's book, *La politique africaine de François Mitterrand,* explores in detail the rapid reversion to business as usual under the French Socialists.

INTERVENTIONISM IN DECLINE

If the objectives and contradictions of French diplomacy in Africa have been fairly constant, the manner of its pursuit has nevertheless softened. Such softening—seen especially in French reluctance to intervene—may show a recognition of the true limits on France's power to control sovereign states as well as to solve their problems. It may also express an equally hardheaded acknowledgment that in economic and political terms French involvement in Africa has high costs and, at best, uncertain returns.[25]

Although France under Giscard d'Estaing resumed an aggressively interventionist posture in western and equatorial Africa, the long-term trend is clearly toward a more cautious and discriminating use of French forces abroad. Indeed, government spokesmen even under Giscard took great care to stress limited objectives and special circumstances. French public opinion, while favorable toward—even proud of—occasional projections of force abroad, is clearly skeptical about the value, for France, of longer-term military involvements in the service of ambitious and complex political strategies.

While Mitterrand has declared his support for continuing France's existing military commitments in Africa, it is clear that actual intervention will occur only in some very specific circumstances and when clearly requested by an African government. France is likely to reserve substantial discretion in responding to such requests. It is unlikely to be drawn into taking sides in domestic power struggles, as was shown when French troops stayed in barracks during the replacement of President Dacko of the Central African Republic in 1981. Also, France will be reluctant to act without the diplomatic—and preferably military—support of African states.[26]

Such caution reflects a reluctance to get burned diplomatically, as happened in 1979 when French troops deposed Bokassa in the then Central African Empire. Although Bokassa's regime had become a byword for cruelty and wastefulness, the sight of French troops, parading openly at Bangui airport—as a recent book puts it—"as if it was the Fourteenth of July" aroused African nationalists and domestic anti-imperialists alike.[27]

Such caution seems to express an accumulating skepticism about the value of any intervention beyond operations aimed strictly at protecting French lives and essential French interests. In the early sixties, Foccart justified French intervention as enabling the survival of those states that France—and specifically his master, de Gaulle—had created.[28] The intervening twenty years have shown the limits on French power to do more than ensure survival—and the case of Chad shows just how tenuous and hollow an achievement that can be. Over the years France's experience of intervention

25. Few French politicians and scholars advocate a complete disengagement from Africa, but the limits and costs of French influence are apparent to observers such as Daniel Bach, who writes: "France's initiatives will produce only limited results. France is ... committed to a costly policy of military and financial support which tends to obstruct the economic reorientations currently required. France remains the prisoner of a sphere of influence inherited from history." "La France en Afrique," pp. 307-10.

26. See Chipman, *French Military Policy and African Security*, pp. 14, 29.

27. Faligot and Krop allege that the French secret service hoped to install Bokassa's successor, Dacko, without it becoming known that French troops had accompanied him. *La Piscine*, p. 345.

28. Grosser, *Affaires extérieures*, p. 177.

in Africa has created a corresponding sense of its powerlessness to shape the forces generating the instability and the discontent that in turn create the crises precipitating intervention. Much the same can be said about the experience of French aid.

The broader problems of characterizing the French-African relationship and of explaining, as one observer put it, "why France gets away with it" lead to similar paradoxes and ambiguities.[29] Critics often present French policy as an extreme case of realpolitik in which diplomats, disdainful of public opinion at home and abroad, pursue the national interest, conceived narrowly as an unceasing quest for the power to dominate competing states. Close examination of French-African relations suggests that in fact the key to French success lies not in its diplomatic skill, but in the breadth of relationships, mainly cultural but also economic, connecting France to its ex-colonies—relationships of the kind to which old-fashioned high diplomacy was mostly indifferent.[30]

The strength of these connections makes it difficult to depict French-African relations in terms of relations between states, as the conventions of analysis and practice in international affairs presume. Such difficulty increases when we look closely at the political traffic flowing between France and Africa. For example, during the 1981 presidential election in France, several African presidents are said to have made significant political contributions to the campaign funds of candidates, notably those of Mitterrand and Chirac.[31] After the election, a vigorous campaign against the African policy of the Mitterrand government began to surface in the French press. The critics consistently reproached Mitterrand for abandoning "friends of France" such as Presidents Bongo, Mobutu, Touré, and Houphouët-Boigny and for encouraging an approach to aid that would dilute the amounts allotted to the Francophone hard core.[32] Whether or not this campaign was inspired by the governments or embassies of the countries concerned is beside the point. The significance of this and the earlier episodes is that they reveal an interpenetration of French and African politics, rather reminiscent of Israeli politicians' forays to New York and Capitol Hill. The difference is that France has to deal with 19 Israels of varying power and determination.

A similar, much better-documented process of interpenetration occurs at the African end. For example, as one scholar has remarked, it is impossible to understand the course of politics in the Central African Republic between 1979 and 1982 without understanding the centrality of French actions and imputed French intentions in the minds of the main participants. French troops intervened to remove one president and by their inaction allowed one to be removed. Some months later, the successor's main rival took refuge in the French embassy

---

29. Tamar Golan, "A Certain Mystery: How Can France Do Everything That It Does in Africa—and Get Away with It?" *African Affairs,* 80:3-11 (Jan. 1981).

30. The cultural bonds tying Africa to France are frequently invoked to explain African acquiescence in relations that would offend most nationalists. Even Lellouche and Moisi, otherwise exclusively concerned with French security policy, remark, "Only the unique community of culture that exists between the French and French-speaking African elites could allow Africa to accept the French mantle without feelings of inferiority." "French Policy in Africa," p. 119.

31. See Bayart, *La politique africaine,* p. 22; Péan, *Affaires africaines,* p. 247.

32. Bayart, *La politique africaine,* pp. 110-21.

after a failed coup, claiming to have been encouraged in his attempt by senior officials of the French Socialist Party.[33]

Such interpenetration confounds simple analysis whether based on the assumptions of realpolitik—the state-to-state model—or inspired by those of dependency theory. As Bayart remarks, before the 1981 election French Socialists firmly believed that the conservative Francophone regimes were essentially puppets of metropolitan French interests and that they lacked roots or legitimacy in their own societies. These regimes, they assumed, could easily be isolated, reformed, or removed. The Socialists therefore reckoned without the capacity for aggressive initiative that these regimes in fact displayed when feeling threatened as fundamentally as they did by the Socialists' accession to power.[34]

33. As Balans remarks, "This series of events demonstrates once again the Central African Republic's dependence on France. Every [domestic] political event inevitably followed the rhythm of French-Centrafrican relations." J.-L. Balans, "La vie politique dans les états francophones en 1981," *Année africaine 1981*, pp. 76-77.
34. Bayart, *La politique africaine*, pp. 125-29. As Bayart remarks later, "Dependence is a two-way street, even if one characterized by inequality. It is not enough to say that African political actors are endowed with a relative independence with regard to France: often, they constrain her." Ibid., p. 142. In a similar vein, John Chipman comments, "French influence in the region has . . . come to be related not only to the nature of power as deployed by French leaders, but also to the definition given that power by the Africans. Indeed, the Africans

In this case, practice confounded theory quite directly. It was the puppets who pulled the strings, so much so that by December 1982 Jean-Pierre Cot, the minister most closely identified with Socialist designs for a fresh start in Franco-African relations, was out of the government.

Episodes of this kind suggest that objective indicators of inequality cannot predict how power will actually be distributed in relations as complex and fundamental as those connecting ex-metropolitan with ex-colonial countries. In the present case, France obviously has immensely greater resources than its African partners. The French state can, if it wishes, exercise great diplomatic and military leverage upon African states. But its evident superiority in resources does not of itself shape French policy or enable any such policy to be effective. The same applies to its diplomatic and military leverage. The problem of analyzing French-African relations is that the relations in question exist between actors who have more sovereignty than the mythology of the Francophone family implies, but also a stronger community of values and a more complex meshing of political processes than the conventions of international relations typically assure.

have to some degree been the determinants of French power in Africa." *French Military Policy and African Security,* p. 2.

ANNALS, *AAPSS,* **489,** January 1987

The Foreign Policy of
the Republic of Zaire

By EDOUARD BUSTIN

ABSTRACT: In many ways, dependency has been the keystone of Zairian foreign policy since independence. Domestic preoccupations—political or economic stability, legitimacy or sheer regime survival—as perceived and interpreted by an oligarchic elite, rather than any ideological premise or any projection of Zaire's role in a global or regional context, have been the only consistent and predictable determinants of Zairian foreign policy. The successive regimes have seldom been able to fully control their domestic environment or even to insulate it from external manipulations. Within a narrowly circumscribed set of options, however, Zairian foreign policy— especially under Mobutu—has demonstrated considerable dexterity at playing off one patron against another, and thus at limiting some of the potentially adverse consequences of the country's lack of a solid power base.

Edouard Bustin is professor, past chairman, and currently associate chairman in the department of political science at Boston University. He is a member of that institution's African Studies Center and Center for International Relations. Formerly affiliated with the University of Liege, in Belgium, the National University of Zaire, and the University of California at Los Angeles, he has conducted research on East, central, southern, and French-speaking Africa. His publications dealing with Zaire include Lunda under Belgian Rule: The Politics of Ethnicity *and several monographs, chapters, and articles.*

TO a greater degree than almost any Third World state, Zaire has suffered from some of the constraints that impede the emergence of a full-fledged foreign policy stance. Whether in terms of the ability to insulate its domestic political processes from external interference, to develop its capacity to choose between plausible alternatives, or to conceptualize national interest in a broader perspective than that of the survival of a self-serving oligarchy, Zaire's foreign policy has been so notoriously deficient as to raise doubts about its credibility.

Zaire's visibility on the international scene, by contrast, has been all too evident. Almost invariably, however, that visibility has existed in a context in which the country was—and was perceived as—a crisis area rather than an autonomous actor, as a prize to be fought over or defended, by a number of leading international actors—in other words, as an object rather than a subject. Indeed, Zaire's initial emergence as a distinct entity—as the Congo Free State—in 1886 and its subsequent avatar as the Belgian Congo in 1908 were also, to an even greater extent than in the case of most other African territories, the by-product of international settlements in which the local populations played absolutely no part.

Similarly, the combination of naive condescension and cynical calculation that presided over Belgium's determination to rush Zaire to nominal independence with only the barest pretense of a transitional period turned its former colony into a travesty of a sovereign state whose basic institutions, not so much inadequate as untested, collapsed within a matter of a few days. Thus Zaire's formal accession to international sovereignty in 1960 coincided with the generalized breakdown of the fundamental ingredients of statehood, thrusting it onto the world scene not as a potential actor but as a crisis area, as a vacuum waiting to be filled, or as a black hole into which the conflicting ambitions, interests, or obsessions of other powers were instantly and inevitably sucked.

INTERNATIONALIZATION OF THE CONGO CRISIS

From the very first days of its accession to independence, the Lumumba government was confronted not only with a host of domestic challenges, but also with an almost complete lack of credibility in the eyes of the international community, which, for the most part, simply declined to treat the Congo as a sovereign state. The pattern was set by Belgium itself through its unilateral military intervention, ostensibly designed to protect European lives, but whose clearest objective effects were to trigger the Katanga secession and to encourage other centrifugal pulls in the direction of a balkanization alternative that had always held strong appeal among some Belgian circles. Though probably not desired by either party, the now-inevitable break between Belgium and the Congo—in July 1960—deprived the latter of the international sponsorship and intercession that other newly independent African countries were able to derive from their privileged relationships with the former colonial power. The urgent and almost simultaneous appeals for assistance that were sent out in mid-July to the United States, the Soviet Union, and ultimately to the United Nations with only the merest amount of concertation hardly added up to a credible foreign policy stance even if they exhibited, in a caricatural way, the aspirations toward nonalignment, the search for linkage diversification, and the preoccupation with internal stability and regime survival that are characteristic of newly independent states.

In the event, the utter helplessness and manifest penetrability of the fledgling Congolese state could not fail but invite outside interference. From the outset, Congolese sovereignty and the constitutional legitimacy of its government were treated by all international actors as negligible quantities, or rather as variables to be manipulated or exploited according to each actor's particular interests, perceptions, and anticipations of other powers' moves. The United States was actively and centrally involved in the overthrow of the Lumumba government, with Belgium and France pursuing convergent moves, albeit for somewhat different reasons. Soviet support for the Lumumba government—and for subsequent claimants to its legal succession—though ostensibly more consonant with the fiction of Congolese sovereignty, also pertained rather transparently to the general pattern of foreign intervention through the deliberate cultivation and manipulation of competing cliques of Congolese clients.

Even the United Nations, reflecting in part the general disregard for Congolese sovereignty as well as the biases of some of its senior officials, chose to interpret its mandatory neutrality as an excuse to treat the Lumumba government as a mere faction whose claims to legitimacy and sovereignty should not be accorded more seriousness than those of rival groups—for example, the Katanga secessionists—and whose initial request for assistance should be superseded by the United Nations' own reading of the crisis as a threat to international peace, a threat that provided the true legal foundation of the United Nations' presence and policies in the Congo. Though not identical, U.N. and U.S. objectives in the Congo were essentially compatible and thanks in part to Dag Hammarskjöld's receptiveness to Western perceptions and inputs, the United Nations provided a convenient international facade behind which U.S.—and, to a lesser extent, Belgian—manipulations of the domestic political processes could proceed unhindered, if not undetected.

It would thus be futile to search for any semblance of a Congolese foreign policy during the 1960-64 period, except in the form of a search by competing factions for outside recognition and support. Given the dubious legality of the September 1960 ouster of the Lumumba cabinet and the transparency of foreign—notably U.S.—influences in this move, as well as in Mobutu's premature attempt to break the ensuing factional deadlock, this quest for legitimacy was especially precarious for the makeshift College of General Commissioners with which Kasa-Vubu, Mobutu, and the members of the emerging clique known as the Binza group sought to fill the political vacuum. Whatever lack of credibility the regime faced in the international arena, however, was only a pale reflection of its lack of domestic authority in the face of the continuing challenges by the Lumumbist countergovernment and of the contagious centrifugal drift primed by the secessionist regimes of Katanga and South Kasai, as well as, paradoxically, by the Lumumbists themselves despite their genuine commitment to the cause of national unity. Meanwhile, the U.N. presence, though powerless to prevent Lumumba's liquidation and the increasingly overt play of foreign influences, continued to cast its shadow over the credibility of the Kinshasa authorities.

The domestic and international backlash triggered by the murder of Patrice Lumumba, in January 1961, briefly drove the Kinshasa regime into the arms of the secessionists who, with tacit French and Belgian support, forced it to accept a virtual blueprint for balkanization at the March 1961 Tanarive conference. The newly inaugurated Kennedy administration, eager to distance itself from the legacy of the Eisenhower years, at least where Africa was concerned, acted to stiffen the resolve of its Kinshasa allies: the centrifugal drift was decisively halted at the May 1961 Coquilhatville (Mbandaka) conference, and the Kinshasa regime responded to American proddings by taking steps to co-opt all dissidents, including the Lumumbists, into a government of national reconciliation. Despite Katanga's refusal, encouraged by France, to take part in this exercise, the reopening of the national parliament—with a strong majority of its Lumumbist members in attendance— and the selection for the premiership of Cyrille Adoula, a relatively unsullied moderate whose ties to the United States—via the International Confederation of Free Trade Unions and U.S.labor circles—were seen as far less objectionable than the Central Intelligence Agency (CIA) connection of other America protégés, provided Zaire with a greater potential for domestic stability and international credibility than it had ever enjoyed since the outbreak of the Congo crisis.

These assets were soon eroded, however, by the Adoula government's failure to negotiate Katanga's peaceful reentry into the national community—ultimately accomplished in January 1963 through a belated show of military muscle by

U.N. contingents—and by attempts on the part of the Binza group to exclude the Lumumbists from any real share of power at the national level. The reintegration of Katanga, which threatened to skew the balance of power even further against the Lumumbists, finally drove them into the wilderness, both figuratively and literally, as the most radical among them again retreated into their provincial strongholds, from which they launched a series of loosely coordinated challenges against the central government. From Kwilu, Kivu, and the Eastern Province, the swell of these rebellions gradually expanded to engulf nearly half of the country, and, by early 1964, the Adoula government had clearly outlived its usefulness.

THE EMBATTLED GOVERNMENT OF MOISE TSHOMBE, 1964-65

Kasa-Vubu's reluctant choice of the implausible Tshombe—self-exiled since the collapse of his secessionist regime— to succeed Adoula indicates the depth of desperation to which the Kinshasa authorities had sunk. Tshombe's chief qualification for the job was, after all, his brazen readiness—amply demonstrated during the Katanga secession— to rely openly on outside military support and particularly on the services of white mercenary units. His notoriety and tarnished reputation could thus be said, without undue cynicism, to represent his greatest assests since they allowed him to embrace overtly policies that Kasa-Vuba and members of the Binza group would only pursue covertly.

At the same time, however, Tshombe's accession to the premiership and the hostile or embarrassed reactions that it elicited from an overwhelming majority of Third World states forced Zaire to confront its international environment in a much more deliberate, if defensive, manner than had ever been the case since independence. Gone was Adoula's pretense of nonalignment, as well as the virtual *deminutio capitis* that Zaire had experienced as a ward of the international community. Tshombe's swearing-in as prime minister coincided, symbolically but not coincidentally, with the United Nations' pullout from the Congo.

Zaire's foreign policy under Tshombe was predicated upon the prime minister's initimate ties with some Western powers, significantly colored by past associations. Belgium, which had—rather successfully, on the whole—managed to reconcile official support for the central government with significant de facto backing for the Katanga secessionists, was in many ways Tshombe's privileged partner and allowed him to score a significant propaganda coup by agreeing— something that they had declined to do with his predecessors—to negotiate with him a settlement—on terms actually more favorable to Belgium than to Zaire—of the intricate set of financial claims and counterclaims (*le contentieux*) resulting from the severance of colonial ties between the two countries. France, which had taken a jaundiced view of the U.N. operation and had, covertly or through its African clients, supported the Katanga secession, was now ready to respond to Tshombe's overtures and to exploit his need for allies—notably by encouraging him to have Zaire join the French-oriented African and Malagasy Common Organization (OCAM).

While this represented the first major breakthrough for French influence in Kinshasa, it did not significantly affect the centrality of the U.S. presence, which rested on four years of consistent involve-

ment and assistance, whether directly or under the cover of the United Nations, as well as on the systematic cultivation of an extensive network of Zairian clients. Indeed, the strength of the U.S. commitment to the Kinshasa regime rather than to Tshombe personally was soon to be tested in the form of the November 1964 set of Belgo-American airborne operations against Stanleyville (Kisangani) and other rebel strongholds in northeastern Zaire. Nor did Zaire's bid to join the OCAM truly solve the controversy of the Tshombe regime's credibility in the wider circle of Afro-Asian states. Indeed, to the extent that OCAM was viewed—not without reason—as a Trojan horse for French influence and as a source of factionalism within the Organization of African Unity (OAU), Zaire's membership in the Francophonic organization only served to exacerbate opposition to the Tshombe government's demands for unqualified recognition and acceptance as a full participating member of the OAU. The open sympathy shown by some Third World states toward the rebel countergovernment provoked Tshombe into vehement denunciations in which "Arabs" and "Communists" were singled out as the "enemies of the Congolese people." Even such a moderate African leader as Jomo Kenyatta was antagonized when his efforts to mediate a settlement between rival Congolese factions were nullified by the concerted Belgo-American onslaught, coordinated with the action of several mercenary units, against the rebel strongholds.

The obligations that Tshombe had earlier incurred on Portugal for allowing his Katanga gendarmes to use Angola for sanctuary—a pattern that recurred in 1966-67, after Tshombe had been driven from power, and then again, in a strikingly different context, in 1977 and 1978—also led him to curtail the activities of Angolan nationalists, to the special detriment of the National Front for the Liberation of Angola (FNLA), whose visibility in the ongoing liberation struggle had been largely dependent on the favored status that it had enjoyed under Tshombe's predecessors, and later regained under Mobutu, vis-à-vis the rival Popular Movement for the Liberation of Angola (MPLA). Tshombe's move canceled the only advantage that the FNLA had derived from its regionalist character, a factor that, in every other respect, had always weighed against its credibility as a truly national movement, and thus indirectly worked to the benefit of the MPLA, which at that same time was thriving in the leftist ambiance of post-Youlou Brazzaville. Never again was the FNLA able to sustain its earlier claim of being the sole legitimate representative of the Angolan people. This development was to have momentous consequences ten years later.

But, even if the Tshombe regime was largely unsuccessful, even if it moved within a relatively narrow range of options and was visibly constrained by a number of predictable determinants, its diplomatic maneuverings nevertheless represented the first sustained attempts by Zaire to achieve an ad hoc foreign policy stance tailored to its idiosyncratic needs. Indeed, during the first years of the Mobutu regime, Zairian foreign policy continued to follow the same fundamental orientations as those of its predecessor, even when it ostensibly seemed to reverse them. That it was able to do so more successfully was due, in no small degree, to its skillful repudiation of those aspects of Tshombe's policy that African and other Third World states had found most objectionable

while relying, in practice, on a slightly reshuffled but basically identical assortment of Western patrons and backers.

By the fall of 1965 Tshombe had clearly outlived his domestic usefulness, itself based, as we have seen, on his unredeemable notoriety. At the same time, his continued presence at the helm was increasingly seen as the sole obstacle to the Kinshasa regime's full acceptance by those states that had been sympathetic to the rebels' claims. But, far from fading away, Tshombe had been engaged for some months in an increasingly overt bid for the presidency, which, under the terms of a new Gaullist-style constitution, offered vastly expanded powers to the future head of state. Tshombe's ambitions thus threatened not only President Kasa-Vubu but also the oligarchic Binza group, which assiduously sought to undermine Tshombe's position by splintering his fragile majority coalition in parliament. When this proved insufficient, Kasa-Vubu dismissed Tshombe from the premiership on 13 October 1965 and immediately proceeded to seek African endorsement for his legal coup, strongly reminiscent of the one he had carried out five years earlier against Lumumba, by personally attending the Accra summit meeting of the OAU, which Tshombe had vowed to boycott in view of the hostile reception he was likely to face.

Kasa-Vubu easily won good marks from his African peers by pledging general goodwill toward all OAU members and support for the Angola liberation struggle without, however, being too specific about which movement his administration would back. He also indicated that Zaire would give up its membership in OCAM and terminate the use of white mercenaries. Such bold pronouncements, even if they could be construed as propagandistic posturing, were nevertheless disturbing for Zaire's Western patrons and for their Kinshasa clients, and they probably played a significant part in Mobutu's decision to seize power shortly thereafter, on 23 November 1965.

CLAIMING A NATION'S BIRTHRIGHT: THE MOBUTU REGIME'S FIRST YEARS

Mobutu, who was in a good position to appreciate the Zairian army's continuing weakness, did not reiterate Kasa-Vubu's vague pledge to get rid of the mercenaries; the mercenaries themselves laid the ground for their own expulsion over the next two years through their adventurist disloyalty to the regime. Mobutu reaffirmed Zaire's membership in OCAM. This sort of backsliding, adding to Mobutu's reputed ties to the CIA and his role in the liquidation of Lumumba, caused a good deal of misgiving among those African states that had been most hostile toward Tshombe. Military regimes were also sufficiently rare at that time to be viewed as deplorable aberrations. Thus the initial African reaction to Mobutu's takeover was a qualified one at best. The principal, if not the only, positive feature that the new regime possessed in the eyes of militant African leaders such as Kwame Nkrumah was the fact that it had sidelined Tshombe and could, to that extent, be regarded as a marginal improvement.

The initial thrust of Zairian foreign policy under Mobutu was accordingly focused on a search for legitimacy and credibility, an external projection, in many ways, of its most serious domestic weaknesses. This search was essentially similar to the unmet goals of the Tshombe regime. A number of factors, however—some domestic and idiosyncratic, others more circumstantial or environmental—combined to enhance the Mobutu regime's image, both internally and externally. Whatever degree of stability Mobutu was able to bring to Zaire was seen as a welcome relief, both by the war-weary Zairian populace and by the international community, including the African states, for whom the seemingly endless Congo crisis had been a constant source of concern and embarrassment. Growing dissensions between the dispirited rebel leaders, now relegated, for the most part, to exile, indirectly enhanced Mobutu's credibility.

So did, after a fashion, the rash of military coups that occurred in the months following Mobutu's takeover. While still in a minority, military regimes could no longer be ignored or treated as temporary aberrations. In Ghana's case, Kwame Nkrumah's overthrow even held the added benefit of removing from the African scene a man whose moral authority had for years stood behind Lumumba and his political heirs and whose endorsement of Mobutu had been lukewarm at best. White Rhodesia's challenge to independent Africa—Ian Smith's Unilateral Declaration of Independence had taken place two weeks before Mobutu's coup—the escalation of the liberation struggle in Mozambique, and Nigeria's drift toward civil war all seemed to claim more urgent attention and combined to relegate Zaire to the back burner.

The next two years were largely devoted to improving the regime's image, both domestically and externally, through a series of moves intended to demonstrate its nationalist militancy and to appropriate some of the charisma ignited by Lumumba's meteoric career. Lumumba's rehabilitation and elevation to the rank of national hero, the breaking of diplomatic relations with Portugal, the Africanization of topographical and personal names in the context of a loudly trumpeted bid for authenticity, and finally the various forms of ostensible economic nationalism culminating with the expropriation of the Union Minière du Haut-Katanga all combined to enhance the regime's credibility. Even the serious military challenges to which it was exposed in 1966 and 1967 ultimately rebounded to its advantage in terms of international—particularly African—support inasmuch as they involved white mercenary units and Katanga contingents that had been integrated into the Zairian armed forces by Tshombe but had never fully transferred their loyalty to his successor.

The successful recasting of the Mobutu regime's image, crowned by the acceptance of Zaire's bid to host the 1967 OAU summit, was all the more remarkable because, despite the *tiers-mondiste* verbiage, Zairian foreign policy—then or later—displayed only the barest signs of nonalignment. Relations with Belgium cooled perceptibly when it became clear that economic nationalism was chiefly aimed at Belgian interests while the admittedly smaller U.S. holdings were being left relatively undisturbed. Nor were relations with Paris particularly cordial through the late 1960s, although this was largely a consequence of France's own tortuous record of seeking to draw Zaire into the French orbit by backing Tshombe both during and after the Katanga secession, by encouraging Zaire's membership in OCAM, or by tolerating the ambiguous maneuvers of mercenary groups led by French agent Bob Denard. U.S. influence, by contrast, was stronger and more direct than ever, and American

tutelage was credited by several observers with the skillful refurbishing of Mobutu's image.

By 1968, the Zairian regime's credibility and acceptability seemed sufficiently assured for its foreign policy to move beyond the reactive or legitimizing patterns that had guided it since independence. Apart from functional ties with Rwanda and Burundi, based on a shared colonial legacy and which Zaire later tried to parlay into a Communauté des états des grands lacs, Mobutu's first bid for regional leadership took the form of the hastily assembled Union of Central African States, linking Zaire with the Central African Republic and Chad. Although Zaire was still nominally a member of OCAM at the time, France took a dim view of Mobutu's initiative and persuaded President Bokassa to withdraw from the projected union, leaving it to wilt as an implausible partnership between two noncontiguous states.

Meanwhile, Zaire was beginning to reap the benefits of its new-found stability. In an attempt to create a favorable climate for foreign investment, Zaire worked out a settlement of the claims arising from the nationalization of Union Minière and, in 1969, published a liberal investment code. By 1970 Mobutu had almost totally reversed his earlier stance of economic nationalism, going so far as to declare that the word "nationalization" was "not part of the Zairean lexicon." Massive direct investments failed to materialize, but Zaire's apparent return to prosperity attracted a swarm of contractors and suppliers buoyed by a generous injection of loans that lined the country's sweet path to eventual bankruptcy.

The personalization of power that increasingly characterized the Zairian regime on the domestic front reverberated on the international scene. Zairian diplomacy in the early 1970s consisted largely of presidential visits and initiatives aimed at projecting an elder-statesman image of the Zairian ruler. In 1971, Mobutu volunteered his good offices to reconcile Idi Admin and Julius Nyerere and to mediate the lingering dispute between Nigeria and the four Biafra recognizers—Gabon, the Ivory Coast, Tanzania, and Zambia. Both offers were declined, but the Zairian leader was included in the team of OAU wise men who were assigned to attempt a negotiated end to Israel's occupation of the Sinai. He also played a significant part in the settlement of the border dispute between Burundi and Tanzania and, despite Nyerere's diffidence, was invited to join the Tanzanian president and Zambia's Kaunda in conversations on the southern African situation.

Still craving acceptance as a genuinely nonaligned country, Zaire multiplied symbolic gestures and contacts. None of these moves were in fact very controversial or likely to jeopardize Zaire's close ties to the West. Pulling out of the moribund OCAM, recognizing the two Germanies after Bonn had shelved the Hallstein doctrine, or establishing diplomatic relations with Peking following Nixon's overture to China hardly caused any eyebrows to be raised in Western capitals, but they enhanced the visibility of Mobutu, whose feverish round of travels peaked in 1973, when he spent 150 days outside Zaire and visited no fewer than 26 countries, including China, India, and 14 African states.

The first real breakthrough achieved by Mobutu's diplomacy, however, came in the fall of 1973. After attending the Afro-Asian summit in Algiers, he announced before the U.N. General Assembly that Zaire was breaking diplomatic relations with Israel. Although Zaire was not, strictly speaking, the first black African country to sever ties with the Jewish state, the fact that it was the first moderate state to take such a stance, combined with the special closeness of its past relations with Israel, attracted considerable attention to Mobutu's decision. In fact, as nearly every other African state followed suit, Zaire found itself, for the first time in its history, in the heady position of a trend setter. The symbolic significance of Zaire's move was duly recognized by the Arab states when they singled out Mobutu as the only black African leader to be invited to the November 1973 Arab summit. The break with Israel was consonant with Mobutu's long-standing efforts to enchance his regime's visibility and to establish Zaire's credibility as an autonomous actor. Apart from the obvious expectation of Arab petrodollars, however, the benefits of the move, when measured in terms of Zairian national interest, were not immediately evident.

MOBUTU IN DECLINE: ANGOLA AND THE ZAIRIAN DEBT PROBLEM

Even if much of it could be dismissed as posturing, Mobutu's assertive pretense of nonalignment, combined with his domestic attacks against the Roman Catholic establishment and with the radicalization measures that rekindled, with dubious results, the fires of economic nationalism, generated a certain amount of mutual annoyance and malaise in Zaire's dealings not only with Belgium—whose relations with its ex-colony were forever alternating between bickering and cordiality—but also, more significantly, with the United States. The assignment to Kinshasa, in early

1974, of Ambassador Deane Hinton to replace Sheldon Vance, who, from 1969 through 1973, had developed extremely close links with Mobutu, ushered in a gradual, if relative, cooling of U.S.-Zairian relations. Mobutu criticized the appointment as assistant secretary of state for African affairs of Nathaniel Davis. Davis, as U.S. ambassador to Chile, was widely credited with having had a hand in the overthrow of Salvador Allende. Mobutu's criticism of Davis's appointment was also directed, by implication, against Hinton, who had served in Chile during the same period. Tension between the two governments culminated in June 1975, when Mobutu accused the CIA of having plotted his overthrow and assassination.

Whatever the truth behind these allegations, and whether or not the CIA had indeed, as a number of observers believed, developed alternative contacts within the Zairian military, independently of Mobutu, the two countries were inescapably tied not only by the past but also by their convergent involvement in Angola. Linkages between Zaire and the FNLA had developed at several levels. Long before the 1961 outbreak of Angola's national liberation struggle, Kongo migrants from northern Angola had sought employment in Kinshasa and in lower Zaire, where ethnic similarity had made adjustment easy. Holden Roberto himself, who since early childhood had continuously resided in Zaire, was an illustration of this pattern of interpenetration. But whereas Kasa-Vubu's own predilection for the cause of pan-Kongo nationalism had been a decisive factor in his early support for the FNLA, Mobutu's ties to Roberto were based on their parallel links to the CIA, later reinforced by the lifelong friendship between Roberto's second spouse and Mobutu's

first wife, who both came from the same village.

Apart from such idiosyncratic factors, however, geopolitical considerations and aspirations to regional leadership—not to mention the tantalizing prospect of possibly gaining control of the oil-rich Cabinda enclave—provided plausible national-interest motivations for Zaire to yield to the temptation of influencing the outcome of the Angola liberation struggle. In the event, Zaire's covert military intervention on the side of the coalition between FNLA and the National Union for the Total Independence of Angola (UNITA) proved to be an unmitigated disaster. Not only did it expose the continuing weakness and unreliability of the Zairian armed forces, thereby causing resentment and demoralization among military circles, but it also exploded in a matter of days the painfully crafted myth of Zaire's nonaligned posture. South Africa's headlong plunge into the Angola civil war decisively tilted Third World opinion in favor of the MPLA. Even China, which had backed FNLA and UNITA out of hostility to the Soviets, now tiptoed off the scene, leaving Zaire in the unenviable position of being unambiguously identified as the apartheid regime's sole African accomplice and as a client of the United States.

In a number of ways, however, by stripping Mobutu's mask of nonalignment the Angola fiasco made it easier for Zaire to claim the full benefits of its now-avowed dependency at a time when Western backing was becoming essential to the regime's survival. By 1975, the combined effects of declining copper prices, corruption, mismanagement, and misguided economic nationalism had brought Zaire to the brink of open bankruptcy. This marked the beginning of an extraordinary decade during which Zaire, basking in the sun of U.S.—and, to a lesser extent, French—protection, managed to defy international financial and monetary circles, to delay or to dilute necessary reforms, and to curb domestic unrest through the recurrent exploitation of its own helplessness.

The cold-war perspective that the United States insisted on applying to the region after the MPLA victory, ironically guaranteeing the entrenchment of Soviet and Cuban forces in Angola, ensured American commitment to the political stability and continued pro-Western orientation of Zaire. All that was needed was for Mobutu to persuade his Western backers that there were no satisfactory alternatives to his regime, and that any major economic or political breakdown would open up a vacuum into which the Soviets and Cubans might be tempted to to step.

The two incursions—Shaba I and Shaba II—launched in 1977 and again in 1978 by the dissident Congolese National Liberation Front, a group organized by former associates of Moise Tshombe who had entrenched themselves in northeastern Angola, appeared to confirm this Manichaean vision. Though the two attacks were limited in scope and had been tolerated rather than instigated by the Luanda government, the fact that they had originated in Angola was sufficient to trigger a swift Western response in the form of the dispatching of French, Belgian, and Moroccan troops with U.S. logistical support. Mobutu naturally tried to present the incursions as instances of Soviet-Cuban subversion, but despite the fact that the Congolese National Liberation Front clearly lacked a nation-wide following, they dovetailed with other signs of domestic discontent to expose the regime's fragility and declining legitimacy.

At the urging of his Western—and particularly U.S.—backers, Mobutu initiated a short-lived period of political liberalization that, by opening some legitimate channels for the expression of dissent, only made it easier for the Zairian leader to identify his most articulate domestic critics and later to suppress them when the newly elected Reagan administration made it clear that it could tolerate authoritarian regimes as long as they were pro-Western.

Pressure for economic reforms was harder to elude. Despite their extraordinary leniency and their repeated willingness to reschedule Zaire's debts after it had become evident that Zaire could not or would not adhere to any repayment schedule, Western creditors finally forced Mobutu to swallow some bitter medicine from the International Monetary Fund and to close off some of the conduits that deflected a good portion of the country's wealth into his own and his cronies' pockets. Making a virtue out of necessity, Mobutu now proclaimed the policy reversals that were being forced upon him as articles of the Mobutist creed—extolling the virtues of free enterprise, privatizing parastatals, and turning over the management of all key sectors of the economy to expatriate technocrats.

Foreign policy also reflected this open-faced realignment and was increasingly geared toward demonstrating Zaire's total reliability as an American ally. Mobutu dispatched troops to Chad in support of the Habré regime, vehemently denounced Qaddafi, allowed Zairian territory to be used for the resupply of Angola's UNITA guerrillas, consistently backed Morocco on the Western Sahara issue to the extent of boycotting the

OAU out of solidarity with King Hassan, and, having lost Arab support when he decided to restore full diplomatic relations with Israel, even proposed to scuttle Afro-Arab unity by suggesting the creation, as an alternative to the OAU, of a league of black African states from which the Arab states of North Africa would be excluded.

The overwhelming predominance of U.S. patronage was tempered only by the closeness of Zaire's links with France, which Mobutu had started to cultivate more deliberately in the mid-1970s as an alternative to the then-ailing American connection. The 1974 election of Valéry Giscard d'Estaing ushered in a marked rapprochement between the two countries. French intervention in the Shaba wars—notably in the form of the spectacular, if somewhat anticlimactic, dispatching of the Foreign Legion to Kowezi in 1978—finally erased the unpleasant memories left by France's ambiguous maneuverings during the 1966-67 Tshombist uprisings.

Zaire now became a regular and valued participant in the annual Franco-African summit conferences initiated by Giscard. Mobutu's misgivings about a possible change of course under Mitterrand were soon put to rest when it became clear that the new Socialist administration was not contemplating any significant reorientation of France's African policy, and Zaire hosted the 1982 Franco-African summit in an atmosphere of renewed cordiality. By and large, Zaire's pro-American and pro-French stances turned out to be quite compatible, but there is no doubt that whenever perceptible differences arose between French and American policies—for example, regarding Chad, Libya, the Middle East, Angola, the Western Sahara, and others—Zairian foreign policy took its cue from Washington rather than Paris.

CONCLUSION: THE USES OF DEPENDENCY

By the mid-1980s, as the economic clouds began to dispel, Zaire's foreign policy remained shackled by some of the same disabilities that had plagued it ever since independence. The only signal advance it could boast was that of having learned to exploit its own weaknesses in order to extract Western backing, however reluctant at times, for what remains its one true priority—regime survival. Zaire's seemingly unending crisis—consisting, in fact, of two protracted crises separated by a seven-year period of relative remission from 1968 to 1975—left it singularly deficient when it came to projecting power or exercising leverage on its environment, even at the regional level. Zaire's contribution or impact on issues affecting Africa or on Third World concerns over the past quarter century has been virtually nonexistent. Within a narrowly circumscribed set of options, Zairian foreign policy, especially under Mobutu, has demonstrated considerable dexterity at playing off one patron against another, the United States, France, and Belgium being, in this context, the three relevant partners. While unable to alter or even to control events occuring in its international environment, it has achieved a certain capacity to limit their consequences as well as some of the potentially adverse effects of its own powerlessness.

Such achievements are not negligible, considering that Zaire lacked—or denied itself—most of the tools with which some small states have at times been able to compensate for their lack of conventional power. The resort to moral suasion, Third World solidarity, ideological assertiveness, or exemplary significance that leaders such as Nyerere, Nkrumah, or Touré—to mention only the Africans—were recurrently able to muster were largely unavailable to Mobutu or to his predecessors—with the brief but inconclusive exception of Lumumba—no matter how strenuously they were claimed.

Zaire never earned recognition on a scale that was commensurate with its size, population, and potential wealth. The magnitude of its problems rather than that of its assets was the true cause of its international visibility. Zaire is, in African terms at least, much too big to be ignored, but its domestic weaknesses have prevented it from effectively performing the regional role, whether as a subimperialist or as an autonomous middle power, that the West or the Third World—operating, of course, from different perspectives—at various times hoped it might fill.

Domestic preoccupations—political or economic stability, legitimacy, or sheer regime survival—as perceived and interpreted by an oligarchic elite, rather than any ideological premise or any projection of Zaire's role in a global or regional environment, have been the only constant and predictable determinants of Zairian foreign policy. The successive Zairian regimes, however, were never able to control the domestic environment fully, or even to insulate it

successfully from external manipulations. The best they could achieve was to ensure that those foreign interveners who had helped them emerge could be persuaded to assist with their self-perpetuation in office.

This, to put it bluntly, amounts to saying that dependency has been, in many ways, the keystone of Zairian foreign and even domestic policies. In fact, the chief use of dependency—or of the regime's ability to secure consistent external patronage—lies with its effects on the domestic scene. In that perspective, even the high visibility of foreign patronage, while it may not enhance the regime's legitimacy, can have and has had the effect of discouraging and demoralizing dissidents. Dependency—whether it be political, military, or economic—has clearly detracted from Zaire's credibility, and capacity to act, as an autonomous actor in the international system. But then again, as this article has attempted to show, the logic of Zairian foreign policy has always been subordinated to such basic domestic considerations as stability, elite entrenchment, and regime survival. Until such time that a formulation of national interest emerges that can supersede and transcend such narrow concerns, the foreign policy of the Republic of Zaire will in all likelihood continue to operate on an ad hoc, short-term, and opportunistic basis.

ANNALS, *AAPSS*, **489**, January 1987

The Politics of State Survival:
Continuity and Change in
Ethiopian Foreign Policy

By EDMOND J. KELLER

ABSTRACT: For more than a century the Ethiopian state has been concerned with promoting the idea in the international community that it is a viable multiethnic nation-state and with having its claimed geographic boundaries accepted as sacrosanct. Irrespective of the 1974 change from a modern imperial regime to a leftist-oriented military government, these foreign policy priorities have been motivated by persistent claims for self-determination expressed by politically subordinate ethnic communities questioning the legitimacy of Amhara hegemony. The weak, dependent character of the state has continued to force Ethiopian leaders to advance their causes through international diplomacy and military force. Thus the state has sought both the role of a spokesman for Africa and the military aid of a big-power patron. The conclusion is that structural requirements for state survival are more important than ideology.

Edmond J. Keller, professor of political science at the University of California, Santa Barbara, specializes in African politics and public policy. He received his doctorate from the University of Wisconsin, Madison. He has lived and worked in Kenya and Ethiopia. He has authored numerous articles on African and Afro-American politics and two books: The Impact of Educational Policy in Kenya *and* Revolutionary Ethiopia. *With Donald Rothchild he edited* Afro-Marxist Regimes.

FROM the very emergence of the modern state of Ethiopia, that country's leaders have been consumed with the twin concerns of establishing the legitimacy of this multiethnic polity as a viable nation-state, and maintaining its territorial integrity. Domestically, public policies have sought to secure and control the acquiescence—if not the genuine support—of disparate ethnic groups. Historically, the Amhara ethnic group has maintained hegemony over more than forty subordinate ethnic groups, some of whom have consistently called for their right to self-determination. For instance, the Somali of the southeast have desired to reunite with their kin in the Republic of Somalia since the early twentieth century; nationalists in the former Italian colony of Eritrea have demanded the right to secede since being incorporated into Ethiopia in 1962; and segments of the Oromo people in the south-central part of the country have pressed for the right to form an independent state of Oromia over the past decade.[1] Faced with such challenges, the boundaries of the Ethiopian state have largely had to be maintained through force.

No matter what the character of the regime, the government has complemented its domestic policies of control with a foreign policy that has relied heavily on strategic military and diplomatic alliances. The ultimate objective has always been to have the world community recognize as legitimate the geographic boundaries of the state as they presently exist. Despite the fact that since 1974 Ethiopia has been governed by a leftist-oriented military dicta-torship, its foreign policy objectives have essentially remained the same. Given the weak, dependent character of the state, no matter what the ideological orientation or organizational form of the regime, leaders have been forced to advance their causes through international diplomacy and defensive military action internally as well as in border zones. The fruits of diplomacy are used to assist the state in maintaining its territorial continuity. What seems to matter most is the state's ability to persist by the most expedient means. In order to understand how the essence of Ethiopia's foreign policy has remained unchanged for more than a century, it is necessary to place this discussion in a historical perspective.

DIPLOMACY AND STATE BUILDING IN IMPERIAL ETHIOPIA

Although the state of Ethiopia can trace its history back more than 3000 years, the modern imperial state did not begin to emerge until the middle of the nineteenth century.[2] At that time, Ras (King) Kasa, who traced his lineage to the house of David and King Solomon, succeeded in consolidating his rule over the Abyssinian core from which modern Ethiopia would flower. The establishment of a link to Solomon's line was important because Ethiopian legend held that this was a prerequisite to establishing one's right to rule as king of kings. Kasa's ascension to power came on the heels of almost 100 years of endemic conflict. Local warlords and traditional nobility competed among themselves and succeeded in fragmenting the state

1. See Edmond J. Keller, "Ethiopia: Revolution, Class and the National Question," *African Affairs*, 80(321):519-50 (Oct. 1981).

2. See Donald N. Levine, *Greater Ethiopia: The Evolution of a Multiethnic Society* (Chicago: University of Chicago Press, 1974).

into numerous mini-kingdoms.[3] By 1855, Ras Kasa had achieved the military capacity and popular support needed to begin the process of reconsolidation.

On being crowned emperor, Kasa took the name Tewodros II.[4] According to one of the religious documents that form the basis of Ethiopian myth and custom, Jesus is said to have prophesied that after a prolonged era of evil deeds among the chosen Ethiopians, a period of divine punishment would ensue. From this chaos would emerge a righteous, just, and popular king, Tewodros, who would rule for 40 years and restore Ethiopia to its former greatness.

Tewodros was predominantly concerned with establishing control over the peripheral parts of his fragile empire and with territorial integrity. He wanted to create a united Ethiopia, but he never quite succeeded. He had to be constantly alert to rebellion in the periphery, and although he succeeded in modernizing and centralizing his army to a degree, Tewodros was never powerful enough to feel secure.

Throughout his reign, Tewodros tried to develop a dynamic foreign policy that reached out beyond the Horn region. He attempted to have his regime recognized on an equal footing with the great powers of Europe. He also appealed specifically to Britain, France, and Russia as fellow Christian nations to assist him in whatever ways possible in his fight against the Turks, Egyptians, and Islam. In neither case, however, was Tewodros's request heeded to his satisfaction. In fact, he was incensed at the apparent lack of respect accorded him by Napoleon and Queen Victoria.

In a fit of desperation in 1865, Tewodros resorted to force in his efforts to gain British recognition of Ethiopia as an equal and the establishment of diplomatic and trade relations. He took as hostage several British subjects who happened to be at his court, including the British consul. At first, Britain tried to negotiate release of the hostages, but failed because it refused to accede to Tewodros's demands for reciprocal relations. Two years later a British military expedition moved from Eritrea into the highland core of Ethiopia, attacking Tewodros's capital of Magdala. Tewodros's troops were outmatched and they succumbed easily. Rather than surrender, Tewodros committed suicide. The British troops withdrew after securing the release of the hostages, and, after a brief power struggle, another king named Kasa claimed the imperial throne. He chose the name Yohannes IV.[5]

As a personality and as a ruler, Yohannes differed from Tewodros as night from day. He was more patient and less impulsive than his predecessor. Although both envisioned a united, Christian Ethiopia, their approaches were in contrast. Yohannes valued order more highly than the rigid centralization that had characterized Tewodros's rule.

Yohannes's most outstanding accomplishments were in the field of foreign policy. Whereas Tewodros had attempted brazenly to demand respect and the recognition of Ethiopia by European powers, Yohannes followed a course of patient diplomacy. This was a time of heightened European interest in Africa as a base for colonial expansion. It was also a period when Sudanese Mahdists

3. See Mordechi Abir, *Ethiopia: The Era of the Princes* (London: Longmans, 1968).

4. Sven Rubenson, *King of Kings: Tewodros of Ethiopia* (Addis Ababa: Oxford University Press, 1966).

5. Zewde Gabre-Selassie, *Yohannes IV of Ethiopia* (London: Oxford University Press, 1975).

challenged Ethiopia on its western border.

Although Yohannes considered Islam a threat, he saw European expansionism as an even greater threat to Ethiopia's political survival. At one point, Yohannes even made an abortive attempt to form an alliance with the Mahdists against a potential European incursion. His worst fears were confirmed in 1885, when Britain, which occupied parts of Eritrea at the time, allowed Italy to take control of the port of Massawa and to expand its presence in the area. Italy immediately made it apparent that it wanted to colonize Ethiopia. In 1889, before he could raise a challenge to Italian encroachment, Yohannes was killed in battle against the Mahdists.

Just prior to Yohannes's death, the Italians had begun to court Ras Menelik II of Shoa, Yohannes's most serious competitor. The Italians looked upon this initiative as preparation for the impending challenge to Yohannes. Menelik saw it as an insurance policy against a possible invasion of his domain by Yohannes. Yohannes died, however, before either of these events could occur.

Only seven weeks after the death of Yohannes, a treaty was concluded between Menelik and the Italians in the small town of Wichale in what is now Wollo Province. The treaty was officially described as the Wichale Treaty of Perpetual Peace and Friendship.[6] Menelik saw this as insurance against foreign as well as domestic enemies. The treaty declared that the state of war that had existed between Yohannes and Italy was officially ended and recognized Menelik as the emperor of all of Ethiopia.

Under the treaty Italian claims to Mas-

sawa were recognized as long as Ethiopia could use the port freely for trade. Ethiopia also agreed to cede part of the Tigre Highlands to Italy and to give the Italians certain commercial, industrial, and judicial privileges in Eritrea. For its part, Italy agreed to give Ethiopia a substantial loan and to continue to supply Menelik with arms. In general, then, both Italy and Ethiopia were guaranteed a measure of security and trading privileges.

Significantly, the treaty was written in two versions, Italian and Amharic, which had profound implications for future relations between the two countries. Both drafts were identical except for one article, Article XVII. The Italian version of this article essentially implied that Ethiopia was a protectorate of Italy. The Amharic version suggested that Ethiopia was free to seek the assistance of the Italians in its dealing with other governments, but it was not obliged to do so. When Menelik realized the discrepancy in the two versions, he tried to have it corrected through diplomacy. After this effort failed, the emperor notified Italy in 1893 that the treaty would be abrogated in one year.

In response Italy prepared for war. Menelik, in anticipation, strengthened his defensive capabilities by purchasing more arms and military equipment from private dealers as well as from such governments as the Russian, French, and British. He already possessed a substantial battery of armaments, which had enabled him to expand his territorial possessions to the north and south even before the demise of Yohannes. In order to secure the popular support he needed to fend off the Italians, Menelik appealed to his subjects, emphasizing Ethiopia's historic reputation for repulsing external enemies. Once again, the threat of a formidable foreign invader seems to

6. Sven Rubenson, *Wichale XVII* (Addis Ababa: Haile Selassie I University, 1964), p. 12.

have coalesced the disparate people who made up the empire.

In early 1895 Italy began its systematic penetration of the highland core. Minor skirmishes between Italian forces and Ethiopian regional armies took place throughout that year. By January 1896, however, Menelik decided that the time had come for a decisive showdown.[7] The Italians had committed 20,000 well-armed troops to this campaign, and Menelik countered with a force of 100,000. After a period of a war of nerves, the consummate battle erupted at Adowa in late February and lasted for six days. The Italians were resoundingly defeated with more than 35 percent of their troops being killed.

The Ethiopian victory at Adowa sent shock waves throughout Europe and caused the reigning Italian government to fall. The vanquished Italians sued for peace, and a treaty was signed that allowed Italy to keep Eritrea while renouncing all claims to the Ethiopian core. For the first time, the European powers realized that Ethiopia was an African power to be reckoned with. Now Britain, France, Russia, and Italy flocked to Menelik's court in order to arrange the exchange of ambassadors and to conclude diplomatic agreements establishing their spheres of influence in the Horn of Africa vis-à-vis Ethiopia. Even Sudanese Mahdists sought to stabilize relations with Ethiopia at this time.[8]

By the end of 1897, Ethiopia's current boundaries—save for Eritrea and part of the western border—had been set, at least on paper. Diplomatic agreements with Britain, France, and Italy established Menelik's exclusive rights to territories bordering the colonial possessions claimed by these powers, respectively. Significantly, these rights made Menelik an active participant in the colonial partition of Africa along with the European powers. It was clear that the emperor was gifted with considerable diplomatic acumen, playing off one power against the other as pawns in an effort to secure the sovereignty of his country. This contributed greatly to the almost mythical image of Ethiopia as the epitome of African independence.

A critical element in Menelik's efforts to establish effective control over the expanded empire was his army. He is credited with professionalizing the armed forces and with creating a standing army. As circumstances dictated, he could raise an army of up to 200,000, with 10,000 to 12,000 men at his direct disposal.[9] Through diplomacy, he secured military technical assistance. European instructors, mainly French and Russian, were invited to his court to assist in military training. That training, however, was confined to weapons use and did not involve strategy and tactics. The first European-style military academy was not established until 1934, four years after Haile Selassie I became emperor.

Menelik introduced the practice of erecting permanent garrison towns throughout the recently conquered periphery to aid not only in defense but also in establishing the administrative presence of the central authorities. Thus military administrators were extremely instrumental in consolidating the physical boundaries of present-day Ethiopia.

7. See Sven Rubenson, *The Survival of Ethiopian Independence* (London: Heinemann, 1976).

8. See Harold Marcus, *The Life and Times of Menelik II* (London: Oxford University Press, 1975).

9. See R.H. Kofi Darkwah, *Shewa, Menelik and the Ethiopian Empire, 1813-1889* (London: Heinemann, 1975), p. 116.

HAILE SELASSIE AND THE
RISE OF THE NATION-STATE

Menelik died in 1913, and it was not until 1930 that the next strong emperor, Haile Selassie I, assumed the throne.[10] The new emperor was dedicated to the creation of a stronger, more modern bureaucratic empire with unquestioned respect in the world community. This was clear as early as 1923, when as Crown Regent Ras Tafari Makonnen, the would-be emperor engineered Ethiopia's entry into the League of Nations.

Haile Selassie's efforts were briefly halted by the occupation of Ethiopia by the Italian Fascists between 1936 and 1941. Ethiopia's joining the League of Nations was clearly instigated by the ever present potential for invasion of the Ethiopian heartland by the Italians. When the Italians did finally invade, the emperor took flight and established a government in exile in London. From there, he journeyed to Geneva, Switzerland, to make an impassioned plea before the General Assembly of the League of Nations for aid in defense to the Ethiopian motherland.[11] Although the League of Nations' charter stipulated that all members were committed to protect the sovereignty of one another, the league ultimately ignored Haile Selassie's plea.

Apparently viewing the League of Nations' inaction as only a temporary setback, the emperor continued to believe in the ultimate value of effective diplomacy. He also recognized Ethiopia's need for a powerful external patron until he could restore the state's administrative capacity for autonomous action.

His diplomatic skills and Britain's own strategic necessities in the area enabled him to elicit the aid of the British in the liberation of Ethiopia.

In the immediate post-World War II period, Ethiopia was extremely dependent on British military, economic, and technical aid. At the same time, the emperor feared that Britain might either declare Ethiopia a protectorate or use the claim that the whole of Italian East Africa—Eritrea, Ethiopia, Somalia—was occupied enemy territory and thus could be partitioned for administrative convenience. Haile Selassie's fears moved him to seek alternative relationships that would allow him to loosen Ethiopia's ties to Britain. This was a period when all the Allied powers were jockeying for leverage in the reordered international political arena. France wanted to return to the prewar status quo; Russia wanted to block Britain from claiming too much of the African spoils; the British wanted to solidify their presence in the Horn; and the United States wanted to establish a new presence in the region.[12]

Through diplomacy, Haile Selassie was able to regain complete administrative control over the territory he claimed—and more—by 1954. In 1952 a U.N. resolution had made possible a federation between Ethiopia and the former Italian colony of Eritrea. Eritrea was to have regional autonomy within the federation, but Haile Selassie was not content with only administrative control. He was not satisfied until he secured the endorsement of both the Eritrean and Ethiopian Assemblies in 1962, which allowed him to incorporate Eritrea fully into the empire, making it a

10. See Leonard Moseley, *Haile Selassie* (London: Weidenfell and Nicholson, 1964).

11. See Haile Selassie I, *My Life and Ethiopia's Progress, 1892-1937*, ed. and annotated by Edward Ullendorff (London: Oxford University Press, 1976).

12. See John H. Spencer, *Ethiopia, the Horn of Africa and US Policy* (Cambridge MA: Institute of Foreign Policy Analysis, 1977), pp. 17-22.

province of Ethiopia instead of a trustee-ship.

These maneuvers took place against the backdrop of the emperor's loosening ties with Britain and establishing new patronage links with the United States. British military aid was withdrawn in 1952, and Haile Selassie moved quickly to firm up relations with the United States. Since the early 1940s, the United States had coveted a base in Eritrea where it could set up a radio tracking station. Haile Selassie viewed the use of such an installation by the United States as having more benefits than costs; that is, he would reap the benefits of being closely allied with the most powerful military power in the world, while being paid rent in the form of military aid that could be used to strengthen the state's military capacity. Two agreements were concluded in May 1953 to formalize this new relationship. As a result, the United States guaranteed Ethiopia's security, which added greatly to the confidence with which the emperor could approach the task of political consolidation.

In addition to the military aid Ethiopia received from the United States over the next 23 years, its armed forces also benefited from the presence of a Military Assistance Advisory Group, which was established in 1954. This group provided training for the Ethiopian forces down to the battalion level. By 1975, the total U.S. military assistance to Ethiopia amounted to almost $280 million. In addition, between 1953 and 1976, 3978 Ethiopian soldiers—more than half the total for Africa—were trained in the United States.[13]

The relationship that developed be-tween the two countries under Haile Selassie is often considered as one of dependency on the part of Ethiopia. I would argue the contrary. A better description is interdependence. At least at the beginning both partners got what they wanted. In the days prior to ad-vances in satellite technology, Kagnew Station in Eritrea provided the United States with a valuable link in its world-wide military communications network. To an extent, American policymakers considered it essential to keep Haile Selassie in power if access to this base was to be preserved. In this sense, the strategic interests of the United States came to intersect with Haile Selassie's domestic and regional interests.

Even though the United States pre-ferred not to become involved in domes-tic politics, on occasion it provided the emperor with the means to put down internal upheavals. On a more consistent basis, the United States contributed to the expansion of the Ethiopian military as a hedge against a Somali threat. It also provided counterinsurgency train-ing and on-the-ground advisers to help to suppress Eritrean nationalism. The scale and character of U.S. military involvement in Ethiopia contributed to a low-intensity arms race in the Horn region. This notwithstanding, Haile Selassie felt the association with the United States was essential not only to his survival but also to the survival of the state itself.

The military dimension was only one part of Haile Selassie's survival strategy. The other involved political diplomacy. On the one hand, under his leadership, Ethiopia became an active member of

13. See Edmond J. Keller, "United States Policy on the Horn of Africa: Policymaking with Blinders On," in *African Crisis Areas and US Foreign Policy*, ed. Gerald Bender, James S.

Coleman, and Richard Sklar (Berkeley: University of California Press, 1985), pp. 178-93.

the United Nations, even going so far as to commit Ethiopian troops for peace-keeping operations in Korea in 1951 as well as the Congo in 1961. He wanted to appear to be a champion of freedom and anticommunism. On the other hand, when the winds of change for African independence began to blow in the 1950s, Haile Selassie belatedly jumped to the forefront of the voices calling for African independence. Until 1958, he had remained silent about European colonialism in Africa. But in April of that year, at the first meeting of the Conference of Independent African States in Accra, Ghana, the emperor pressed for a resolution in which the signatories agreed to observe each other's territorial integrity.[14] He thereby avoided Ethiopia's being branded an African imperialist for its role in the partition of Africa during the period of European colonial expansion.

From this point on, Haile Selassie recognized the value not only of participating in international organizations, but also of taking the lead in the interest of the voices of moderation. Such consideration prompted him to extend an invitation to host the 1963 meeting of the Conference of Independent African States. There he proposed that priority be given to spelling out the meaning of the concept of African unity and to its operationalization. This meeting resulted in the founding of the Organization of African Unity. Due to his role, Haile Selassie secured the mantle of patriarch of African unity. Even more important, he ensured that Ethiopia's territorial integrity would not be questioned by other African states.

14. See Peter Schwab, *Haile Selassie I* (Chicago: Nelson-Hall, 1979), pp. 101-14.

REGIME CHANGE, IDEOLOGY, AND FOREIGN POLICY

The reign of Haile Selassie came to an end in September 1974. The emperor was deposed by a military coup d'état. The new regime at first did not attempt to alter the country's foreign policy significantly. In fact, priority was initially given to addressing the long-standing problem of underdevelopment that had characterized Haile Selassie's rule. An equally pressing problem from the perspective of the Provisional Military Administrative Council (PMAC) was a resolution of the nationalist insurgency in Eritrea that had been raging since the early 1960s and that by 1974 had intensified. Even though Eritrea had been annexed only in 1962, the new regime, as the one before it, asserted that Ethiopia's claim to the region could be traced to antiquity. With the aid of a newly formed people's militia in alliance with units of the regular armed forces, the PMAC tried to secure a military solution to the problem.

Simultaneously, the new government liberalized the political atmosphere and allowed relatively free and open exchange of political ideas. Wanting to carve out a vanguard role for the PMAC in the creation of the new society, it actually opened the door to civilian criticism of its dictatorial and antidemocratic tendencies. Consequently, urban guerrilla warfare erupted, involving civilian groups that supported the vanguard role of the men in uniform, those who opposed it, and the politicized military itself.

Although the United States had decided not to renew its lease of Kagnew Station—land-based communications facilities were no longer needed—it wanted to maintain a presence in Ethiopia to block Soviet expansionism in Africa. The Ford administration wanted to avoid an embarrassment similar to what it experienced in Angola in 1974, when covert United States aid to anticommunist forces failed to dislodge the pro-Moscow Popular Movement for the Liberation of Angola. Yet it was uneasy with the growing leftist tendencies and political excesses of the regime.

The United States began to express concern about violations of human rights in Ethiopia as early as November 1974, when 60 political prisoners were executed. Concern was heightened two months later when the struggle for Eritrea reached a crisis level. By June 1975, the government had 30,000 to 40,000 troops poised in the Eritrean region, most of whom were poorly trained and poorly armed militiamen.[15] The Eritrean forces attacked them in their own camps before they could launch an offensive and decimated them. The United States then appealed to the PMAC to halt its use of the militia in the Eritrean campaign, threatening to withhold needed military aid. Presidential candidate Jimmy Carter, noting growing human rights violations throughout the world, vowed to make human rights the centerpiece of his foreign policy in the event of his election. When he assumed office, Carter moved swiftly to make good on his word. On 25 February 1977, it was announced that because of continued gross violations of human rights by the governments of Ethiopia, Argentina, and Uruguay, U.S. military aid to those countries would be reduced in the new fiscal year.[16]

In the face of the worsening Ethiopian-U.S. relations, the Soviets moved to take advantage of an opportunity to become Ethiopia's new big-power patron. By April it was clear that the PMAC had decided to shed its unreliable patron and to replace it immediately with a new partner. As head of the PMAC, Colonel Mengistu Haile Mariam demanded that the United States close down Kagnew, all operations of the Military Assistance Advisory Group, and most other U.S. installations within 72 hours. By then, the Soviets had begun to provide military arms and equipment to replace lost American aid.[17]

Sensing that the regime was in desperate trouble, internal and external enemies began to take action to hasten its demise. Most important, civilian opposition groups began to intensify the urban guerrilla campaign, and Somalia committed regular troops to assist ethnic Somali in the Ogaden in their efforts to separate from Ethiopia. The Somali government expressed concern over the growing Soviet and Cuban presence in Ethiopia. Until then Somalia had been a client of the Soviet Union. Although the Soviet Union continued to supply aid to Somalia, after the Ogaden invasion in June 1977, it began to withdraw its personnel until by September no more than 400 remained out of 1000. In November, Somalia announced the abrogation of the 1974 Treaty of Friendship and Cooperation with the Soviet Union. In addition, diplomatic relations with Cuba were suspended. This cleared the way for the unconstrained entry of the Soviet Union into Ethiopia.

15. See Haggai Erlich, *The Struggle over Eritrea, 1962-1978: War and Revolution in the Horn of Africa* (Stanford, CA: Hoover Institution Press, 1983), pp. 71-78.

16. Sandra Vogelgesan, "What Price Princi-

ple?—U.S. Policy on Human Rights," *Foreign Affairs*, 56(4):833 (July 1978).

17. Gary D. Payton, "The Soviet-Ethiopian Liaison: Airlift and Beyond," *Air University Review*, 31:66-73 (Nov.-Dec. 1979).

In late November the Soviets launched a huge air and sea lift of arms and equipment to Ethiopia.[18] In addition, over the next several months more than 11,000 Cubans and 1000 Soviet military personnel arrived in the country and were sent to the Ogaden front. This aid was decisive in turning the tide in favor of Ethiopia by early 1978. As this drama unfolded in Ethiopia, the United States and other Western allies rallied to the side of Somalia.

As a result of the split between Ethiopia and the United States, tension mounted throughout the whole region. Beginning in May, clashes occurred between Sudan and Ethiopia on their common border, and Egypt committed troops to help guard the eastern border of Sudan. The United States eventually began to pursue systematically an encirclement strategy intended to isolate Ethiopia by entering into military relationships with its neighbors. Countries such as Egypt, Sudan, Kenya, Somalia, and Oman were asked to allow their territories to be used as staging grounds for the U.S. Rapid Deployment Force, which could be used to project U.S. military power into the Middle East and Persian Gulf.[19] These developments caused Ethiopia, South Yemen, and Libya to come together in a show of solidarity and resolve jointly to repulse any efforts by the United States or its proxies to intervene in their affairs. The U.S. policy in the Horn was continued and even extended by the Reagan administration, which by 1986 was attempting to smooth the way for covert aid to opponents of the Afro-Marxist regime.

The broader implication of these developments was an escalation of the regional arms race in the Horn. The Soviets and Americans jockeyed to check one another; the Ethiopians and Somali tried to outfox each other. The consequences were momentous. The size of the Ethiopian military jumped from 65,000 in 1976 to almost 300,000 in 1986. Somalia's army swelled from 31,000 to about 54,000 in the same period. Domestically, Ethiopia's opposition groups, although temporarily contained in 1978, had achieved the military capacity to cause serious problems for the regime by the mid-1980s, particularly in the Eritrea and Tigre regions. Between 1974 and 1982 Ethiopia's military expenditures grew more than tenfold to $381 million.[20] By then, the Soviets had provided over $2 billion in military aid in comparison to less than $300 million provided by the United States over a 22-year period. What is more remarkable is the fact that both Somalia and Ethiopia now spend almost 10 percent of their gross national products for military purposes in spite of being among the poorest countries in the world.

As did the previous regime, the present Ethiopian government has accorded its international image and territorial integrity the highest priority in its foreign policy. Domestically its approach to foreign policy has resulted in the growing regimentation and militarization of society. Opposition groups have forced the regime to rely extensively on the Soviet Union to maintain itself in power and to preserve the country's territorial integrity. Critics suggest that this deepening association has resulted in Ethio-

18. Ibid.

19. Henry F. Jackson, *From the Congo to Soweto: U.S. Foreign Policy toward Africa since 1960* (New York: William Morrow, 1982).

20. U.S., Arms Control and Disarmament Agency, *World Military Expenditures and Arms Transfers, 1985* (Washington, DC: Government Printing Office, 1985).

pia's becoming a Soviet pawn. I, however, would question this. Although the regime consistently sides with the Russians in the international diplomatic arena, it has on numerous occasions demonstrated its independence in the area of domestic policy and international economic policy.[21] For instance, the PMAC took its time in setting up a vanguard party in spite of Soviet pressure. When the party was formed, it was dominated by military personnel, again contrary to Soviet wishes. In economic policy, Ethiopia has close aid and trade relations with the West and pursues a pragmatic investment policy. Clearly, then, the new regime takes an opportunistic approach to its dealings with the big powers. To be sure, it is heavily dependent on the Russians for military aid, but it cannot do without the West for economic development aid. Ironically, this places the current regime in a stronger position than the previous one. It can use its necessarily diversified aid sources as leverage, playing one big-power bloc off against the other, although within limits.

Ideologically, the PMAC is oriented toward the Soviet Union, but this has made little difference in the fundamental essence of its foreign policy. It continues to strive to have its commitment to the principles of nonalignment, self-reliance, and self-determination accepted as genuine. For instance, in 1974 at Ethiopia's invitation, the Organization of African Unity decided to make Addis Ababa the permanent site not only for its headquarters but also for its annual summit. By emphasizing its leadership role in the Organization of African Unity, the regime reinforces its definition of the Ethiopian nation-state.

One subtle change aimed at enhancing Ethiopia's international reputation is its leader's repeated claims of solidarity not only with the other peoples of Africa, but also with all progressive forces throughout the world, including the West.[22] To legitimize its position, the regime quotes the charters of the United Nations and the Organization of African Unity and pledges endorsement of the principle of peaceful coexistence. Significantly, the rhetoric emphasizes peace and friendship, not proletarian internationalism and class struggle.

By 1985, in spite of problems caused by drought, famine, and internal war, the PMAC was beginning to resolve at least temporarily some of its regional foreign policy problems. After the overthrow in Sudan of President Jafar Muhammad al-Nimeiry in April of that year, the regime that replaced him began to express a desire to secure Sudan's border with Ethiopia and to tighten surveillance of cross-border operations by Ethiopian and Eritrean opponents of the regime.[23] More remarkably, about the same time Ethiopia and Somalia began to move toward détente. A historic meeting between Mengistu and Mohamed Siad Barre of Somalia was held at the inaugural meeting of the Intergovernmental Authority on Drought and Development. A joint communiqué, issued after extensive talks, stated that the aim of these preliminary contacts was to create the "conditions for the normalization of relations and the estab-

21. See Edmond J. Keller, "Revolutionary Ethiopia: Ideology, Capacity and the Limits of State Autonomy," *Journal of Commonwealth and Comparative Politics*, 23(2):133 (July 1985).

22. See "Ethiopia's Foreign Policy," *Yekatit Quarterly*, 8(1):30-32 (Sept. 1978).

23. "Foreign Policy and National Interest," *Omdurman Domestic Service in Arabic*, 0430GMT, 28 Apr. 1985.

lishment of lasting peace" between the two countries.[24]

CONCLUSION

The fundamental essence of Ethiopia's foreign policy has not changed over the past century despite the change in regime. Although the imperial regime has been displaced by a military Afro-Marxist government, the main focus of the country's foreign policy continues to

be the desire to have the multiethnic character of the nation-state internationally accepted as legitimate and to defend its territorial integrity. As in the past, these goals are pursued with the military aid of a big-power patron. The identity of the patron has changed, but the reason for the alliance has not. The ideological character of the new regime is less important for what it is than for what it does. It provides the government with the needed military wherewithal to ensure the survival of the state as well as the regime.

24. Pramila Bennett, "The Horn: Burying the Hatchet," *Africa,* no. 175, pp. 36-37 (Mar. 1986).

Anglophonic Variants:
Kenya versus Tanzania

By DAVID F. GORDON

ABSTRACT: The East African countries of Kenya and Tanzania provide an interesting comparative context for examining the evolution of African foreign relations. In the past decade both countries have significantly broadened the range of issues on their foreign policy agendas in response to changes in both regional and international environments. Tanzania has shifted its trade and aid relations away from the European powers and has become heavily involved in the diplomacy surrounding southern African conflicts. Kenya has become a significant exporter of goods to other Third World countries. Relations between the two countries deteriorated sharply in the latter 1970s, but, since 1983, have entered a new period of cooperation. Tanzania has maintained a policy of strict nonalignment, while Kenya has developed close strategic ties to the United States. International financial institutions, especially the International Monetary Fund (IMF), have been increasingly involved in both countries. IMF relations with Tanzania have been highly conflictual; Kenyan-IMF relations, while cordial, have also had their problems. In sum, both countries have been relatively successful in utilizing foreign relations to promote national goals.

David F. Gordon is associate professor of international relations at James Madison College, Michigan State University, and a member of the senior research staff at the Center for Research on Economic Development at the University of Michigan. Dr. Gordon was educated at Bowdoin College and the University of Michigan. He has been on the staff of the Department of History at the University of Nairobi and has traveled widely in East Africa. He is the author of Decolonization and the State in Kenya.

T HE foreign relations of Kenya and Tanzania shifted dramatically in the late 1970s and early 1980s as both countries responded to a rapidly changing regional context, the heightened importance of Africa in the global geostrategic considerations of the world's superpowers, and the onset of severe domestic economic difficulties. Between independence and the mid-1970s, there was a remarkable continuity in both the issues that Kenya and Tanzania faced in their foreign relations and the manner in which they responded to those issues. The legacies of colonial rule and narrowly defined regional issues dominated the agendas of both countries. Kenya's foreign policy during that period has been described as one of "quiet diplomacy,"[1] cautious and pragmatic in its articulation. While Tanzania was always more outward looking, it also played an essentially low-key role in foreign affairs.

Since the late 1970s, both countries have become much more actively involved in foreign affairs, and the issues that make up their foreign policy agendas have been transformed. Forming the background of this transformation are the following elements: the breakup of the East African Community (EAC); superpower involvement in the conflicts in northeast Africa; the emergence of southern Africa as a major focal point of global political interest; the overthrow of Idi Amin in Uganda and the subsequent continuing instability in that country; the growing conflict between economically strapped Third World nations and international financial institutions such as the International Monetary

Fund (IMF) and the World Bank; and the growing interest of the United States in playing a more direct role in the Indian Ocean as a response to the fall of the Shah of Iran and the Soviet invasion of Afghanistan.

This article will explore the evolution of the foreign relations of Kenya and Tanzania since independence, the changing goals of both, and why these changes have occurred. I will first examine the broad global economic dimension of Kenyan and Tanzanian foreign relations, then discuss the evolution of their regional diplomacy, and finally examine how each has responded to the increasing role of the great powers and of international financial institutions in African affairs.

Until 1967, Kenya and Tanzania responded quite similarly to their inherited colonial legacies. Both countries recognized and accepted their structural dependence on the global economy while, at the same time, attempting to reform their domestic structures and to diversify and improve their positions in the international economic order. In 1967, Tanzania turned to the Left, concluding that self-reliance and socialism provided the only path forward for underdeveloped African countries.[2] How have Tanzania and Kenya fared in their efforts to reorganize their relations with the international economic system? While the answer to this question should consider domestic issues, this discussion will be limited to the international dimension, in particular to trade and aid.

---

1. John Okumu, "Kenya's Foreign Policy," in *The Foreign Policies of African States*, ed. O. Aluko (London: Hodder and Stroughton, 1977), p. 136.

2. For a discussion of the broad strategic choices available to African governments, see Donald Rothchild and Robert L. Curry, Jr., *Scarcity, Choice and Public Policy in Middle Africa* (Berkeley: University of California Press, 1978), pp. 115-16.

TRADE AND AID: TANZANIA

The striking features of Tanzania's trade since independence are the dramatic increase and subsequent decrease in the level of imports from China, the demise of bilateral trade with Kenya, and the reemergence of the Western countries as the major suppliers of foreign goods to Tanzania. Increased trade with China was a result of Tanzania's need to repay China for money lent for the construction of the Tanzania-Zambia (Tazara) railway. With the completion of the railway in 1974, China's share of Tanzania's imports declined sharply. The demise of trade with Kenya was the result of the closure of the Kenya-Tanzania border in 1977. Between 1967 and the mid-1970s, Tanzania had sought to limit imports of goods from the industrialized countries. One by-product of the border closure with Kenya was the reemergence of Western countries as Tanzania's most important trading partners, on both the import and export sides.

Perhaps the most important features of the evolution of Tanzania's foreign trade are its overall decline and a growing gap between exports and imports. In the second decade of its independence, its foreign trade, in real terms, diminished; imports shrank by about 1 percent per year and exports decreased by 8 percent per year. Between 1961 and 1968, Tanzania had exported goods worth more than those imported, but since 1970 this pattern has reversed, and since 1978 the value of imports has more than doubled those of exports.[3] The growing balance-of-trade deficit was at first paid for by Tanzania's foreign exchange reserves,

but, for all intents and purposes, these had run out by 1981. The imbalance must now be covered by foreign assistance and borrowing. This has resulted in a substantial drop in real imports since 1980. Foreign assistance has increased rapidly in recent years; by the early 1980s it equaled exports as a source of revenue and foreign exchange.[4]

Tanzania has greatly diversified its sources of foreign assistance, moving away from its initial dependence on Britain, by maximizing aid from the smaller industrialized countries. Countries that have been particularly important lenders to Tanzania are Sweden, Canada, Norway, Denmark, Finland, the Netherlands, and, more recently, West Germany.

Tanzania has also received large-scale loans from the World Bank and its concessional window, the International Development Association, although Tanzania's conflict with the IMF has caused delays in the disbursement of these funds in recent years. Very little aid has been received from the Soviet-bloc countries, although Yugoslavia was a major donor in the 1970s.[5] Never a major source, the United States ceased its assistance in 1982 when Tanzania was over a year in arrears on repayment of a prior bilateral loan.

Tanzania's growing dependence on loans calls into question President Nyerere's self-reliance approach. Its successful diversification of aid, however, which has vastly reduced Great Britain's role in Tanzania and limited the influence of any major global power, under-

3. Data are taken from International Monetary Fund, *Direction of Trade Annual* (Washington, DC: International Monetary Fund, various years).

4. Organization for Economic Cooperation and Development, *Geographical Distribution of Financial Flows to Developing Countries* (Paris: Organization for Economic Cooperation and Development, various years).

5. Ibid.

lines Tanzania's continued commitment to nonalignment.

TRADE AND AID: KENYA

In contrast to Tanzania, Kenya's trade and aid relations show a more gradual evolution and, while also becoming increasingly diversified, do so in a quite different way. While Kenya has run into balance-of-trade difficulties in the past few years, they have been less serious than those of Tanzania. Kenya's trade with Britain has shown a slower, smaller, but steadier drop-off. While Tanzania's imports from Britain dropped from 38 percent of all its imports at independence to 13 percent in 1982, Kenya's dropped from 31 percent to 18 percent. Two recent trends are the growing share of imports from oil-producing countries, which reached over 30 percent of total imports following the second oil shock of 1979-80, and the almost total loss of imports from Tanzania and Uganda, which once accounted for 10 percent of all imports.[6]

On the export side, the overall trend is toward greater diversification away from Britain to industrialized countries and toward an increasing importance of markets in developing countries as compared to industrialized countries. In the early 1980s, Kenyan exports to developing countries—both African and non-African—virtually equaled Kenyan exports to the industrialized West. The division between Kenya's exports to industrialized and developing countries, however, is substantially out of the control of the Kenyan government. During periods of high international prices for coffee, the proportion of Kenya's exports to industrialized countries increases; during periods of low coffee prices, Kenya's overall export levels diminish, with the result that exports to developing countries, though relatively steady in volume, increase as a proportion of the total.

In real terms, Kenya's volume of trade stagnated in its second decade of independence, after growing very rapidly in the first. But Kenya's experiences in this regard were not as bad as Tanzania's. While Kenya has always had a negative trade balance, it has been balanced historically by the revenue and foreign exchange generated by tourism and foreign investment. But the double blow dealt by the second oil shock and the international recession put Kenya into a serious balance-of-payments crisis in the early 1980s.

Kenya's foreign assistance record also evolved differently from Tanzania's. Virtually all of Kenya's foreign assistance has come from Western industrialized countries and from multilateral institutions closely tied to them such as the European Economic Community, the World Bank, and the IMF. Kenya has, however, diversified its aid resources among the industrialized countries. Britain continues to be an important source of aid, although not as predominantly since the middle 1970s.[7] The most important trend in Kenya's foreign assistance is the recent emergence of the United States as the largest single aid source. Prior to this, Kenya, like Tanzania, did not allow either of the two superpowers to play a large role in development assistance.

KENYAN-TANZANIAN RELATIONS

Relations between Kenya and Tanzania have been marked by a combination

6. International Monetary Fund, *Direction of Trade Annual.*

7. Organization for Economic Cooperation and Development, *Geographical Distribution.*

of cooperation and suspicion that go back to the early days of colonial rule. Under colonialism, the British created fiscal arrangements and infrastructural services for all of East Africa. Even then, the Tanzanian government distrusted white-settler-dominated Kenya and argued that interterritorial arrangements did not equally distribute the benefits of cooperation. At independence, Tanzania insisted that a new basis of cooperation be found that could better serve the interests of all the newly independent East African states. The Kenyans, preoccupied with the struggle for independence and domestic conflicts over both power and policy, gave little attention to the details of regional cooperation. In the first years of independence, the leaders of both countries took regional cooperation for granted, accustomed as they were to cooperating in the anticolonial struggle. They failed to perceive that independence would make regional integration more, rather than less, difficult once separately defined national interests and national development came to the fore.

The Kampala Agreement of 1964 was intended to provide the basis for more balanced cooperation between Tanzania, Kenya, and Uganda, the last being the third former British colony in East Africa. It sought to limit trade imbalances and to reallocate investment so as to enhance industrialization opportunities for Tanzania and Uganda. The arrangements were never effectively implemented because the changes involved were more difficult than had been foreseen. In the years following the Kampala Agreement, regional cooperation continued to falter while Kenya's predominance in intraregional trade increased. The three countries tried to overcome the difficulties by setting up a

new system of regional cooperation in June 1967—the EAC. The EAC sought to "strengthen and regulate industrial, commercial and other relations of the partner states in order that there must be accelerated and sustained expansion of economic activities within East Africa, the benefit of which shall be equally distributed."[8] Four autonomous corporations were set up to manage the railways, harbors, airways, and ports together with telecommunications. Their headquarters were divided among the participant states, and the EAC's overall administrative headquarters was established in Arusha, Tanzania.

Although cooperation in the EAC was encouraging in the initial years, relations between the member countries began to deteriorate by the early 1970s. Despite elements of the treaty favorable to Uganda and Tanzania, Kenya continued to dominate interterritorial trade. This led the other two partners to take steps to protect their own interests. In 1972, exchange controls and import restrictions were reimposed, diminishing the effectiveness of the common market and dissolving the common monetary area. Restrictions were also imposed by member states that limited the efficient functioning of the four service corporations.

The demise of EAC cooperation was given further impetus by Idi Amin's coup against Uganda's President Obote in 1971. President Nyerere detested Idi Amin and refused to meet with him. Thus the EAC's highest body, the East African Authority, which consisted of the presidents of the three member countries, did not meet after 1971. This

8. United Nations, *Survey of Economic Conditions in Africa, 1971* (New York: United Nations, 1972), p. 197.

absence precluded any high-level negotiations to rectify problems in the community. At the same time, Uganda's economic collapse under Amin made cooperation and planning all the more difficult.

While the Amin coup was the decisive event in the downfall of the EAC, the immediate cause of its breakup in 1977 was failed brinkmanship by both Kenya and Tanzania. In 1976, the four common service corporations faced overwhelming difficulties due to the cumulative impact of interstate financial restrictions and political conflicts. By the end of 1976, only East African Airways remained operational as a community venture. In January 1977, the airline was grounded and Kenya, not expecting Tanzanian retaliation, immediately set out to form its own national airway, using equipment from East African Airways to make up its core. Tanzania, incensed at what was viewed as a lack of goodwill by Kenya, hit back in the only way it could— by closing its border with Kenya to cut off Kenyan exports. Bilateral relations sharply deteriorated, removing any basis for continuing the EAC, and in June 1977 the community officially died.

Both Kenya and Tanzania paid substantially for the demise of regional cooperation. In absolute terms, Kenya was hurt more. Exports to Tanzania dried up, and the border closure made trade with Zambia, which had become a significant importer of Kenyan goods, all but impossible. The lack of a secure regional market has been a major factor behind Kenya's failure to sustain foreign private investment. On the other side of the border, Tanzania's tourist trade was devastated since its most spectacular game parks are located near the Kenyan border and have historically depended on Kenyan tour operators for their supply of visitors. Tanzanian consumers also lost their access to many commodities for which there were no consistently supplied alternatives. In general, the border closure encouraged smuggling, increased prices, and limited employment opportunities in both countries.

The closure of their common border and the collapse of the EAC led Kenya and Tanzania to reorient their regional relations. For Kenya, this meant improving political ties and expanding economic links to Ethiopia and the Sudan. It also meant a search for new markets in the Middle East and a subsequent shift in attitude toward Israel. Although Kenya had broken official relations with Israel in the aftermath of the 1973 Arab-Israeli war, solid commercial and intelligence links between the two countries had continued. In the late 1970s and early 1980s, however, Kenya became much more pro-Arab in political orientation, and its exports to Middle Eastern countries expanded.

By the end of 1977, efforts were under way to normalize relations between Kenya and Tanzania. This process proved to be very difficult until 1983, when a number of factors combined to produce a settlement. Until then, the situation on the ground was one of protracted stalemate. Each country maintained preconditions for negotiations that the other country found unacceptable.

Just as Idi Amin's successful coup was a key event in the collapse of regional cooperation, his removal improved the possibility for Kenyan-Tanzanian détente. Until Amin's fall in April 1979, the Tanzanians felt that continuing Kenyan trade with Uganda, particularly the supply of oil from Kenya's refinery in Mombasa, was propping up Amin. Kenya, for its part, was wary of Nyerere's intentions in moving militarily against Amin and feared that the post-Amin regime would be closely tied to Tanzania. In fact, Tanzanian influence in post-Amin Uganda has not been extensive. Political stability has not been reestablished in Uganda and the several governments of the post-Amin era have all sought close ties to Kenya as well as to Tanzania.

Improvements in Kenyan-Tanzanian relations resulted from shifts in the Kenyan political scene, most significantly Daniel Arap Moi's succeeding Jomo Kenyatta after the latter's death in 1978. Also in 1978, Bruce McKenzie, minister of agriculture and the architect of Kenya Airways, was killed in an aircrash. He had been one of the two politicians most hostile to Tanzania. The other, Charles Njonjo, former attorney general and close adviser to both Kenyatta and Moi, fell into political disgrace in 1983.

In mid-1983, Tanzanian Prime Minister Edward Sokoine signaled a new Tanzanian initiative to resolve the dispute when he publicly stated that the border should be reopened and Kenyan-Tanzanian relations normalized. This initiative stemmed from Tanzania's very severe economic crisis and its desire to present international donors, especially the IMF, with a pragmatic image. The pieces of the East African puzzle were finally falling into place. In November 1983, the presidents of Kenya, Tanzania, and Uganda, meeting in Arusha, the former headquarters of the defunct EAC, announced agreement on the major issues in dispute between them. Nearly seven years after its closing, the border between Kenya and Tanzania was reopened.

In the short period since the agreement, relations between Kenya and Tanzania have improved slowly but steadily. Regional cooperation is likely to continue to be less formal and institutionalized than in the old EAC. The most probable format for broadened economic cooperation will be the Preferential Trade Area for Eastern and Southern Africa, which the U.N. Economic Commission for Africa has been attempting to create in recent years. The general economic decline of the states to be covered by the Preferential Trade Area makes cooperation more imperative, but also more difficult.

KENYA'S REGIONAL DIPLOMACY

In Kenya's relations with neighboring countries, three themes—national consolidation, territorial security, and economic development and integration—have predominated. Kenya has attempted to maintain friendly and stable relations in the region, but has had a difficult time in doing so. In the late 1970s Kenya became increasingly isolated due to ideological trends, political upheavals, and conflicts of interest with neighboring countries. Kenyan policymakers sometimes overestimated their ability to influence neighboring states and lacked sensitivity to the possible costs of isolation. In recent years, with growing great-power involvement in northeast Africa, regional diplomacy has become even more complex and difficult. But by the mid-1980s, the threat of isolation had subsided and Kenya was becoming more active, and astute, in its regional diplomatic dealings. While President Moi's efforts to mediate in the 1985 Ugandan civil war did not succeed, the effort itself was noteworthy.

Of Kenya's neighbors, only Somalia has posed serious and direct threats to Kenyan security. The northeastern portion of Kenya is populated by ethnic

Somali and was claimed by Somalia after the end of colonial rule. During the early years of independence, the Kenyan army fought a low-level counterinsurgency war against *shifta* rebels supported by Somalia. In 1967 a détente was negotiated between the two countries, but relations again worsened after the socialist military regime took power in Mogadishu in 1969 and established close military ties with the Soviet Union. Somalia also claimed the Ogaden region of neighboring Ethiopia, and the shared perception of threat created a strong bond between Kenya and Ethiopian Emperor Haile Selassie.

The year 1977 marked a turning point in Ethiopian-Somali relations that posed serious policy dilemmas for Kenya. During the mid-1970s, a military creeping coup had overthrown the imperial feudal oligarchy in Ethiopia and had turned Ethiopia toward Moscow and Marxism. Russian efforts to creat a *Pax Sovieticus* between Somalia and Ethiopia failed. Somalia expelled the Russians and adopted a pro-Western stance. In 1977, war broke out between Somalia and Ethiopia in the Ogaden, nationalist fervor ran high inside Somalia, and the conflict spread into Kenya. In Nairobi, geopolitical logic outweighed ideological considerations and Kenya strengthened relations with the revolutionary government of Ethiopia, despite the presence there of Soviet advisers and thousands of Cuban troops. The increased tension with Somalia also prompted Kenya to expand its hitherto very small military budget and led to the first important agreement with the United States for the supply of military hardware. Kenya decided to increase its ties to Washington in hopes of gaining American leverage against any Somali efforts to threaten Kenya more actively.

In the early 1980s, Kenya's relations with the antagonists in the Horn began to shift. Its growing military ties to the United States antagonized Ethiopia, and Kenya became more convinced of Washington's willingness and ability to restrain Somalia from acting on its designs on northeast Kenya. In late 1981 Kenya and Somalia reached agreement on a new détente. Kenyan officials now believe that Somalia has renounced its claims on parts of Kenya.[9] Somalia, for its part, made no effort to exploit the uncertainty in Kenya immediately following the failed coup attempt in August of 1982. Kenya clearly hopes that an overall easing of tensions in the Horn might provide an opportunity to establish broader, more stable relations with all of its northern neighbors.

TANZANIA'S
REGIONAL DIPLOMACY

Issues of political principle, in particular the assertion of meaningful national and continental independence in a more equitable global community, have been central to Tanzania's foreign relations. It is the seriousness of Tanzania's purpose and the insistence that President Nyerere had brought to this task that has given Tanzania an international significance far beyond what its size, resources, and location would warrant. The top priority in Tanzania's foreign relations has been the ongoing struggle against colonialism and apartheid in southern Africa. Tanzania emerged in the mid-1970s as a spokesman for the Front Line States (FLS) and as a leader in the regional integration activities of majority-ruled nations in southern Africa. Continual and consuming involvement in southern Africa led Presi-

9. *Standard* (Nairobi), 8 Sept. 1981.

dent Nyerere to conclude that African states weaken their ability to gain international support for the struggle against racial oppression in southern Africa by their unwillingness to criticize oppressive leaders and regimes in black Africa. His own conflict with Ugandan dictator Idi Amin, which culminated in the Tanzanian army's invasion of Uganda and overthrow of Amin in 1979, raises profound issues for Africa's international relations and for the meaning of pan-Africanism.

From the early days of its independence, Tanzania has played a major role in supporting liberation struggles in southern Africa. Dar es Salaam has been the headquarters for the Liberation Committee of the Organization of African Unity (OAU) and has provided temporary or permanent bases for many liberation groups, including the Front for the Liberation of Mozambique, the Popular Movement for the Liberation of Angola, Namibia's South West Africa People's Organization, and South Africa's African National Congress. Tanzania played a particularly significant role in the struggles leading to the independence of Mozambique and Zimbabwe. Tanzania provided training facilities and military bases for the Front for the Liberation of Mozambique, as well as schools and social services for Mozambican refugees. Since Mozambique became independent in 1975, trade between the two countries has expanded and a very close bilateral political relationship has emerged.

The Rhodesian crisis, which began in 1965, led Tanzania to develop close ties to Zambia in order to assist the latter in overcoming its dependence on transportation routes through southern Africa to maintain its foreign trade. In addition to the construction of the Tazara rail-

way, during the early 1970s, the two countries cooperated in the construction of an oil pipeline and an all-weather paved road between Dar es Salaam and Lusaka. Throughout the 1970s cooperation between the two countries increased, but their bilateral relationship has not been without serious tensions. Due to the collapse of international copper prices, Zambia has been unable to keep up with payments due Tanzania for upkeep of the Tazara railway. In the past several years, the railway has become inefficient and costly. The Lusaka-Dar es Salaam axis has, thus far, not lived up to the hopes of either country nor to its potential.

Tanzania's role in the Zimbabwe conflict was somewhat different from its role in Mozambique, but no less important. While Tanzania did provide important material support for the liberation movements in Zimbabwe, its more important role was diplomatic, in relation both to the Western powers and to the conflicting factions among the Zimbabwean liberation movements. President Nyerere was one of the architects of the FLS's strategy of combining assistance to and support for the guerrilla struggles with diplomatic pressure on Western powers to play an active role in seeking a negotiated settlement leading to majority rule.[10] Guerrilla warfare was to be encouraged as the lever with which to pressure Western governments, especially those of Britain and the United States.

This strategy proved successful. Zimbabwe gained its independence in April 1980 following a negotiated cease-fire

10. See David F. Gordon and Ali A. Mazrui, "Black African States and the Struggle for Southern Africa," in *Southern Africa since the Portuguese Coup*, ed. J. Seiler (Boulder, CO: Westview Press, 1980), pp. 183-94.

and internationally supervised elections. President Nyerere had played a substantial role in this process through his influence on Western leaders, especially President Carter, and on the leaders of the guerrilla movements, especially Robert Mugabe. Two forceful interventions by Nyerere had kept the negotiated settlement on track. In early 1979 he had urged the United States and Britain to reject recognition of the internal-settlement regime of Bishop Muzorewa. Later that year, he had urged Mugabe not to walk out of the Lancaster House negotiations and resume the armed struggle.

Tanzania has built upon its role in the FLS to become actively involved in regional cooperation initiatives in southern Africa. The first meeting of the Southern Africa Development Coordination Conference (SADCC) was held in Arusha, Tanzania, in 1979. It brought together representatives of Angola, Mozambique, Botswana, Lesotho, Swaziland, Zambia, Malawi, Tanzania, and, upon its independence, Zimbabwe. At the meeting four main development objectives were agreed upon: (1) reduction of economic dependence, particularly on the Republic of South Africa; (2) forging links to create a genuine and equitable regional integration; (3) mobilization of resources to promote the implementation of national, interstate, and regional policies; and (4) concerted actions to secure international cooperation within the framework of SADCC's strategy for economic liberation.[11]

Because SADCC's goals are extensive and long term, the group's short-term achievements have been limited. Access to large amounts of international funding has not been forthcoming. SADCC goals have been vulnerable to South Africa's regional destabilization activities. Finally, many states find it difficult to put current resources into projects and plans the payoffs of which are so far in the future. For example, Tanzania has been given responsibility within SADCC for regional industrial development, a task for which it is hardly prepared. Despite its concern for liberation in southern Africa, the potential for effective Tanzanian leadership in SADCC is poor. While ideological sympathies and political ties have reoriented Tanzania's efforts to the south, economic and geographical realities will continue to draw it back to East Africa.

As mentioned previously, one factor that drew Tanzania away from East Africa originally was Nyerere's keen distaste for Ugandan dictator Idi Amin. In October 1978, Ugandan forces invaded and occupied the Kagera salient in Tanzania, with Amin declaring it to be a part of Uganda. Nyerere, infuriated, vowed to drive the Ugandan troops out of Tanzania and to get the OAU to condemn Uganda's aggression.

While the Tanzanian army mobilized for the first task, Nyerere had a series of meetings with other African leaders after the OAU took up the dispute. The OAU's attempt to mediate the conflict, rather than condemn Amin, enraged Nyerere. Other than Tanzania's partners in the FLS, only Ethiopia among the OAU states was willing to vote for condemnation. The OAU's refusal to act convinced Nyerere that unilateral Tanzanian action to remove Amin was justified.

In January 1979, Tanzanian troops entered Uganda. At the same time, several anti-Amin Ugandan exile groups

11. Arne Tostensen, *Dependence and Collective Self-Reliance in Southern Africa* (Uppsala: Scandinavian Institute of African Studies, 1982), p. 96.

put together a force to march on the Ugandan capital of Kampala. Tanzania hoped to play only a limited role in the overthrow of Amin. But when Amin lost Soviet military support and advisers, Libya stepped in to provide him with large-scale military assistance. Tanzania then decided to throw all of its military weight into the struggle; 40,000 Tanzanian troops marched into Uganda, and in April 1979 Idi Amin fled and his regime collapsed.

Just as it was impossible to remain minimally involved in the effort to topple Amin, so it was very difficult for Tanzania to extricate itself from Uganda afterwards. The Tanzanians could not help but become the de facto authority in Uganda. A year after Amin's fall, over 15,000 Tanzanian troops remained in Uganda. While Kenya feared that Tanzania wished to set up a puppet state in Uganda, Tanzania was being bankrupted by its inability to extricate itself from Uganda without leaving it in total chaos. Estimates of the cost to Tanzania are upwards of $500 million, almost half in foreign exchange.[12]

Tanzania's military involvement in Uganda has been followed by more limited military engagements in other regional conflicts. In the mid-1980s, Tanzanian forces were sent to Mozambique to help the Front for the Liberation of Mozambique's government stave off the South African-backed rebels of the Mozambique National Resistance Movement and to the Seychelles to provide general security support for that country's Left-leaning regime, which had been the target of a coup by South African mercenaries. The continuing

12. Precise figures are impossible to obtain. Tanzanian officials claim that the ongoing costs are greater than $500 million. The World Bank has used that figure in some of its reports.

willingness of the Tanzanian government to commit its forces to neighboring countries, despite the severe financial and economic crisis Tanzania faces, is an indication of the high priority the regime puts on broader continental issues.

KENYA, TANZANIA, AND THE SUPERPOWERS

In recent years Africa has played an increasing role in the global competition between the United States and the Soviet Union. Northeast Africa and the Indian Ocean constitute one geographical focal point of this competition. There, the United States has sought closer relations and an expanded military presence in response to the rise of the Soviet Union's global reach, the fall of the Shah of Iran, the Soviet invasion of Afghanistan, and general instability in the Persian Gulf area. The Soviet Union, for its part, became a major supplier of military equipment to a number of countries in the area and attempted, along with Cuba, to form an anti-imperialist front among them. Kenya and Tanzania have responded very differently to the increasing role of the two superpowers in the region.

Kenya has substantially increased its ties to the United States and has become more openly identified with the United States on East-West Issues. As mentioned, one source of this shift was Kenya's concern about expanded U.S. military support for Somalia. Increasing ties to the United States and more open identification with the West were also congruent with Kenya's bucking of the leftist ideological trend in East Africa. After Kenya's 1979 election, the first held under President Moi, Kenya's pro-Western shift became more pronounced.

For example, Kenya participated in the United States-sponsored boycott of the Moscow Olympics in 1980 to protest the Soviet invasion of Afghanistan.

In 1980 Kenya concluded a treaty with the United States that, in return for expanded economic aid and more military equipment, provided the United States with access to air and naval facilities in Kenya. The United States sought the treaty with Kenya as part of its overall strategy of expanding its ability to rapidly project military force in the Persian Gulf-southwest Asia quadrant. The Kenyans saw the treaty as an inexpensive opportunity to expand its relatively limited military capacity while at the same time gaining protection under the U.S. security umbrella at a time when the Soviet capacity to intervene in Africa was expanding.

Kenya's close ties to the United States provide a range of benefits in the short term. The United States has played a major role in arming and training the Kenyan air force and has undertaken port and airport expansion in Mombasa. U.S. military assistance to Kenya, as of 1985, is $20 million per year. The United States also provided increased development assistance and food aid following the abortive coup attempt in August 1982. But the more intimate links with the United States create long-term risks for the Kenyan government. The highly visible American presence and incidents of conflict between U.S. military personnel and Kenyan nationals have promoted anti-U.S. and antigovernment feelings. Too close a relationship with the United States might be detrimental to Kenya's overall goal of expanding its influence both in Africa and elsewhere in the Third World.

Unlike Kenya, Tanzania sees increased superpower involvement in Africa as providing an even greater need for strict nonalignment. Nyerere criticized the Soviet Union for supporting Idi Amin, and he criticized Washington for "intimidating and threatening" Indian Ocean countries in its efforts to obtain military bases following events in Iran and Afghanistan. In a speech in 1980, Nyerere reiterated his long-held belief that "non-alignment is the only basis on which a small and weak state like ours can maintain its political independence."[13] He criticized both the United States and the Soviet Union for viewing all events in the world through the lens of East-West conflict.

In recent years, Tanzanian-Soviet relations have improved as a result of the fall of Idi Amin, less extensive ties between Tanzania and China, and the increasingly active role of Tanzania in southern Africa. Tanzanian relations with the United States grew substantially in the first half of the Carter administration. American officials saw Nyerere as a crucial figure in their efforts to achieve negotiated settlements of the conflicts in southern Africa. But, by the end of the Carter administration, with its shift to a concern about building up U.S. power in the Indian Ocean, relations between Tanzania and the United States began to sour. Under the Reagan administration, these relations have continued to weaken. Tanzania has been vocal in its criticism of the constructive-engagement policy toward southern Africa, while some Reagan administration officials have been openly contemptuous of Tanzania's continuing adherence to a socialist development strategy.

13. Quoted in Colin Legum, ed., *Africa Contemporary Record 1980* (London: Rex Collings, 1981), p. 334.

RELATIONS WITH THE IMF

The IMF has only recently emerged as an important actor in sub-Saharan Africa. Since 1979 the IMF has been locked in a struggle with the Tanzanian government that is likely to presage similar conflicts with other African states given the endemic economic crisis of the 1980s and given the differences between the IMF and African policymakers in their perceptions about the causes of and cures for that crisis. Kenya's relations with the IMF have also included a great deal of conflict, an interesting outcome given that Kenya's rather conservative government and market-oriented economy appear to make it a natural for a cooperative relationship with the fund.

The year 1979 was calamitous for Tanzania's economy. The second oil shock sent the cost of petroleum skyrocketing, and bizarre weather conditions played havoc with Tanzania's crops. These exogenous shocks coincided with major domestic problems, most important, growing anarchy in the state-run agricultural marketing system and a total lack of budgetary realism. Price management became less and less effective; black market activity increased substantially. Available foreign exchange was so low that high-priority needs could not be met.

To meet this crisis, Tanzania sought bridging finance from the international community. It was at this point that the conflict between Tanzania and the IMF began. The IMF proposed a series of stabilization measures, including a large-scale devaluation of the Tanzanian shilling. The Tanzanian government responded with a much more limited reform package.

In a speech on 1 January 1980, Nyerere condemned "the attempt by the IMF to exploit" Tanzania's difficulties and accused it of trying to impose conditions upon Tanzania that were inconsistent with its socialist development strategy and that were of dubious technical relevance.[14] Nonetheless, in September agreement was reached on a lending program that set conditions on credit ceilings, a reduction of external payment arrears, and a reduction of government deficit. But the continuing costs of the Uganda invasion pushed Tanzania's budget even further into deficit. The IMF suspended its lending and the conflict resumed.

Throughout 1981 and 1982, Tanzania's economy continued to deteriorate despite a series of government initiatives to increase exports, give more incentives to agricultural producers, limit government spending, and increase the utilization of existing capacity. In the face of these conditions, the Tanzanian government and the IMF agreed on two points: (1) that large-scale external finance would be needed to break the vicious circle of economic deterioration; and (2) that a significant program of structural adjustment must occur if the external funds were to be used effectively. But conflict continued over two issues that made reaching complete agreement very difficult.

The first disagreement was over the cause of Tanzania's economic decline. The IMF argued that while external shocks made adjustment very difficult, Tanzania's problems were mainly caused by domestic policy errors, including overexpansion of the government's role in the economy and an overvalued currency. Tanzania argued that, while there

14. Ibid., p. 325.

had been serious policy problems, external factors were a more important cause of its economic decline.

The second disagreement, following from the first, was over what kind of domestic adjustments would be most appropriate. The IMF argued for a major overhaul of domestic policy. The Tanzanians continued to believe in the viability of their overall socialist self-reliance approach. They were also firmly opposed to what they believed would be ceding their sovereignty to the IMF by agreeing to its conditions. On the other hand, recognizing the need for IMF funds, Tanzania has put greater emphasis on economic prudence in recent years. In July 1983 a 20 percent devaluation was announced. Tanzania has also further reformed its domestic pricing and marketing structures. In mid-1986, there were signs that an agreement between Tanzania and the IMF was forthcoming. Whether or not it can be sustained, however, is less evident.

Kenya's relations with the IMF have been of a fundamentally different nature from those of Tanzania. Kenya has not had the conflicts of basic principles and assumptions that Tanzania has had. Relations with the fund have not been intensely politicized, and interactions between Kenyan financial officials and fund personnel have remained cordial. Nevertheless, each of the several agreements reached between Kenya and the IMF between the middle-1970s and the early 1980s broke down without fully effective implementation. Generally, the reason for the breakdowns has been the unwillingness of Kenyan officials to undertake the full range of demand-management steps set down in agreements with the fund.[15]

15. Tony Killick, "Kenya, the IMF and the

Kenya's failure to maintain fund programs is significant since, unlike Tanzania, it has not had major conflicts over devaluation nor have its policymakers' assumptions varied radically from those of the fund staff. The Kenyans view the IMF as far too short-term in approach, setting politically unrealistic targets that are not met, but that almost inevitably are recalculated. One of the biggest problems with this approach from the Kenyan side is the need for much high-level manpower to spend a great deal of time either preparing material for the IMF or in actual negotiations with IMF personnel. If the IMF-Tanzania debate reveals African relations with international financial institutions at their most contentious, Kenyan difficulties with the IMF suggest that, even under the best circumstances, relations between Africa and these institutions will be uneasy.

CONCLUSION

Both Kenya and Tanzania have substantially expanded their foreign policy activities since the mid-1970s, moving beyond the postcolonial phase when foreign relations were largely dominated by issues relating to the legacies of colonial rule. Kenya has become a major exporter to other developing countries, has broad links with the states of the European Economic Community, and strong strategic bonds to the United States. Tanzania has become a major actor in the international politics of southern Africa, and Julius Nyerere is an articulate spokesman for developing countries in the North-South debate.

Unsuccessful Quest for Stabilization," in *IMF Conditionality*, ed. John Williamson (Washington, DC: Institute for International Economics, 1983), pp. 381-414.

Both countries have developed a set of characteristic policy styles that have given consistency to their foreign relations.

Have Kenya and Tanzania been successful in their foreign relations? In terms of their own stated goals, each has had both successes and failures. President Nyerere played a major role in achieving a negotiated settlement of the Zimbabwe conflict. He has also succeeded in garnering large amounts of foreign aid for Tanzania, but given Tanzania's policy of self-reliance should that be considered success? Kenya has become a focal point for foreign investment in Africa as well as an increasingly important center for international organizations. Both countries have maintained their territorial integrity and have been free from major external intervention.

On the negative side, both Tanzania and Kenya bear responsibility for the breakdown of East African cooperation, to which each nation was committed in principle. Kenya's policymakers, moreover, were sometimes guilty of overestimating their country's importance. Tanzanian policymakers must take at least a large share of the blame for allowing Tanzania's relations with the IMF to deteriorate to the point where the livelihood of many of its people is threatened. Because of this, Tanzania faces a more serious immediate challenge than does Kenya in its foreign relations.

Despite the schisms of ideology, national interest, and political style that drove Kenya and Tanzania apart in the 1970s, they remain each other's natural partners. The reopening of their common border and their likely participation in the Preferential Trade Area will provide mutual benefits and draw them into a closer bilateral relationship. Kenya and Tanzania face daunting economic and political challenges; political normalization and mutually beneficial economic cooperation are two areas in which both governments can positively affect their own destinies.

ANNALS, *AAPSS,* **489,** January 1987

Security versus Growth: The International Factor in South African Policy

By ROBERT M. PRICE

ABSTRACT: A key feature of South Africa's political dynamics is the linkage between its domestic affairs and its international relations. South Africa's access to international markets for vital capital and technology is threatened by the nature of its domestic socioeconomic and political systems. In its efforts to maintain white rule, the South African government has, over the past 25 years, sought to deal with this threat by uncoupling its domestic affairs from its foreign economic relations. The methods utilized to attempt this have varied. Pretoria has altered its domestic sociopolitical arrangements in ways that it believed, and hoped, would make South Africa more acceptable internationally. It has fashioned its foreign policy so as to attempt to reduce the international consequences of its stigma of racial rule. It has sought to reduce its vital dependence on the international economic system through policies that would increase the autonomy of the South African economy. And, most recently, it has sought to diversify its foreign sources of capital and its trading partners toward countries whose governments and firms are likely to be less sensitive about South Africa's system of white supremacy.

Robert M. Price is associate professor of political science at the University of California, Berkeley. He is the author of Society and Bureaucracy in Contemporary Ghana; U.S. Foreign Policy in Sub-Saharan Africa: National Interest and Global Strategy; *and numerous journal articles and symposium volume contributions dealing with South African domestic and foreign policy, and U.S. policy toward southern Africa. He is also coeditor of* The Apartheid Regime: Political Power and Racial Domination.

MORE than any other state in the contemporary world, South Africa's international situation and its domestic politics are inextricably linked. The dynamics of this linkage have shaped and driven the most important of Pretoria's policies with respect to both South Africa's internal sociopolitical arrangements and its foreign relations.

In its efforts to maintain white minority rule, the government of South Africa has, at least since the end of World War II, been challenged by a fundamental contradiction between its international and domestic requirements. Internationally, South Africa requires access to markets for the export of its minerals and, increasingly, for its manufactured goods, as well as the opportunity to import vital capital, technology, and producer goods. These are prerequisites for the health, growth, and development of its modern industrial economy. But the nature of South Africa's domestic system of white supremacy and the efforts government is required to make in order to maintain it threaten such access to global markets and thus directly place in jeopardy economic growth and development.

This contradiction between domestic and international requirements is a dynamic one: the greater the government's use of overt repression against the black majority, the greater its problems with its international environment. Active political pressure by the majority and its counterpoint, repressive action by the minority government, render the nature of the South African system visible to the world and thus serve as a catalyst for international reactions. Conversely, in periods of political quiescence, Pretoria's international problem remains largely hypothetical. It is when the majority makes its political opposition felt and

visible, and thus when the need of the white government to make its domination manifest is greatest, that the international threat becomes real.

It is, of course, quite common for states to coerce their populations with little adverse effect on their global economic relations. South Africa, however, is afforded no such luxury, and its system of racial domination is the reason why. Since the defeat of nazism, there has been general agreement in the international community on the odiousness of a political system based upon racial classification and stratification. Consequently, Pretoria has experienced increasing diplomatic isolation. This has meant not only frequent votes of condemnation at the United Nations, an international arms and oil embargo, and a sports competition boycott, but, more important, an environment in which public attention focused on South Africa's domestic arrangements translates easily into blocked access to global markets for capital and technology. When black opposition and government repression raise the international salience of South Africa's system of white supremacy, Western governments, international banks, and multinational corporations find themselves unwilling or unable to resist pressures to reduce their economic ties to the South African economy.

DOMESTIC AND INTERNATIONAL LINKAGE

The first clear manifestation of Pretoria's security contradiction is found in the international reverberations set in motion by Sharpeville. On 28 March 1960, in the black township of Sharpeville, a peaceful demonstration against South Africa's pass laws was attacked by police, who shot and killed 69 Africans and wounded another 178. To mourn the dead, the African National Congress (ANC) called a general strike that paralyzed the country for nearly three weeks. In response the government cracked down on the African opposition movement: a state of emergency was declared; thousands were detained; and the main African political organizations were outlawed.

Images of the Sharpeville massacre, carried abroad by the news media, galvanized international attention on the South African system of apartheid and on the efforts of resistance and repression that followed in its wake. Pretoria found itself diplomatically isolated, and faced with threats to its future security and economic growth. At the United Nations the General Assembly, by a massive majority of 96 to 1, passed a resolution that requested all states "to consider taking such separate and collective action as is open to them, . . . to bring about the abandonment of [the apartheid] policies."[1] This resolution represented the first occasion on which the General Assembly called for action against Pretoria, in contrast to earlier resolutions, which had merely condemned apartheid and exhorted the South African government to change course. It initiated a three-year period in which repeated attempts were made to persuade member states to move against the white regime. In 1962 a resolution asking for economic and diplomatic sanctions as well as an arms embargo was passed by a vote of 67 to 16, with 23 abstentions. Although not binding on member states, this resolution produced efforts that led in early 1964 to a partial embargo on weapons sales to Pretoria.[2]

However significant Sharpeville's impact on Pretoria's diplomatic situation, the really dramatic effect of Sharpeville occurred in the behavior of international capital. Foreign investment has been a considerable factor in South Africa's economic development, from the growth of mining after the discovery of diamonds and gold in the nineteenth century, to the industrial maturation associated with the growth of a manufacturing sector in the years after World War II. Between 1946 and 1959 there were only two years when South Africa was not a net importer of capital.[3] But in 1960 Sharpeville created a crisis in South Africa's access to foreign capital. Despite a healthy economic outlook and a favorable trading situation, the years 1960-64 witnessed a huge capital outflow. In 1960 and the early part of 1961, the capital loss was at the rate of R12 million per month, creating a balance-of-payments crisis more severe than any experienced since 1932.[4] Total capital outflow reached R183 million in 1960 and averaged R101 million per annum through 1964.[5] In contrast, during the eight years after World War II, 1947-54, South Africa had experienced an average annual capital inflow of R176 million.[6]

The security measures adopted by Pretoria after Sharpeville had their intended effect. The banning of the ANC

2. Ibid., pp. 513-15.
3. D. Hobart Houghton, *The South African Economy* (Cape Town: Oxford University Press, 1973), pp. 180-81.
4. Ibid., p. 184.
5. Ibid., p. 277.
6. Houghton, *South African Economy* (1964), p. 242.

1. Jack Spence, "South Africa and the Modern World," in *The Oxford History of South Africa,* ed. Monica Wilson and Leonard Thompson (Oxford: Oxford University Press, 1971), 2:513.

and Pan-African Congress, a state of emergency in which over 10,000 persons were detained, the arrest of the entire underground ANC leadership in 1963, as well as the introduction of security and apartheid laws intended to deny to blacks any opportunity for autonomous organization or political expression, ushered in a decade of political quiescence.

Such domestic peace had its international benefits, both diplomatically and economically. The most dramatic gains on the diplomatic front occurred with respect to the United States. After the election of Richard Nixon, U.S. policy tilted toward the white regime.[7] Reasoning that white power in South Africa was stable and invincible, Nixon and his secretary of state, Henry Kissinger, opted to work with Pretoria rather than encourage its opponents.[8] They ended U.S. support for condemnatory resolutions at the United Nations, the U.S. arms embargo was partially lifted, and U.S. business was encouraged to increase its investments in the South African economy.[9] The international capital market can also be said to have tilted toward South Africa once its domestic scene had become more tranquil. In 1965 foreign capital began once more to flow into South Africa. After six consecutive years in which more private capital

left South Africa then entered, the movement of capital in the six years beginning with 1965 was continuously positive, averaging a net annual inflow of R261 million.[10]

The flow of foreign investment into South Africa continued at a high level during the first half of the 1970s. Net capital inflow averaged over R700 million per year.[11] Then in the spring of 1976, the political peace that had existed after the Sharpeville eruption was abruptly shattered. Beginning in the black township of Soweto, and rapidly spreading to the townships of South Africa's larger white cities, the urban black youth rose in rebellion, demonstrating against apartheid policy and attacking symbols of government authority. The Soweto Uprising lasted through the spring of 1977 and was countered by state repression similar to what had been experienced during Sharpeville. Approximately 1000 urban Africans, mostly youths, were killed by the police; black student and cultural organizations were outlawed; black leadership was detained, imprisoned, tortured, or driven into exile.

The international repercussions of Soweto were a replay, in a more intense form, of what had followed the Sharpeville shootings. South Africa was once again thrust into a diplomatic deepfreeze. The greatest diplomatic estrangement of Pretoria from the West in that country's history was experienced.[12] The

7. See Robert M. Price, "U.S. Policy toward South Africa," in *International Politics in Southern Africa,* ed. G. Carter and P. O'Meara (Bloomington: Indiana University Press, 1982), p. 46.

8. See National Security Study Memorandum 39, reprinted in *The Kissinger Study of Southern Africa,* ed. Mohamed A. El-Khawas and Barry Cohen (New York: Lawrence Hill, 1976), p. 105.

9. See Donald Rothchild and John Ravenhill, "From Carter to Reagan," in *Eagle Defiant,* ed. K. Oye et al. (Boston: Little, Brown, 1983), p. 340.

10. See Houghton, *South African Economy* (1973), p. 277.

11. *Quarterly Economic Review,* annual supps (London: Economist Intelligence Unit, 1971-76).

12. See Robert M. Price, "Apartheid and White Supremacy: The Meaning of Reform in the South African Context," in *The Apartheid Regime,* ed. Robert Price and Carl Rosberg (Berkeley: University of California, Institute of International Studies, 1980), p. 313.

U.N arms embargo was expanded and made mandatory, with the approval of Western governments. The U.S. government, under newly elected President Jimmy Carter, took the lead in criticizing Pretoria and, for the first time, demanded a system of majority rule in South Africa. On the international economic front, the flow of direct investment into South Africa slowed to a trickle. The multinational corporations, either because they had doubts about the long-term stability of the republic or because they were under pressure from their shareholders or their home governments, or for a combination of these reasons, no longer considered South Africa a particularly attractive place for investment purposes. Some of the largest foreign corporations announced they would not expand their South African investments and explicitly linked this decision to the country's domestic political and social arrangements. Thus the General Motors Corporation, in announcing that it had no intention of further expanding its South African facilities, stated, "The single most important factor in the creation of a more promising investment climate in South Africa is a positive resolution of the country's pressing social problems, which have their origin in the apartheid system."[13]

As the flow of new foreign capital into South Africa slowed, foreign-owned firms began to repatriate an unusually large proportion of their local earnings. As a result the country's capital flow experienced another dramatic turnabout. Within six months of Soweto, South Africa's capital account, which

had recorded a positive net inflow each year for a decade, swung into reverse. In 1977 there was a net outflow of R810 million, and in 1978 an even more dramatic outflow of R1370 million.[14]

The effective repression of the Soweto Uprising seemed to have the same impact on South Africa's international economic posture as had the crushing of opposition groups in the wake of Sharpeville a decade earlier. It restored a surface peace to the townships, which apparently prepared the way for the South African economy's return to international capital markets. In 1982, according to statistics of the International Monetary Fund, South Africa once again experienced a positive net inflow of direct foreign investment after six continuous years of negative foreign investment flow.[15] At the same time South African-based firms turned successfully to the international banking system, and loan capital replaced direct investment as a source of foreign funds. Unlike the situation in the mid-1960s, however, Pretoria had not been able to sustain the reversal in the international effects of Soweto. In the fall of 1984, unrest returned to South Africa's black townships, and in a form more intense, sustained, and widespread than ever before. The international reverberations were not long in coming.

Reacting to the renewed township unrest and police repression, the anti-apartheid movement in the United States was, by the spring of 1985, successfully pressuring large institutional investors to reduce their holdings in companies with South African ties, and the Con-

13. Quoted in Timothy Smith, "U.S. Firms and Apartheid: Belated Steps Analyzed," *Africa Today*, 24(2):29-33 (1977).

14. *South Africa, Barclay's Country Report*, 3 May 1979; see also *Africa Research Bulletin*, p. 4402 (15 Aug.-14 Sep. 1977).

15. *International Financial Statistics* (various issues, 1977-85).

gress of the United States was poised to enact a law mandating a series of economic sanctions against Pretoria. In early August, international banks, following the lead of Chase Manhattan, called in their short-term loans to South Africa. On 9 September 1985, President Reagan announced limited economic sanctions. The European Economic Community followed suit one day later. The South African economy found itself virtually shut out of the international capital market, and multinational enterprises and banks sought to reduce their South African exposure. Thus total direct investment by U.S. companies, which stood at $2.6 billion in 1981, had been drawn down to $1.8 billion in 1984, and to $1.3 billion by the end of 1985.[16] Some 28 U.S. firms sold their South African assets and withdrew in 1985, up from 7 that did so in 1984, while an increasing number of banks have begun to ban new loans to either private or government borrowers in South Africa.[17]

The dynamic quality of Pretoria's fundamental security dilemma—the contradiction between its needs with respect to maintaining white rule at home while preserving access to markets abroad—is revealed by the interrelated events of the 1960-86 period. Both the contradiction and dynamic interaction have become especially intense since 1976. Isolated internationally because of its system of racial rule, Pretoria finds that when its domestic situation is characterized by visible black resistance, Western govern-

16. Statement by James Kelley, U.S. deputy assistant director of commerce for Africa, before House Foreign Affairs Subcommittee on Africa, reported in *Weekly Mail* (South Africa), 25 Apr.-1 May 1986, p. 4.
17. Bill Sing, "Exodus of U.S. Firms Quickens in South Africa," *Los Angeles Times,* 7 June 1986.

ments are unwilling or unable to resist taking steps against it. Likewise, under these circumstances, multinational corporations and international banks come to recognize significant costs in an expanded, or even continued, presence in South Africa. International isolation is transposed into blocked access to capital and technology markets. Difficulty in obtaining new direct investment from abroad, in importing the latest technology, and in gaining access to international bank loans threatens South Africa's long-term economic growth. Without economic growth, the prospects for domestic tranquility and security decline, for unemployment and downward pressure on wages serve to increase black anger and to make militant political responses more likely. A violent and seemingly unstable domestic situation, in circumstances of diplomatic isolation and hostility, serves to undermine South Africa's foreign economic relations further, by increasing the likelihood of embargoes and sanctions and by reducing the attractiveness of South Africa's investment climate. Such developments in South African foreign economic relations, in turn, threaten economic growth, jobs, and income, producing more alienation and threats to domestic security, in a continuing cycle of economic decline and political unrest.

This cycle, the dynamic reflection of the fundamental security contradiction facing white-ruled South Africa, is schematically represented in Figure 1.

PRETORIA'S RESPONSE

Faced with a security contradiction in which its internal political needs undermine its external economic requirements, Pretoria continuously seeks to uncouple its domestic environment from

FIGURE 1
POLITICAL UNREST AND ECONOMIC DECLINE

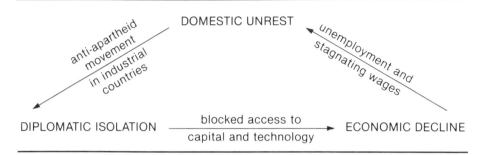

its international environment. On the one hand, it seeks to break out of its status as an international pariah. It strives to be dealt with as a normal country, in which efforts to maintain domestic security do not immediately impact negatively on international economic and political relations. On the other hand, Pretoria adopts measures to increase economic autarky, so as to buffer itself from the threats and costs of international economic withdrawal, sanctions, and embargoes. Although building autonomy from the international community through autarkic economic policy would seem the most effective means to uncouple South Africa's domestic problems from international threats, the costs of such a strategy, and the real limits to what is feasible, render it a second-best strategy to that of achieving international normalcy.

International acceptability

Pretoria has sought to obtain normal status internationally by a combination of two methods. It has altered its domestic sociopolitical arrangements in ways that would supposedly bring South Africa into line with international standards, and it has designed its foreign policy so as to attempt to reduce the international consequences of its stigma of racial rule.

Domestic reform. One of the great ironies of contemporary South African history is that separate development policy—apartheid's political cornerstone—was developed as a means to avoid international pressure for an end to white rule. Separate development involved the ultimate partition of South African territory so as to create nine independent South African states, along with white South Africa. All black South Africans were assigned citizenship in one of these new homelands by the government, using a loose set of criteria based on ethnic ties, linguistic abilities, family history, and the like.

For the architects of apartheid, separate development would perform two basic functions with respect to preserving white rule in South Africa. Domestically, it was intended to contribute to the security of white rule by dividing the African majority and directing its political attention away from racial rule in the South African heartland. At the same time separate development was seen as a way to adapt South Africa's system of white minority rule to a changing international environment. No less an authority than Dr. Hendrik Verwoerd, prime minister from 1958 to 1966 and principal architect of apartheid, provides direct evidence for this view. Defending his separate development policy to his followers within the National Party, Verwoerd declared that "[we] cannot govern without taking into account the tendencies in the world and in Africa." "We must have regard to them."[18]

The tendency alluded to by Verwoerd was the postwar movement away from political systems based upon domination by racial minorities, a tendency reflected in the dismantling of the European colonial empires. With the independence of Ghana and Nigeria in the late fifties, and the imminent arrival of majority rule to the rest of colonial sub-Saharan Africa, the disenfranchisement of the majority of South Africa's population on racial grounds appeared increasingly untenable. Thus, according to Verwoerd, "we can only take them [the tendencies in the world] into account and safeguard the White man's control over our country if we move in the direction of separation... in the political sphere."[19] This point was driven home to the Afrikaner leadership by the diplomatic isolation and international economic pressures they experienced in the wake of Sharpeville. They were pushed to expand the notion of separate development, from the creation of distinct homeland institutions operating within a South African state to the goal of actual partition of South Africa's terri-

tory.[20] Verwoerd explained this new conception of separate development by direct reference to the Sharpeville-related international pressures to which Pretoria was being subjected.

The Bantu will be able to develop into separate states. That is not what we would have liked to see. It is a form of fragmentation that we would not have liked if we were able to avoid it. In the light of the pressure being exerted on South Africa, there is however no doubt that eventually this will have to be done, thereby buying for the White Man his freedom and the right to retain his domination in what is his country.[21]

Separate development, defined as partition, sought to reduce the international problems associated with South Africa's disenfranchised racial majority by simply eliminating that majority through legal definition. Africans would become citizens of the independent states to be created out of the homelands, within which they could exercise their political rights; those found in white South Africa could then be considered temporary sojourners in search of employment. Thus separate development would have the effect of legally transforming the members of the African majority into citizens of other independent countries. As such they would have no more legitimate claim to participate in the governance of South Africa than Turkish guest workers have to participate in the governance of West Germany or

18. From a speech to the South African House of Assembly, 27 Jan. 1959.

19. Ibid.

20. See Jeffrey Butler, Robert Rotberg, and John Adams, *The Black Homelands of South Africa* (Berkeley: University of California Press, 1977), pp. 30-31.

21. Quoted in André du Toit, "Ideological Change, Afrikaner Nationalism and Pragmatic Racial Domination in South Africa," in *Change in Contemporary South Africa*, ed. Leonard Thompson and Jeffrey Butler (Berkeley: University of California Press, 1976), p. 41.

Mexican migrant laborers in the governance of the United States. By this means the South African system could be brought into line with the standards of Western civilization. Moreover, the entire exercise could be explained, justified, and defended—that is, sold to the world—in terms to the two values that were at the core of postwar liberalism: equality and self-determination. Thus the cabinet minister in charge of Bantu affairs defended separate development in this manner:

Every people in the world finds its highest expression and fulfillment in managing its own affairs and in the creation of a material and spiritual heritage for its prosperity. We want to give the Bantu that right also. The demand for self-determination on the part of the non-white nations is one of the outstanding features of the past decade. . . . If the white man is entitled to separate national existence, what right have we to deny that these People have a right to it also? Nationalism is one of the forces which has led to the most beautiful deeds of idealism. . . . Should the Bantu not have it? It will always be my task not only to respect these things of the Bantu, but to assist them to develop it as something beautiful.[22]

While the Afrikaner political elite adopted separate development so as to make South Africa's domestic arrangements more internationally acceptable, their efforts failed to have the desired effect. The international community rejected separate development, refusing to accept it as an instance of genuine self-determination. Not a single government has accorded diplomatic recognition to the four African states thus far created by Pretoria. Rather than providing international acceptability, separate development came to be viewed as one of the most odious aspects of apartheid and as a focus for continued international pressure on South Africa.

As already noted, a second, more intense and prolonged period of international pressure on Pretoria followed the Soweto Uprising of 1976-77. As was the case after Sharpeville, the South African government responded by seeking to alter its domestic arrangement so as to bring them more into line with what would be considered acceptable internationally. By 1978, the South African prime minister had sketched the broad outlines of a reform package that, he said, rendered "apartheid dead." Although international considerations were not solely responsible for the initiation of reforms—structural problems in the economy and the need to deal with domestic black opposition were very significant—it is clear from what has been altered, from the pace at which changes have been introduced, and from the manner in which reforms are announced that for Pretoria the international community is a very important audience for its reform program. The basic thrust of the reform effort initiated in 1978, and slowly implemented and extended since, has been to reduce as much of officially mandated racial separation and discrimination as is consistent with the maintenance of white control of the political system and with what the prime minister calls "the maintenance of white identity." Thus the National Party government has permitted local authorities and private individuals, such as theater owners, to desegregate social amenities such as beaches, parks, and cinemas. It has added multiracial cars to its state-owned railroads, and it has decriminalized interracial marriage and

22. Great Britain, *Hansard*, 18 May 1959, col. 6006, quoted in C. Dunbar Moodie, *The Rise of Afrikanerdom* (Berkeley: University of California Press, 1975), p. 268.

sexual relations by the abolition of the Immorality and Prohibition of Mixed-Marriages Acts.

The elimination of these aspects of what is termed petty apartheid does not affect the system of economic and political domination and consequently is not viewed by black political groups as especially significant. The main audience for these reforms, however, is probably not at home, but abroad, where the stigma of official racism has been costly to Pretoria. Since much of the international criticism of South Africa is focused on its official segregationist practices and on racialist laws such as the Immorality and Prohibition of Mixed-Marriages Acts, their elimination involves a step toward creating a more enlightened international image for the country, without undermining the basis of white control.

In addition to deracializing official and public life, the government's reform effort has sought to achieve economic, geographic, and political control of the black majority by substituting decentralized and indirect means for the coercive apparatus of the central state. Thus the government has attempted to devolve a variety of control and law-and-order functions that had been performed by white officialdom to town councils, whose members are drawn from, and elected by, the residents of the black urban townships. It also hopes to rely increasingly on market mechanisms as a means of control and social separation, rather than on direct state controls. Thus, instead of relying on apartheid's bureaucratically imposed system of influx control and pass laws to regulate the movement of Africans from rural to urban areas, the government appears to be ready to rely on the availability of jobs and housing in urban areas to

accomplish the same function. The switch from state to market mechanisms of control and separation is nicely captured in an Afrikaans-language newspaper commentary on the elimination of state-mandated hotel segregation:

With the unconditional opening of hotels and other licenced business premises for consumers of all races, another step away from the constitutional discrimination has been taken.

The reservation of the right of admission and prices are now the methods with which criteria will be maintained . . . who will determine the criteria? The answer is that criteria are determined according to what people can afford and circumstances in which they feel at home.[23]

The underlying logic of Pretoria's reform program can be summarized as an intention to substitute indirect rule—blacks controlling blacks—and the invisible hand of the market for the fist of the white state. If successful, such efforts would not only reduce the friction between white officialdom and the black population, but would also render South Africa more palatable internationally by reducing the explicitly and visibly racial aspects of its system of domination.

Despite a great deal of effort to package its reform program for foreign consumption and to broadcast its reformist message to the international community, Pretoria has found, to its great and public consternation, that international economic and diplomatic pressures have increased. The primary reason for the increase is that the South African government has been unwilling to tackle the core of its political problem—the white minority's monopoly of

23. *Die Vaderland*, 10 Apr. 1986, reprinted in *South African Digest*, 18 Apr. 1986, p. 342.

political power. The urban black population, increasingly militant over the past decade, is demanding an end to white political supremacy, not just the dismantling of apartheid. Thus militant and violent opposition has continued in the townships, despite real changes in the system of apartheid. It is clear that in the current era the international community, in both its governmental and business guises, is taking its lead from the black population. Domestic reform, unless it demonstrably satisfies the aspirations of South Africa's blacks, is unlikely to be effective in gaining international acceptability for Pretoria.

Regional policy. As Dr. Verwoerd correctly predicted, the end of colonial rule in sub-Saharan Africa did not bode well for white South Africa. The one foreign policy issue upon which all of the newly independent states have agreed is that priority should be given to completing the abolition of white rule on the African continent. They have pursued their efforts to eliminate South African apartheid and minority rule in the United Nations, where, since the period of Sharpeville, they have spearheaded the campaign for an arms embargo and for economic sanctions. More important, from Pretoria's vantage point, they have contributed indirectly but significantly to South Africa's diplomatic isolation from the Western industrial countries. The Western nations, and particularly the Europeans, have been concerned about being able to maintain and expand their trade relations with Africa and, more generally, with the Third World. Yet a close relationship to Pretoria, under conditions of intense and united hostility toward South Africa on the part of the governments of black Africa, could harm the long-term economic interests of an industrial country. It is this concern with the reaction in black Africa that is probably responsible for the international failure of separate development, that is, for the unwillingness of a single country to offer diplomatic recognition to the Pretoria-created homeland states.

South African officials, from Verwoerd to the present, have recognized the relationship between the diplomatic hostility and ostracism they have received from Africa and the insecurity and isolation that have developed in their relations with the industrial countries of Europe and North America. As a result, a major preoccupation of South African foreign policy has been to break the united front of African hostility. During the late 1960s and early 1970s Pretoria pursued a policy toward the newly independent states of black Africa that it termed détente. Essentially, South Africa sought to exchange the provision of economic resources for diplomatic recognition and friendly relations. Although several of the most conservative African leaders flirted briefly with the idea of a relationship with Pretoria, détente never succeeded as a strategy for breaking down Africa's united opposition. More recently, Pretoria has focused its African policy on the states of the southern African region.

Since the late 1970s, Pretoria has pursued a policy that seeks to establish what I elsewhere called a "regime of regional hegemony."[24] It seeks to obtain

24. See Robert M. Price, "South Africa and Afro-Marxism: Pretoria's Relations with Mozambique and Angola in Regional Perspective," in *Afro-Marxist Regimes: Ideology and Policy*, ed. E. Keller and D. Rothchild (Boulder, CO: Lynne Reinner, forthcoming). See also idem, "Southern African Regional Security: Pax or Pox Pretoria?"

public and de jure acknowledgment from African neighbors of its dominant role in the region and of its ability to direct their internal and foreign policies on matters affecting South Africa globally and domestically.

To achieve this objective, Pretoria has deployed its superior military might and dominant economic position in the region. Usually referred to as a destabilization policy, this method of imposing hegemony has a number of distinct elements. These are summarized in Table 1. First, the South African military has launched cross-border attacks. These have taken the form of large-scale air and ground assaults, as have occurred regularly into Angola since 1979, or commando raids, as have been directed against Mozambique, Botswana, Lesotho, and Zimbabwe, as well as Angola. Second, South Africa has provided extensive assistance to insurgent movements in Angola and Mozambique. The provision by Pretoria of military equipment, logistical and communications assistance, training, and, in the case of Angola, direct air force and ground troop support, have helped the Resistencia nacional moçambicana in Mozambique and the National Union for the Total Independence of Angola, in Angola, develop militarily to the point at which they can threaten the survival of the governments of their respective countries. The third component in Pretoria's effort to establish hegemony involves the use of South Africa's pivotal position in the regional economy. The landlocked

countries of the region depend on the South African transportation and port network for at least two-thirds of their imports and exports. South African mines employ several hundred thousand migrant workers from neighboring countries, who remit a portion of their earnings home in the form of foreign exchange. Pretoria has been able to take advantage of these, and other dependencies, in order to squeeze the economies of her neighbors. Mozambique, Lesotho, and Zimbabwe have been particular targets for South Africa's economic leverage.

The campaign of military, political, and economic pressure serves a number of purposes for Pretoria. The most immediate goal is to eliminate the ANC from southern Africa. What is being sought, however, is not simply the expulsion of the ANC cadre and organizational infrastructure. Rather, Pretoria seeks to force regional states into signing formal treaties of nonagression, the key provision of which is the establishment of a joint security commission. In January of 1986, the South African state president proposed creating a regionally based "permanent joint mechanism for dealing with matters of security."[25] "Security," in this context, must be understood as a code word for eliminating the ANC in all its guises. According to President Botha, should his proposal for a joint security mechanism "be ignored or rejected," Pretoria "would have no choice but to take effective measures in self-defence."[26] In other words, it would continue its regional policies of military attacks, support for

---

World Policy Journal, 2(3):533-54 (Summer 1985); idem, "Creating New Political Realities: Pretoria's Drive for Regional Hegemony," in *African Crisis Areas and U.S. Foreign Policy*, ed. Gerald J. Bender, James S. Coleman, and Richard L. Sklar (Berkeley: University of California Press, 1985), pp. 64-88.

25. See "Text of State President's Speech upon Opening of 1986 Parliament," *South African Digest*, 7 Feb. 1986, p. 100.
26. Ibid.

TABLE 1
IMPOSITION OF REGIONAL HEGEMONY POLICY

Country	Destabilization (Support for Insurgent Movements)	Military Attack	Economic Pressure
Angola	Support for UNITA,* 1976 to present	Invasion, intermittent, 1977 to present Air attack, intermittent, 1980 to present Occupation of Cunene province, 1979-85	
Botswana		Commando raid, June 1985 Commando raid, May 1986	Delayed Customs Union payments
Lesotho	Support for LLA† Support for coup, January 1986	Commando raid on ANC‖ houses, December 1982 Commando raid on ANC houses, December 1985	Border closure, 1983, 1986 Delayed Customs Union payments
Mozambique	Support for RENAMO,‡ 1979 to present; reduced support after Nkomati Accord of 1984	Commando raid on ANC houses, January 1981 Air strike against ANC houses, May 1983	Cut employment of mine workers Reduced use of railroad and port facilities
Zimbabwe	Support for ZAPU§ and Ndebele dissidents, 1979-81	Commando raid on airfield, July 1982 Commando raid, August 1982 Commando raid, May 1986	Petrol cutoff, 1981

*National Union for the Total Independence of Angola.
†Lesotho Liberation Army.
‡Resistencia nacional moçambicana, which is also known as Moçambique resistencia nacional (MNR)
§ Zimbabwe African People's Union.
‖ African National Congress.

insurgent movements, and economic pressure.

The emphasis on formal treaties and joint security mechanisms can be understood in terms of Pretoria's drive for international acceptability. If African countries are seen to be engaged diplomatically with Pretoria, and, more significantly, if their security forces are actively cooperating with their South African counterparts in cooperative security efforts, then a sharp break in the Africa-wide consensus on the need to ostracize South Africa will have been achieved. With Africa divided on the issue of cooperative engagement with Pretoria, the way would presumably be open for Western countries to reduce the pressure on, and improve their relations with, South Africa. As one South African newspaper put it, nonaggression pacts with regional neighbors represent "the beginning of a new road which would, if followed ... lead South Africa back into Africa and through Africa back into the world."[27] Consequently, when Mozambique signed such a pact

27. *Sunday Times* (Johannesburg), 18 Mar. 1984, reprinted in *South African Digest*, 23 Mar. 1984, p. 19.

with South Africa in the spring of 1984—the Nkomati Accord—the occasion was hailed in South Africa as a major breakthrough with respect to the country's most pressing global concerns. "A completely new . . . game is under way," wrote one South African media commentator, "and with so many new teams in the league it should be clear to all but the most dense of overseas observers that there is just no place on the field for purveyors of sanctions, boycotts, and disinvestment."[28] A more restrained *Sunday Times* of Johannesburg opined, "The new alliances in Southern Africa will have a valuable spin-off benefit in the international arena by making the prospect of economic sanctions against South Africa—ever present for two decades—more remote."[29]

With the signing of the Nkomati Accord in March 1984, Pretoria's regional strategy for achieving international acceptability began to bear fruit. Within a month, P.W. Botha was invited for official visits to Portugal, Germany, and Great Britain. The prime minister's tour, which eventually involved stops in six countries, was the first time in over twenty years that a South African head of government had paid an official visit to Europe. Success, however, was short-lived.

When Nkomati was signed, it had been almost seven years since the end of the Soweto Rebellion. South Africa was once again characterized by a surface tranquility; the large-scale township unrest had seemingly run its course. Thus South Africa's domestic situation, in early 1984, had created a context in which a diplomatic breakthrough was possible. But within six months of Nkomati, urban unrest erupted once again, spreading from the townships of the Transvaal to engulf eventually nearly every black urban residential area in the country. The international benefits of a regional policy of hegemony imposition quickly evaporated. With images of the daily confrontations between township residents and police beamed nearly instantly to the outside world, and with the death toll from police actions mounting each day, the posture adopted by Western governments toward Pretoria was increasingly determined by its domestic, rather than its regional, policies. Diplomatic relations with the industrial states became more strained than ever, and economic pressure from sanctions, embargoes, and disinvestment, both actual and threatened, mounted.

The shifting fortunes of Pretoria's regional policy during 1984-85 reveal the severe limits of foreign policy as a means to establish international acceptability or normalcy, as long as South Africa is ruled by a racial minority. Sensitive to the corrosive effect that its domestic arrangement has on its diplomatic and global economic relations, Pretoria seeks to uncouple its international from its domestic environments by building international acceptability. This effort, however, is continually short-circuited by the very coupling it seeks to avoid. Neither domestic reform nor foreign policy has been able to create acceptability because a volatile domestic situation prevents the consolidation of a global perception of South Africa as a normal country.

International autonomy

For South Africa, autonomy from the international economic system is an

28. *Natal Mercury*, 5 May 1984, reprinted in *South African Digest*, 11 May 1984, p. 21.
29. *Sunday Times*, 18 Mar. 1984, reprinted in *South African Digest*, 23 Mar. 1984, p. 21.

alternative to international acceptability as a means to reduce the cost of maintaining white political control. Autarkic economic policies, if successfully pursued, would increase South Africa's self-reliance and thus reduce its vulnerability to international economic pressures. Such policies have already been adopted in certain limited areas, and with some notable success. As it finds that international and domestic environments cannot be uncoupled through a combination of domestic reform and foreign policy, Pretoria is likely to look increasingly to strategies of self-reliance.

As indicated at the outset, South Africa is dependent on the international economy in essentially three ways: the international economy serves as a customer for its mineral exports; as a provider of capital for industrial expansion and modernization; and as a source of machinery and components, which are the sinews of its manufacturing industry and which embody the advanced technologies required for development. The extent of South Africa's dependency and of its vulnerability to international pressure differs for each of these three dimensions.

Dependency is probably the greatest with respect to South Africa's exports, but, ironically, vulnerability is least in this area.[30] The mining sector is South Africa's primary earner of foreign exchange; in 1980 it accounted for nearly 70 percent of total export earnings.[31] If the sales of South Africa's minerals abroad were blocked, it would constitute a severe blow not only to the mining sector, which contributed 26 percent to

gross domestic product in 1978[32] and about one-third to government tax revenue in 1980,[33] but also to manufacturing, which depends on the foreign exchange earnings of mining to import essential machinery.

A significant international boycott of South Africa's minerals is, however, very unlikely. There are at least three reasons for this. First, nearly three-fourths of South Africa's exports are raw or slightly processed materials that enter the world market with few, if any, markings that would distinguish their South African origin. It would be extremely difficult for boycotters to target and trace the movement of specificially South African minerals in international markets. This is especially true for gold, which accounts for over 50 percent of the value of mineral exports and which can be moved virtually invisibly because of its very low bulk-to-value ratio.

Second, for many minerals, of which gold is again preeminent, South Africa is such a large producer—60 percent of world production and 50 percent of world reserves—that a reduction of its supply on world markets, or even a threat of a significant reduction, would increase world prices. South Africa would then have to sell less of its minerals in order to earn the same, or even more, than before the boycott was attempted.

Third, South Africa is the non-communist world's main supplier of certain industrially critical minerals—in particular, chrome, antimony, and vanadium, which are essential in the production of corrosion-resistant steels. Since the industrial economies of Western Europe, North America, and Japan cannot do

30. See Richard C. Porter, "International Trade and Investment Sanctions: Potential Impact on the South African Economy," *Journal of Conflict Resolution,* 23(4):587-88 (Dec. 1979).

31. *Economist,* 16 May 1981, p. 8.

32. Ibid.
33. Ibid.

without these minerals, and since the only plentiful supplier outside of the Soviet Union is South Africa, a boycott of industrially essential minerals from South Africa is highly improbable.

The second dimension of South African economic dependence on the international system is the net inflow of capital. This has traditionally performed three functions for the South African economy—as direct foreign investment it has supplemented domestic savings in the process of industrial expansion; when transferred by multinational corporations, it has been packaged with advanced technologies; and it adds to foreign exchange reserves, allowing for high levels of imports.

International pressures on the capital-dependency dimension could take the form of either a severe reduction in new capital inflow, through private corporate actions or through governmental imposed prohibitions, or a withdrawal of capital already invested, that is, disinvestment. With respect to the former type of action, Pretoria could reduce its vulnerability by increasing domestic savings to make up for unavailable foreign capital. In this manner Pretoria has the ability to maintain capital formation, without foreign inputs, but at real cost in terms of government and private consumption. With regard to disinvestment, it is unlikely that the South African government would permit a massive withdrawal of capital equipment or of the funds raised by the sale of such equipment. For a period after Sharpeville, when faced with a situation of capital flight, Pretoria imposed exchange controls, which prohibited the repatriation of capital.[34] These required

the foreign corporation seeking to withdraw capital from South Africa to deposit its funds in government securities, which would mature and be paid off over a period of time.[35] In essence, Pretoria forced the disinvestors to invest their funds in the South African government.

It is likely that, should the disinvestment crises of the mid-1980s intensify, Pretoria would reimpose a similar ban on the export of capital. The major constraint for Pretoria is the negative effect such a ban has on the willingness of new capital to enter South Africa. In 1985, Pretoria reintroduced a dual exchange rate system as a means to stem the movement toward disinvestment while simultaneously avoiding the negative effects on potential investors of a total ban on capital repatriation. Foreigners wishing to export their capital can buy so-called financial rands, which are sold at a heavy discount vis-à-vis the commercial rand. Financial rands can, in turn, be sold abroad to individuals or firms interested in investing in South Africa. This system thus makes it possible for people to move their capital out of South Africa, while discouraging them from doing so by a heavy financial penalty, and simultaneously offers a financial incentive to new investors.

The potential costs to South Africa of a withdrawal of multinational corporations goes beyond the question of the ability to retain already invested capital. In addition, withdrawal could also mean the withholding, from the multinational corporation's erstwhile South African subsidiary, of intermediate inputs, specially designed machinery, and technological information. The extent of South

34. See Houghton, *South African Economy* (1973), p. 184.

35. *Quarterly Economic Review: Southern Africa*, annual supp. 1967 (London: Economist Intelligence Unit, 1967), p. 18.

Africa's vulnerability to this form of sanction depends on the availability of substitutes from other sources, foreign or domestic. And that relates to the third dimension of South Africa's economic dependency, its reliance on imports. It is here that South Africa is both heavily dependent and vulnerable. South Africa imports virtually all of its basic capital equipment and a major share of its intermediate industrial inputs. One systematic study, conducted in the late 1970s, concluded that "if sanctions were to cut off South Africa from capital equipment, South Africa's growth ... as a modern, industrialized economy could be dramatically interrupted."[36]

The obvious means to reduce vulnerability to import embargoes is a strategy of import substitution—to produce at home what was previously purchased from abroad. In the two areas in which South Africa has been subject to import embargoes—oil and arms—Pretoria has pursued such an import-substitution strategy as a means to reduce its international vulnerability. These cases provide an indication of both the strengths and limits of import substitution for the South African economy.

South Africa depends on petroleum to meet approximately 25 percent of its energy needs, but it lacks any significant oil deposits within its territory. In the mid-1950s, the South African government began on a small scale to respond to this strategic vulnerability by developing technology for the synthetic production of petroleum, utilizing the country's abundant resources of coal. When an Arab oil embargo and the fall of the Shah of Iran cut off South Africa's main dependable sources of imported oil,

Pretoria rapidly and substantially increased the capacity of its synthetic fuel industry. It is widely estimated that by the mid-1980s the three government-owned oil-from-coal plants of the South African Coal, Oil, and Gas Corporation were supplying about 50 percent of South Africa's petroleum requirements. While the synthetic oil is reportedly expensive—estimated at about $35 per barrel[37]—the increased cost has bought considerable autonomy from potential international pressures. The portion of South Africa's oil needs that is not currently met by domestic processing continues to be imported. Paying premium prices, and using clandestine means to purchase and ship the petrol, Pretoria has been able to circumvent the oil embargo imposed upon it.[38]

The oil case indicates that, at least when resource endowment is favorable and technological knowledge is locally available, Pretoria can successfully utilize an import-substituting strategy to counter and reduce its international vulnerability. Moreover, it shows how international economic sanctions can have the ironic effect of making South Africa stronger through stimulating policies that reduce dependence on the external world. Finally, the oil case also shows how difficult it is to stop the flow of imports into a sophisticated economy such as South Africa's. As long as a commodity is available from many sources, and Pretoria is willing to pay above-market prices, there is likely to be someone willing to sell. Moreover, given South Africa's extensive maritime bor-

36. Porter, "International Trade and Investment Sanctions," p. 590.

37. "Sasol's Success," *Science*, 2(1):63 (Jan.-Feb. 1981).

38. See Martin Bailey, "Fleet of Supertankers Is Busting Arab Oil Embargo on South Africa," *Observer*, 18 Jan. 1981, p. 8.

ders, the heavy sea traffic in the area of the Cape of Good Hope, and the volume of minerals shipped from South Africa's ports, it is probably impossible to trace what commodities are moving in and out of South Africa or to identify their destination or origin.

The U.N. ban on the sale of arms to South Africa has served to stimulate an import-substituting strategy, as did the oil embargo. In response to the voluntary arms embargo of 1964 and, more dramatically, to the mandatory embargo imposed by the Security Council in 1977, Pretoria has developed its state-owned armaments corporation, Armscor, into the third largest industrial group in South Africa, employing some 16,000 people and producing equipment that in 1982 was valued at $1.4 billion.[39] By 1985, South Africa's arms industry was ranked as the tenth largest in the world and reportedly fulfilled 85 percent of South Africa's armaments needs. In addition, by the early 1980s Armscor had become an active exporter of its locally developed weapons, allowing it to recoup some of its development costs through foreign exchange earnings.[40]

As with oil, Pretoria's response to the arms embargo shows that import substitution can successfully increase self-sufficiency and thus reduce international vulnerability. But it also reveals the very real limits of such a strategy for the South African economy. While greatly increasing Pretoria's self-sufficiency in weapons, by its own account Armscor is unable to supply all of South Africa's weapons requirements. What it cannot provide is the advanced high-tech weap-

onry—the complex guided missile systems and, most important, aircraft. With respect to the capital requirements of research and development, engineering, and manufacturing, the cost of producing this type of weaponry is prohibitive, given the small production runs necessary to fulfill Pretoria's needs. Even if the technical know-how were to exist locally, which is highly unlikely, the inability to capture economies of scale, given the small South African market, makes a domestically oriented aerospace industry infeasible.

The arms-industry case offers an important general lesson with respect to the limits of import substitution for the South African economy. Of South Africa's imports, 80 percent are intermediate inputs and capital goods.[41] As has already been noted, in the process of its industrialization South Africa has come to rely almost totally on foreign sources for the machinery and equipment that are the basis of manufacturing. The more technologically advanced the industry, the more complete is the foreign dependence. It is in the nature of basic capital goods industries that, like aerospace, they require large investments of capital, research, and engineering knowledge. Consequently, they need to be able to take advantage of economies of scale in order to be feasible. The small size of the South African economy denies such possibilities for large production runs that can spread capital and research-and-development costs over many units of production. The South African government may be able to absorb the costs of small-scale production in a few industries, but could hardly do so across the entire gamut of indus-

39. Joseph Lelyveld, "South Africa Tries to Sell Its Arms," *New York Times*, 5 Dec. 1982.

40. Glenn Frankel, "U.N. Arms Ban Proves Costly to South Africans," *Washington Post,* 24 Jan. 1985.

41. Porter, "International Trade and Investment Sanctions," p. 589.

TABLE 2
PERCENTAGE OF TOTAL IMPORTS TO SOUTH AFRICA,
BY TYPE OF COUNTRY

	1974	1975	1976	1977	1978	1979	1980	1981	1982
Established industrial country	88.0	90.3	88.9	88.1	90.4	89.4	64.5	66.8	68.7
Other	12.0	9.7	11.1	11.9	9.6	10.6	35.5	33.2	31.3

SOURCES: International Monetary Fund, *International Financial Statistics, Supplement on Trade Statistics* (Washington, DC: International Monetary Fund, 1982), p. 99, and idem, *Direction of Trade Statistics*, yearbook, 1985 (Washington, DC: International Monetary Fund, 1985), p. 357.

trial production. In other words, import substitution has a real, but limited, utility for a South African government seeking to free itself from international vulnerability. If South Africa is to maintain its industrial economy, and certainly if it is to grow, it will have to continue to import technically advanced producer goods. An autarkic strategy will not be sufficient to protect the South African economy from international sanctions and embargoes.

The limits of an autarkic strategy will require a South African government that is intent upon maintaining white power to search for ways to circumvent international embargoes and sanctions. This involves finding nontraditional foreign suppliers who are, because of self-interest or politics, less likely to comply with a sanctions campaign than South Africa's traditional Western trading partners. In this respect, South Africa's circumstances have been fortuitously enhanced by the economic achievements of the newly industrialized countries (NICs) of Asia and Latin America. The NICs—of which South Korea, Taiwan, and Brazil are the most significant— have a strong export orientation and need to capture markets at the expense of firms from the older industrial countries. They are likely to find the South

African market, if it is abandoned by established suppliers, an attractive opportunity. The domestic politics of the NICs is also less sensitive than that of the Western democracies to South African domestic affairs, and so there are likely to be few constraints on their taking advantage of market opportunities created by disinvestment, sanctions, and embargoes. Trade statistics indicate that South Africa has already begun to reorient its trade toward these nontraditional sources.

Table 2 reveals that in 1980 a major shift in South Africa's imports occurred, away from America, Europe, and Japan and toward the countries of the Third World. Table 3 indicates the countries involved in this reorientation and reveals the prominence of the NICs as new import sources. During the period of international attention on South Africa that followed the Soweto Rebellion, imports from the established industrial countries either grew more slowly than South Africa's overall import growth, as was the case for France, the United Kingdom, and Germany, or kept pace with South Africa's import growth, as in the U.S. and Japanese cases. In contrast, imports from Israel and South Korea grew at twice the pace of overall import growth rates, imports from Brazil grew

TABLE 3
CHANGE IN SOUTH AFRICAN IMPORTS
FROM SELECTED COUNTRIES, 1978-84

	Change in Value of Imports (percentage)
Total South African imports	+107.4
Imports from	
France	+3.8
United Kingdom	+38.3
Germany	+59.5
Japan	+104.2
United States	+108.9
Israel	+196.4
South Korea	+229.4
Brazil	+275.7
Taiwan	+495.1

SOURCES: International Monetary Fund, *Direction of Trade Statistics*, yearbook, 1985; Republic of China, Ministry of Finance, *Monthly Statistics of Export and Import*, no. 189 (May 1985).

by almost three times the overall rate, and from Taiwan they expanded by nearly five times.

One can expect that in the years ahead, should Western economic pressure for change in South Africa increase, the reorientation toward nontraditional suppliers and particularly the NICs will intensify. Whether the NIC economies will grow rapidly enough and in a sufficiently diversified manner to meet South Africa's external requirements remains to be seen. Although they clearly offer a means to reduce Pretoria's vulnerability to Western economic pressure, they can hardly be expected to offer an alternative to everything previously available from the West. Thus Pretoria will find that while it can reduce the costs of the coupling of its domestic arrangements to its international situation, it cannot reduce them to anything approaching zero.

ANNALS, *AAPSS,* **489,** January 1987

The Eagle and the Bear in Angola

By GERALD J. BENDER

ABSTRACT: The United States and the Soviet Union have supported opposing sides in Angola for more than a quarter of a century. Both superpowers have been stymied by their lack of control over their respective Angolan allies and frustrated by their lack of impact on determining events. Each of the superpowers has also been an unreliable patron for their Angolan clients. One important result is that, not surprisingly, most Angolans—no matter what side they are on—are highly skeptical and cynical about both the United States and the Soviet Union. While superpower intervention is usually justified in ideological terms, few Angolans are fighting for, let alone familiar with, any ideology. The war in Angola is hopelessly stalemated; neither side can possibly defeat the other and there seems to be no prospect for a military solution. Thus it becomes increasingly clear that only a political solution can end the war, but neither superpower is posturing for peace or seriously pursuing political solutions.

Gerald J. Bender, director of the School of International Relations, University of Southern California and the recent past president of the African Studies Association, received his B.A. from the University of Minnesota and his M.A. and Ph.D. degrees from the University of California at Los Angeles. In addition to living in Portugal and Angola (1967-69), he has spent part of every year in Angola since 1976. He is the author of the book Angola under the Portuguese *(1978) and is coeditor of* African Crisis Areas and U.S. Foreign Policy *(1985).*

NOTE: An early version of this article was presented at the Third Joint American-Soviet Conference on Contemporary Sub-Saharan Africa, Institute of International Studies, University of California, Berkeley, 29 May 1986.

THE United States and the Soviet Union have supported opposing sides in Angola for more than a quarter of a century. Generally throughout this period, both superpowers have been stymied not only by a lack of control over their respective Angolan allies but also by the minimal impact they have had on determining the desired outcomes of their support. Another critical aspect to U.S. and Soviet activity in Angola has been their unreliability as patrons for their respective Angolan clients. Not surprisingly, most Angolans—no matter which side they are on—are highly skeptical and cynical about both superpowers.

While global strategists in Washington and Moscow consult their scorecards and tabulate statements by Angolan leaders under categories of pro and con, the preferred course of action for most Angolan leaders is to follow a path that will not deeply offend either of the two powerful and dangerous giants. In today's world, such a policy can be extremely difficult, if not at times impossible, to carry out. Perhaps that is why inaction has so often been the *modus operandi* of Angolan decision makers.

With slogans such as "freedom fighters" and "internationalist solidarity" dominating the East-West dialogue, it often appears that no one realizes how precious few Angolans are fighting for, let alone are more than vaguely familiar with, any ideology. Too many in the East and West have forgotten, or never learned, Amilcar Cabral's adage about the unimportance of ideas and ideology in a revolutionary struggle. Cabral, founder of the African Party for the Independence of Guinea and Cape Verde, the independence movement in Guinea-Bissau, told his cadres in a 1965

party directive, "Always bear in mind that the people are not fighting for ideas, for the things in anyone's head. They are fighting to win material benefits, to live better and in peace, to see their lives go forward, to guarantee the future of their children."[1]

Too many have also forgotten or prefer to ignore other realities of the Angolan context in which an imposed East-West struggle continues to simmer. American polemicists, in addition to President Reagan and part of his cabinet, are fond of charging that the Soviets and/or Cubans have colonized Angola. Given the infinitesimally small impact that either the Soviets or the Cubans have had on Angolan culture or society, such a charge can only be considered ridiculous. One need only look at the record of the Portuguese after 500 years in Angola. In the early 1970s, for example, a highly sophisticated survey of rural Angolans, which included about 80 percent of the entire African population in the country, revealed that very few Angolans had any knowledge at all of the Portuguese language, history, leaders, or geography.[2]

PERCEPTIONS AND MISPERCEPTIONS

For centuries Angola was an enigmatic, unknown quantity on the African

1. Amilcar Cabral, *Revolution in Guinea: An African People's Struggle* (London: Stage 1, 1969), p. 70.
2. In 1970-71 only 6.5 percent of the rural heads of families named Salazar, Caetano, or Americo Tomas as the "Chief of the Portuguese Government" and less than 1 percent identified Lisbon as the capital of Portugal. Moreover, 85.0 percent could not answer the question, "What is Mozambique?" Only 0.6 percent identified Mozambique as a Portuguese territory. See Franz-Wilhelm Heimer, *Educação e sociedade nas areas rurais de Angola* (Luanda, 1972), 1:347-58. See also Gerald

continent.[3] Its history under Portuguese colonialism was learned by outsiders largely through the eyes of Lisbon, a vision basically taken at face value. Even in the mid-1950s, John Gunther observed that Angola was the least known big country in Africa, adding that scarcely a half dozen journalists had visited the territory during the previous two decades.[4]

With the outbreak of the war of national liberation in 1961, a number of journalists, scholars, and diplomats began to visit and write about Angola. Yet understanding still seemed to elude most of them, and diametrically opposed interpretations of Angola's colonial state were common. In addition, the fact that three major liberation movements evolved during the independence struggle—the Popular Movement for the Liberation of Angola (MPLA), the National Front for the Liberation of Angola (FNLA), and the National Union for the Total Independence of Angola (UNITA)—further served to confuse attempts to understand Angolan realities. Each movement naturally claimed preeminence over the others and produced outside experts who, after on-the-spot trips, supported their respective host's contention of controlling major portions of Angola.

The Angolan civil war in 1975-76 resulted in a plethora of publications whose interpretations and facts were so contradictory that it was often hard to

J. Bender, *Angola under the Portuguese: The Myth and the Reality* (Berkeley: University of California Press, 1978), pp. 221-22.

3. This section draws from Gerald J. Bender, "Angola: The Continuing Crisis and Misunderstanding," *International Affairs Bulletin,* 7:5-6 (1983).

4. John Gunther, *Inside Africa* (New York: Harper & Brothers, 1953), pp. 585-99.

believe they referred to the same country and the same war. Almost all writers were partisans who selected facts according to their political preferences. Common to most was the notion that the struggle was between good and evil, between villains and heroes, with the only difference being the party to which these appellations were given.

Part of the confusion and misunderstanding over the Angolan civil war resulted from the political and ideological diversity of the support the two sides attracted. The FNLA-UNITA alliance received assistance not only from the United States, France, and Britain, but also the People's Republic of China, Rumania, North Korea, and South Africa. Some, like Henry Kissinger, saw this alliance as pro-Western, while others called it pro-Chinese. The MPLA, on the other hand, secured support ranging from that of the Soviet Union and Cuba to Sweden, Denmark, Nigeria, and the former Katangese Gendarmes, once loyal to Moise Tshombe. To many, this was the pro-Soviet side, while others considered it to be the non-aligned side.

Whereas the overwhelming tendency was to define and characterize the competing parties by the source of their external support, the diversity of that support, for both sides, was such as to preclude meaningful characterizations. In fact, none of the three movements could be legitmately or intelligently defined by the ideology of their outside patrons. Instead, each was more an expression of internal Angolan differences—for example, ethnolinguistic, regional, racial, and other domestic factors. Nevertheless, both internal and external perceptions of the competing parties have been based primarily on selective perceptions of external patrons. Moreover, this pattern, established during the civil war, has persisted until today. In it, the favored party is portrayed as enjoying broad ethnic and national support, while the other side is depicted as being a puppet of foreign powers—for example, the Soviet Union or Cuba, on the one hand, or the United States or South Africa, on the other.

These distorted perceptions have not only stymied a negotiated settlement of the civil war, but they have inhibited efforts toward national reconciliation since Angola's independence on 11 November 1975. The MPLA and its supporters view UNITA as a puppet or creature of South Africa and assume that it will wither away once its umbilical link to Pretoria is severed. UNITA and its supporters portray the MPLA as a Soviet or Cuban puppet that will collapse as soon as Havana's troops leave Angola. The truth is that neither would UNITA perish without South African support nor would the MPLA be overrun were Cuban troops to be withdrawn. No amount of propaganda on any side can alter these facts.

THE UNITED STATES AND THE SOVIET UNION: UNRELIABLE ALLIES

While the Soviet Union began to assist the MPLA almost five years before the United States began its support of the Union of Angolan Peoples, the predecessor of the FNLA, neither provided sufficient aid for its side to win. The support was extremely low level, both financially and technically. Once Portugal regained almost total control of the country in 1962, the amount of aid was further reduced on both sides. American support for the FNLA was severed altogether with the advent of Richard Nixon's presidency.[5]

The United States was always torn between its support for national liberation in Angola and its assistance to Portugal, an ally in the North Atlantic Treaty Organization. This was already apparent in the Kennedy administration, when the policy of supporting anti-Portuguese resolutions at the United Nations and guerrilla fighters in Angola was severely attacked from within the administration. The detractors argued that the United States needed Portugal more than the liberation of Africans in Angola and that a choice must be made between the two. Under President Johnson the move to reduce support for the FNLA and raise military assistance for Portugal was clear; Kissinger and Nixon later made the choice definitive.[6]

Portuguese officers received training in the United States, while Washington supplied Portugal with airplanes, equipment that could serve either civilian or military purposes, over $400 million in credits and loans, napalm, herbicides, and, most important, moral support. There were always sophisticated explanations of how each example of U.S. aid could be interpreted in two ways, but the sum total of American actions left no doubt about which side the United States actually supported in the war for independence. The United States placed its bets on the tenacity of the Salazar-Caetano regime and the white settlers—and lost.

5. Apparently Holden Roberto, the FNLA leader, continued to receive $10,000 to $20,000 a year during the Nixon administration for intelligence he provided. This is not the same, however, as aiding the FNLA itself.

6. See Richard D. Mahoney, *JFK: Ordeal in Africa* (New York: Oxford University Press, 1983); Witney Schneidman, "American Foreign Policy and the Fall of the Portuguese Empire" (Ph.D. diss., University of Southern California, 1987).

Soviet support for African liberation in Angola was never compromised by a Lisbon or colonial connection. The Soviets were always on the morally correct side of all U.N. votes concerning Portuguese colonialism. Nevertheless, Soviet support for the MPLA did waver at times, as in 1962, 1968, and 1973-74—when it appeared that Moscow had lost confidence, if not all hope, in an MPLA victory.

The MPLA was a mass movement, not a disciplined party, and contained very few Marxists or strong ideologues of any persuasion. What united MPLA members was their opposition to Portuguese colonialism. The party was not easily controlled from within or without. The emergence of at least three distinct factions within the MPLA on the eve of the Portuguese coup underscored Agostinho Neto's inability to control the affairs of his party, as well as Moscow's impotency in influencing developments within the party. Certainly this must partially explain the Soviet Union's decision to cut off the MPLA altogether in March 1974, just one month before Caetano was overthrown. That assistance remained frozen for roughly six crucial months following the coup. When Moscow did resume its support, it was originally directed to one of Neto's principal rivals, Daniel Chipenda, who, when he failed in his attempt to take over the MPLA, joined the FNLA.[7]

Both superpowers paid lip service to the transitional government established in January 1975, but they actually helped to undermine that government with their exclusive support for one of the three partners.[8] During the first half of 1975,

the United States ignored UNITA altogether. Discovering it later in the year, the United States provided outmoded weapons, which offered little protection for the UNITA soldiers. For the United States, Angola was a no-win war in which UNITA was treated as little more than cannon fodder and useful cover for South African military forays into the country.[9]

Soviet support for the transitional government was much stronger than that of the United States, perhaps because Moscow was doubtful that the MPLA could prevail militarily over its two rivals. In fact, some top MPLA leaders remain bitter today about Soviet insistence on a coalition government as late as a week before independence. Clearly, the Soviet Union neither planned nor anticipated a scenario, even at that late date, which had Cuban troops playing the decisive role in projecting the MPLA exclusively into power.[10]

"Kissinger in Angola: Anatomy of Failure," in *American Policy in Southern Africa: The Stakes and the Stance,* 2nd ed., ed. Rene Lemarchand (Washington, DC: University Press of America, 1978), pp. 65-143; idem, "Angola: A Story of Stupidity," *New York Review of Books,* 21 Dec. 1978, pp. 26-30.

9. John Stockwell, former Central Intelligence Agency head of the Angolan operation, discusses this in greater depth in his book, *In Search of Enemies* (New York: W. W. Norton, 1978), pp. 138-90.

10. The latest account to suggest that the idea for the large-scale Cuban operation in Angola originated in Havana, not Moscow, can be found in Arkady N. Shevchenko, *Breaking with Moscow* (New York: Ballantine Books, 1985), pp. 362-65. Shevchenko was startled when he discovered this fact. He manifests a very hawkish, anti-Soviet attitude toward Moscow's Africa policy, which makes his revelation about the Havana role all the more credible. He clearly would have preferred to blame the Soviet Union exclusively for what happened in Angola in 1975.

7. Chipenda visited Luanda in early 1986 and apparently plans to return home after living a number of years in Portugal.

8. See, for example, Gerald J. Bender,

Some of Moscow's moral credits for consistent opposition to Portuguese colonialism began to dissipate soon after independence. Soviet support for the bloody regimes of Amin in Uganda, Macias in Equatorial Guinea, and Bokassa in the Central African Empire, or Republic, raised doubts about whether Moscow was not just another opportunistic superpower. The *volte-face* in the Horn further exacerbated these concerns. But none of these actions compared in terms of negative impact to the support that the Soviet Union provided to President Neto's chief rival for power within the MPLA, Nito Alves.

According to a confidential MPLA report on the attempted coup of 27 May 1977, the plotters (*fraccionistas*) were encouraged and supported by "the Soviet Union, and two other Eastern European countries," which were never named. The expulsion of the Soviet ambassador following the coup attempt marked the nadir in relations between the Soviet Union and the MPLA.[11] This could have resulted in a major setback for the Soviet Union if the cold warriors in the Carter administration, led by Zbigniew Brzezinski, had not come to Moscow's rescue. In the spring of 1978, while the MPLA was still hurting from the attempted coup, which had eliminated one quarter of the party's central committee, the Central Intelligence Agency (CIA) and the National Security Council developed a plan for the United States to intervene in Angola on the side of UNITA.[12]

Carter ultimately rejected the plan in May 1978, but the damage had been done. Despite the encouraging statements from top officials in the Carter administration about the desirability of improving relations with the MPLA government, the uncovered plot to support UNITA drove a number of MPLA officials, who were still angry over Moscow's support of Nito Alves, back to the Soviet bosom for protection. Relations were strained again the following year, however, when President Neto died on the operating table of a Moscow hospital. Some members of the Central Committee remain convinced that Neto did not die of natural causes.[13]

Despite these tensions between Moscow and Luanda since independence, the Soviets have not wavered in their commitment to support the MPLA against all external threats, especially from South Africa. Given the aggressive behavior of Pretoria against independent Angola, especially after 1980, it can be said that Soviet and Cuban support have been major factors in discouraging another South African attempt to overrun Angola. Undoubtedly, South Africa would have massively intervened in Angola to overthrow the MPLA government if it had not feared facing Cuban and Soviet soldiers on the battlefield. This effective deterrence against South Africa has engendered great

11. An extended discussion of this coup attempt can be found in Gerald J. Bender, "Angola, the Cubans and American Anxieties," *Foreign Policy*, no. 31, pp. 23-26 (Summer 1978).

12. At a seminar I presented to Columbia University's Research Institute on International Change on 25 March 1986, Zbigniew Brzezinski

denied that the National Security Council had drawn up any plans to intervene in Angola on the side of UNITA while he was national security adviser. He was either unaware that his deputy, David Aaron, had helped to draw up such a plan or he did not see any of the newspaper articles on this issue, or he may simply have forgotten.

13. While I have always believed that Neto died of natural causes, I am aware of a report— never released—drafted by some top MPLA officials that accuses the Soviet Union of murdering Neto.

appreciation among a large segment of the MPLA leadership.

The United States, for its part, has been an even less consistent ally for its Angolan clients than has the Soviet Union. The Clark Amendment effectively precluded any meaningful support until its repeal in 1985. Even if the Clark Amendment had not been in place, however, it is not clear that the United States would have supported UNITA. American official attitudes about UNITA have covered the full spectrum in recent decades. Prior to 1974, the party was viewed almost as an enemy, since it opposed an ally in the North Atlantic Treaty Organization. During most of the transition period, 1974-75, UNITA was essentially ignored. The spurt of military aid near the end of the civil war was given very cynically since the CIA knew that it could not reverse the military situation but could only raise the level of deaths on both sides.

The Carter administration adopted a policy toward UNITA of benign indifference. During Savimbi's visit to Washington in 1979, the highest member of the government to see him was the State Department desk officer for Angola—a marked contrast to the UNITA leader's triumphant visit to the United States in early 1986, when he saw the president, secretaries of state and defense, director of the CIA, and other top officials in Washington. During most of the Reagan administration, the attitude toward UNITA could be labeled schizophrenic. Chester Crocker, in an article he published just prior to assuming the job of assistant secretary of state for Africa, argued that the United States should admit publicly "the legitimacy of the UNITA struggle," but he cautioned that if the United States were to back UNITA outright "it is not obvious how this path would lead to reconciliation. . . . It could

produce an escalation of conflict, and it would probably rule out responding to frequent hints from the MPLA of a desire to reduce sharply its Soviet-Cuban ties."[14]

Some of Crocker's close advisers viewed UNITA as more of a nuisance factor—which could undermine the policy of linkage—than an ally. One even presciently confided in 1982 that UNITA could be the Achilles' heel of constructive engagement. By the mid-1980s, however, Crocker and the State Department had lost control over Angola policy. The congressional repeal of the Clark Amendment in July 1985 opened the floodgates for the right wing to seize the initiative on Angola. Their influence peaked during Savimbi's carefully orchestrated visit to Washington in January and February 1986 and the military aid that followed in the spring. Suddenly, the Reagan administration dropped all caveats and began to hail Jonas Savimbi in unrestrained superlatives as a modern hero. Once again, Washington stepped into the Angolan quagmire with all of the predictable results.

RESULTS OF U.S. AID

What has Washington bought for $15 million dollars of aid to UNITA?

1. It bought a major setback in the negotiations over Namibia when Luanda rejected a continued solo role for the United States as an intermediary in early March of 1986.

2. It bought into a perceived military alliance with South Africa, automatically

14. Chester Crocker with Mario Greznes and Robert Henderson, "A U.S. Policy for the '80s," *Africa Report,* 26(1):9-10 (Jan.-Feb. 1981). See also Chester Crocker, "African Policy for the 1980s," *Washington Quarterly,* pp. 72-86 (Summer 1982); *idem,* "South Africa: Strategy for Change," *Foreign Affairs,* 59(2):324-51 (Winter 1980/81).

associating the United States with Pretoria's destabilizing activities against neighboring states in southern Africa.

3. It bought the wrath of the membership of the Organization of African Unity, which strongly condemned U.S. support for UNITA, and many other nations around the world, including some allies in the North Atlantic Treaty Organization.

4. It bought another no-win military policy that will certainly lead to what the world will perceive as a defeat for the United States. Both the CIA and the State Department argue that success is not possible with the present program.[15]

5. It bought the responsibility for sabotaging the Namibia negotiations, which not only leaves South Africa squarely ensconced in Namibia, but leaves its Western allies in the Contact Group looking foolish for having trusted the Reagan administration to play the role of an honest, neutral broker over Namibia.

6. Finally, it also bought the responsibility for UNITA's and South Africa's conduct of the war. The mines laid by CIA operatives in the Managua harbor, which caused such a big scandal some time ago, are child's play compared to the activities that UNITA and South Africa carry out in Angola. UNITA has claimed to have downed three civilian aircraft and to have kidnapped hundreds of foreign missionaries, blew up a Trans-America plane killing an American crewman, and participated with South Africa in trying to attack Gulf oil installations in Cabinda in May 1985. No

15. It should be noted that while the Defense Intelligence Agency (DIA) does hold out some prospect for the success of this program, their fundamental premises are so flawed that their conclusion does not merit serious consideration. See David Ottaway and Patrick Tyler, "DIA Alone in Optimism for Savimbi," *Washington Post,* 7 Feb. 1986.

sooner had the Stinger missiles been shipped than UNITA kidnapped over 200 foreign nationals near the diamond mines and announced they were going to march them over 1000 kilometers to the Namibian border. Not surprisingly, the Reagan administration quietly persuaded UNITA in March 1986 to release the hostages in Zaire before an international campaign against American complicity in terrorism could be launched.

The Reagan administration, in fact, bought so many negative consequences for its paltry aid to UNITA that one wonders whether Moscow has a mole in the White House urging these policies. Would rational policymakers purposefully shoot themselves in the foot by joining in a tacit military alliance with South Africa on the Angolan battlefield in 1986? But policymaking in Washington is not always rational, so it is not necessary to resort to conspiratorial theories about moles to explain the Reagan Angola policy.

The vicissitudes and schizophrenic nature of American policy toward UNITA over the past two decades obviously have had an impact on Savimbi and other party leaders. He is distrustful of the United States, as he indicated in a 1985 speech at his headquarters in Jamba that was shown on Portuguese television:

I also don't want to leave without [correcting some errors]. The leaders of UNITA cannot create illusions. The West is not our ally. This is a lie. There are interests which coincide, but this is different. You know that it took a long time for the articles of UNITA to be published in the Western press. They are not our allies! And for this very reason [it must be clarified for those] who say that UNITA is pro-West. This is wrong! I am not pro-West. I am pro-Angola. I fight for Angola and we only love Angola.

We want to have good relations with America but who is it that doesn't want to have good relations with America. But it is necessary that America does not try to make Angola into another state of the United States.[16]

The present policy of the Reagan administration virtually guarantees another victory for the Soviet Union in Angola. If Angola represents a victory for the Soviet Union, some Soviets must wonder how many more such victories Moscow can endure; nevertheless it will be counted as a victory on the global scorecard.

CONCLUSION

The war in Angola is hopelessly stalemated; neither side can possibly defeat the other. Despite all of the attention and concern expressed about MPLA offenses, there is no prospect for a military solution of the war. From the MPLA point of view, the military situation has steadily deteriorated during the 1980s as UNITA has incrementally expanded its zones of operation and scale of attacks. Yet UNITA is not any closer to military victory.

Nor can the MPLA hold realistic hopes for victory through winning the hearts and minds of the peasants in the countryside. There are many explanations for the state of the Angolan economy, with the fault divided between government inefficiency and incompetence and factors beyond the government's control, such as the destruction of the colonial distribution system, droughts, floods, and South African and UNITA attacks. But the end result is that the Luanda government has basically failed to deliver even minimal essentials to the countryside. With the

16. Bracketed phrases are the author's paraphrasing of portions on the recording that were not clear enough for a literal translation.

expansion of the war into the rich food-producing central highlands and the dramatic drop in the price of petroleum, it appears impossible for the government to improve significantly on its delivery of goods and services to the interior.

Thus, as the struggle continues, it becomes increasingly clear that only a political solution can end the war. But a political solution requires courage and sacrifice on all sides. There are clearly domestic Angolan constraints on the prospects for reconciliation, but this will require another article to discuss. Therefore, the focus in this conclusion is on the possible constraints to reconciliation presented by the United States and the Soviet Union.

Political reconciliation for the MPLA requires a fundamental trust in the intentions of South Africa and the United States. Pretoria's violations of the Nkomati and Lusaka accords of 1984 and of the understandings with Washington not to attack its neighbors without justifiable provocation do not inspire trust in any quarter. In fact, there may even be more cynicism and skepticism in Washington today than in Luanda about South Africa's intentions vis-à-vis Angola.

Developments in the United States do not inspire trust in Luanda. The right wing's usurpation of Crocker's Angola policy in 1985-86 raises serious questions about future American intentions. Will those in the administration and Congress who support military assistance to Savimbi accept political reconciliation or will they seek an outright military victory? If Nicaragua is any indicator, many of Savimbi's American supporters will not be content until the MPLA is overthrown. Will they be the ones guiding American policy in the future?

The most vociferous attacks on constructive engagement have come, ironically, from the Right, not the Left. The Right opposes linkage because it precludes a military victory in Angola that, they argue, could not only drive the Cubans out but prevent the South West Africa People's Organization (SWAPO), the main Namibian nationalist party, from ever replacing South Africa in Namibia.

One of the most outspoken advocates of this position has been Patrick Buchanan, President Reagan's influential director of communications. He wrote that he opposes linkage and favors backing UNITA to a military victory because "a Savimbi victory in Angola would mean a reversal for the Soviet empire on the scale of Mr. Sadat's expulsion of the Russians from Egypt." He also argued that a UNITA "victory would leave the Marxist guerrillas of SWAPO . . . without a base camp, without a strategic rear. SWAPO would die on a severed vine."[17]

Savimbi, likewise, has strong reasons to be distrustful of the United States and South Africa. Pretoria says that it will never abandon him, but the South African government has abandoned other allies in the past and would not hesitate to drop UNITA as well, if that served its purpose. Moreover, he cannot count on the present government in Pretoria to run that country indefinitely. The surprise agreement between Angola and Zaire in 1978, which resulted in President Mobutu sending tens of thousands of former FNLA supporters back to Angola, is a sufficient reminder of how fleeting alliances are in this part of

the world. The fickleness of the United States toward UNITA is not only legendary, but a new chapter will be written if the Democrats gain the presidency in 1988.

And what about Soviet intentions and goals in Angola? The prospects of Namibian independence and reconciliation in Angola cannot be seen in Moscow as necessarily desirable outcomes. They would certainly result in a marked decline of Soviet influence in the region and may even call into question the *raison d'état* for anything more than a normal presence. Soviet models and recommendations in the economic and military fields in Angola have basically failed, at least in the eyes of the overwhelming majority of the Angolan people. "Socialism has failed, let's try something else" is a phrase heard with increasing frequency.

There will never be peace in Angola if Moscow continues to place all bets on illusory military solutions that have failed in the past and will fail again in the future. Nor can there ever be peace with the United States' introducing sophisticated weapons on the battlefield. Neither of the two superpowers is posturing for peace. On the contrary, both are presently pursuing policies that will prolong the war. There is little incentive for either to change since it is a relatively cheap war for both, and those maimed and killed on the battlefields are not Americans or Soviets, but Angolans. So it appears that Moscow and Washington will continue to send messages to each other via the Angolan battlefield. It would be so much better if they spoke directly to each other about ways for bringing about peace in Angola, rather than continuing the bloodshed.

---

17. Patrick Buchanan, "Selling Savimbi down the River," *Washington Times,* 29 Feb. 1984.

ANNALS, *AAPSS,* **489,** January 1987

The Organization of African Unity and Intra-African Functionalism

By G. AFORKA NWEKE

ABSTRACT: The Organization of African Unity was the product of a compromise between African statesmen who wanted political union of all independent African states and those who preferred functional cooperation as a building block toward the construction of an African sociopsychological community. As embodied in the Charter of the Organization of African Unity and put into operation, the inherent contradictions of the ideas, behaviors, and interests of member states, in conjunction with the dynamics of international politics, brought practically all efforts at functional cooperation to naught. In order to revamp Africa's commitment to functionalism, the Lagos Plan of Action was adopted in April 1980. But it remains to be seen how practicable it will be for Africans, relying on themselves, to achieve the goal of an African Common Market by the year 2000, as envisaged in the plan.

G. Aforka Nweke is associate professor of political science at the University of Nigeria, Nsukka, and, since 1983, he has been president of the Nigerian Society of International Affairs. He holds a B.S. with honors from the University of Lagos, an M.S. from the London School of Economics, a Ph.D. from Boston University, and a postdoctoral M.A. in Middle Eastern studies from Harvard University, where he lectured in 1977-78. From 1978 to 1982 he was a lecturer at the University of Lagos. He has authored three books and numerous articles.

THE Organization of African Unity (OAU), since its formal establishment at Addis Ababa, Ethiopia, in May 1963, has existed as a continental institutional expression of over six decades of the African struggle for collective identity and security. Although in theory and practice the OAU falls far short both of the orthodox functionalist model of "a working peace system"[1] and of a neofunctionalist supranational body offering appropriate outlets for a plurality of interests,[2] its commitment to functionalism is reflected not only in the politics of African unity,[3] but also in its Charter[4] and in the fact that it is seen as a precursor to that end dream of an African sociopsychological community. Mitrany stresses the point that "economic unification would build up the foundation for political agreement";[5] and Haas, in his scheme of international integration, argues that a "political community exists when there is likelihood of peaceful change in a setting of contending groups with mutually antagonistic aims."[6]

1. David Mitrany, *A Working Peace System* (Chicago: Quadrangle Books, 1966).

2. Ernst B. Haas, *Technocracy, Pluralism and the New Europe,* Reprint no. 18 (Berkeley: University of California, Institute of International Studies, n.d.), from *A New Europe?* ed. Stephen R. Granbard (Boston: Houghton Mifflin, 1964), pp. 71-78.

3. See, for instance, Chimelu Chime, *Integration and Politics among African States: Limitations and Horizons of Mid-Term Theorizing* (Uppsala: Scandinavian Institute of African Studies, 1977), pt. 2, pp. 117-99.

4. Ian Brownlie, ed., *Basic Documents on African Affairs* (Oxford: Clarendon Press, 1971), pp. 1-16. See also Zdenek Cervenka, *The Organization of African Unity and Its Charter* (London: C. Hurst, 1968), chap. 3, pp. 30-84; T. O. Elias, *Africa and the Development of International Law* (Leiden: A. W. Sijthoff, 1972), chaps. 7-9, pp. 121-76.

5. Mitrany, *Working Peace System,* p. 97.

6. Ernst B. Haas, "International Integration:

The OAU is unique as a regional organization in that it is an attempt to maintain a delicate balance in the transition from functional cooperation in economic, social, cultural, technical, and defense spheres to "a political community" in which supranationality or "the supremacy of welfare-dominated policies is assured."[7] This assertion should not, however, be interpreted to mean that the establishment of the OAU implies that the most fundamental functionalist and neofunctionalist theses have been realized in the African continent. On the contrary, the theories were formulated not with the backward African states in mind, but with particular reference to the modern industrial states of Europe where traumatic experiences of war, followed by the establishment of the European Economic Community (EEC), appeared to suggest the tendency toward the decline of the nation-state.[8]

The argument of this article is that the OAU symbolizes a positive attack on the problem of intra-African cooperation, achieved through a tenuous compromise by shifting the focus of African diplomacy from divisive political and ideological issues to relatively noncontroversial economic, social, cultural, and technical fields in which African states share a common interest. This is the *raison d'être* of the OAU. Whether, and to what extent, it has been able to fulfill or justify this functional existence is directly related to the central argument.

The European and the Universal Process," in *International Stability,* ed. Dale J. Heknis, Charles C. McClintock, and Arthur L. Burus (New York: John Wiley, 1964), p. 230.

7. Haas, *Technocracy, Pluralism and the New Europe,* p. 71.

8. Haas, "International Integration," p. 229.

THE FUNCTIONALIST IDEA
IN THE POLITICS
OF AFRICAN UNITY

The character of the OAU's system of functionalism derives directly from the politics of the pan-African movement in Africa after 1958. Although the ideological stream of thought underlying the pan-African movement was overwhelmingly inspired by hatred of the slave trade and colonialism and the desire to establish an independent sovereign "Africa for the Africans,"[9] by the late 1950s and early 1960s, the situation had changed considerably and Africa had become bitterly divided into different political and ideological streams. The emergence of Ghana (1957), Guinea (1958), and several former British and French territories (1960) as independent states, coupled with the Algerian (1958-62) and Congo (1960-63) crises, created in the African continent an atmosphere of hope and confusion, and among African statesmen a certain sense of urgency regarding the need for African integration to resolve these problems.

At the root of the politics and diplomacy over the form of African integration were two diametrically contrary propositions. On the one hand, there were those such as Kwame Nkrumah of Ghana who advocated a political union as an inevitable first step toward a prosperous African community and world peace. In opposition to the idea of a political union in one fell swoop, others proposed functional cooperation at regional levels to serve as building blocks toward a higher level of organic unity. It is a remarkable feature of intra-African functionalism that these two tendencies were not only reflected in various experiments at integration prior to the establishment of the OAU, but were also projected onto the OAU's system of functional cooperation.

Political union:
its proponents and
their arguments

It has been suggested by Colin Legum that the idea of political union was an idea of which Nkrumah became the leading, if not the only, prominent exponent in Africa.[10] As an integration scheme, however, the idea was bought by such radical statesmen as Sékou Touré of Guinea and Modibo Keita of Mali, and, to some extent, formed the basis of the Ghana-Guinea Union, established in 1959, and the Ghana-Guinea-Mali Union, established two years later. Ghana, Guinea, and Mali met at Casablanca in January 1961, along with Morocco, the United Arab Republic, Libya, and the Algerian Provisional Government, and bound themselves under a charter[11] to what became known as the Casablanca Powers.

Although a common revisionist stream of thought with regard to African politics and international relations seemed to unite the Casablanca Powers, functional cooperation was never far from their minds. Membership in the Ghana-Guinea Union was thrown open to all independent African states, provided they adhered to the principles upon which the union was based. One of the key principles was the building of "a free and prosperous African Community in the interests of its peoples and world peace." There was, however, an impor-

9. Colin Legum, *Pan-Africanism: A Short Political Guide,* rev. ed. (New York: Praeger, 1965), p. 22.

10. Ibid., p. 57.
11. Ibid., pp. 205-15.

tant caveat to the effect that "members will decide in common what portions of sovereignty shall be surrendered to the Union in the full interest of African Community."

This adroit juxtaposition of the elements of functional cooperation and political union was the essence of the Ghana-Guinea-Mali Union and the Charter of the Casablanca Powers. The aims of the former, known as the Union of African States, were, among others, "to strengthen and develop ties of friendship and fraternal co-operation between Member States politically, diplomatically, economically and culturally" and "to harmonize the domestic and foreign policy of Members." But the main emphasis of the Union of African States' activities was on the political, diplomatic, and defense spheres, to the extent that economic and social functions seemed almost lost. In the Charter of Casablanca, the proposal for the establishment of an African Political Committee and Joint African High Command was balanced with that for an African Economic Committee and African Cultural Committee. Nkrumah emphatically and repeatedly argued that "the future of Africa lies in a political union—a political union in which the economic, military and cultural activities will be co-ordinated for the security of our Continent."[12]

*Functional cooperation:
  its proponents and
  their arguments*

The importance of the colonial legacy in the history of functional cooperation in Africa prior to the OAU cannot be overemphasized. In East Africa, for

example, Britain laid the foundation for a "closer union" between Kenya, Tanganyika, and Uganda,[13] which, at independence, developed into one of the most successful experiments in economic integration—the East African Community.[14] Similarly, France engineered the formation of the Union africaine et malgache (UAM).[15]

While the three East African states played a relatively small role in the debates prior to the OAU's formation,[16] the impact of the original 12—later 14—UAM states was considerable. Two major contributions of the UAM states were particularly relevant. First, apart from formally institutionalizing the UAM into a functional organization, with articulated economic, postal, and air services—the Organisation africaine et malgache de coopération économique, the Union africaine et malgache des postes et telecommunications, and Air afrique, respectively—at independence the UAM states reconstituted themselves into a neofunctional organization known as the Union of African States and Madagascar, referred to as the Brazzaville Powers.[17] Although national security remained the primary consideration,

13. Edward A. Brett, "Closer Union in East Africa," in *Inter-State Relations in Africa,* ed. Dennis Austin and Hans N. Weiler (Freiburg i. Br.: Arnold-Bergstraesser-Institut für kulturwissenschaftliche Forschung, 1965), pp. 51-67.

14. Arthur Hazlewood, "Economic Integration in East Africa," in *African Integration and Disintegration: Case Studies in Economic and Political Union,* ed. Arthur Hazlewood, (London: Oxford University Press, 1967), pp. 69-114.

15. Keith Panter-Brick, "The Union Africaine et Malgache," in *Inter-State Relations in Africa,* ed. Austin and Weiler, pp. 68-84.

16. See D. K. Chisiza, *Realities of African Independence* (London: African Publications Trust, 1961).

17. Hella Pick, "The Brazzaville Twelve," *Africa South in Exile,* 5(3):76-84 (Apr.-June 1961);

12. Quoted in ibid., p. 57.

proposals were also laid down for inter-territorial cooperation in economic, social, transport, and research fields.

The second major contribution of the UAM to the development of intra-African functionalism was the willingness of its member states to collaborate with the three sponsors of the May 1961 Monrovia Conference—Liberia, Nigeria, and Sierra Leone—in the search for a consensus on the institutional form of African integration. If until the Monrovia Conference intra-African functionalism as such was not yet organized into an elaborate body of principles, the conference provided broad guidelines on which consensus by a majority of independent African states was possible. The consensus was to establish "a loose form of association . . . based upon the principles of economic, cultural, scientific and technical co-operation."[18]

More important in the context of intra-African functionalism, the conference's 22 participating states—including Ethiopia and Libya, a Casablanca renegade—agreed that "economic and technical development, both within their respective territories and on [an] intra-African basis, should take precedence over political union."[19] The possibility of an African political integration emerging at an unspecified distant date was not ruled out, but in the prevailing circumstances of the time, economic and social cooperation should precede political union. "The unity that . . . is aimed to be achieved at the moment," declares the sixth principle of the conference resolution, "is not the political integration of sovereign African States, but unity of aspirations and of actions considered from the point of view of African social solidarity and political identity."[20]

Addis Ababa
compromise: The OAU

Protagonists of neofunctionalist theories of integration, especially Haas, have contended that the construction of an international community in which state sovereignty is gradually eroded can be achieved through deliberate and voluntary decisions by actors or through unintended consequences of such decisions, but never by force.[21] Neither the Monrovia group as a whole nor the UAM nor even the radical Casablanca Powers ever advocated force as a means toward the goal of African unity. All the other founding fathers of the OAU, in particular Dr. Nnamdi Azikiwe and Sir Abubakar Tafawa Balewa of Nigeria, Houphouët-Boigny of the Ivory Coast, Leopold Sedar Senghor of Senegal, and William Tubman of Liberia, stood for gradualism as opposed to revolutionary change. Although Nkrumah advocated positive action, such action was never interpreted to mean the application of physical coercion.

Thus the functionalist idea in the politics of African unity appeared to have evolved as if in strict conformity with some of the key prescriptions of orthodox functionalism and neofunctionalism. The Casablanca, Monrovia, and UAM groups mentioned earlier

Thomas Hodgkin and Ruth Schachter, "French Speaking West Africa in Transition," *International Conciliation*, no. 528, pp. 375-436 (May 1960).

18. Elias, *Africa and the Development of International Law*, p. 122.

19. Ibid.

20. Legum, *Pan-Africanism*, app. 17, p. 216.

21. Ernst B. Haas, "International Integration," *International Encyclopedia of the Social Sciences*, p. 522.

existed as one of the many partly competing and partly overlapping groups of African states that, from 1958 onward, formed and reformed in kaleidoscopic fashion until, in 1963, all were finally united in the OAU.[22] The essence of the OAU compromise was the mutual agreement among the contending groups to harmonize their positions into a unified document on African integration. The OAU Charter was the product of this understanding, as well as the blueprint of intra-African functionalism.

THE OAU's SYSTEM OF FUNCTIONAL COOPERATION

The OAU Charter specifies clearly the end goal, purposes, principles, fields of cooperation, institutions, and specialized commissions that, taken together, constitute the framework of intra-African functionalism.

The end goal

The Charter's preamble contains some of the most fundamental postulates of functionalism. The end goal is the common determination to promote African cooperation "in a larger unity transcending ethic and national differences." In order to translate this collective aspiration into "a working peace system," the preamble specifically mentions three contingent requirements: that conditions for peace and security must be maintained; that all African states should henceforth unite so that the welfare and well-being of their people can be assured; and that it has become imperative to reinforce the links between African states by establishing and strengthening common institutions.

22. Panter-Brick, "Union Africaine et Malgache," p. 68.

These postulates must be viewed not so much in terms of abstract theorizing on integration as in terms of the practical experiences of the problems confronting African states as new actors in the international system. Apart from the practical realities of African independence, there was also an element of fear that the enormous natural resources of the continent, without a strong technical manpower and military base to exploit and safeguard them, could provide grounds for neocolonialism and a gradual encroachment upon national sovereignty.

Purposes and principles

Article II of the Charter specifies the OAU's purposes and indicates areas of intra-African cooperation. The purposes derive directly from the postulated end goal and are as follows:

—to promote the unity and solidarity of the African states;

—to coordinate and intensify their collaboration and efforts to achieve a better life for the peoples of Africa;

—to defend their sovereignty, their territorial integrity, and their independence;

—to eradicate all forms of colonialism in Africa; and

—to promote international cooperation, having due regard for the Charter of the United Nations and the Universal Declaration of Human Rights.

The OAU's principles derive from the postulated purposes in the same way as the latter derive from the end goal. They are as specified in Article III:

—the sovereign equality of all member states;

—noninterference in the internal affairs of member states;

—respect for the sovereignty and territorial integrity of each state and for its inalienable right to independent existence;

—peaceful settlement of disputes by negotiation, mediation, conciliation, or arbitration;

—unreserved condemnation, in all its forms, of political assassination as well as of subversive activities on the part of neighboring states or any other state;

—absolute dedication to the total emancipation of the African territories that are still dependent; and

—affirmation of a policy of nonalignment with regard to all blocs.

The main features of these principles, some of which are peculiar to the African situation, must be mentioned. First, more than half—the first four—which have already found expression in Article 2 of the United Nations' Charter, reflect an attempt to project U.N. ideals onto the new African organization and to associate intra-African cooperation with such ideals. Second, the principles reflect the great emphasis accorded to functional cooperation in contradistinction to political integration. In this respect, the principle of peaceful settlement of disputes appears to be based on the assumption that peace is necessary both to ensure the progressive fulfillment of mutual cooperation for development and to counter the perennial incidence of African conflicts arising from boundary disputes and sociocultural differences.

The principal institutions

Article VII names the four principal institutions as the Assembly of Heads of State and Government (AHG), the Council of Ministers, the General Secretariat, and the Commission of Mediation, Conciliation and Arbitration.

The AHG is "the supreme organ of the Organization" and the final decision-making authority. It is not, however, a sovereign political organ, so that its decisions or resolutions, particularly on sensitive issues affecting the national interests of member states, often remain unimplemented. In fact, the powers of the AHG are circumscribed by its functions, the most pertinent of which are to discuss matters of common concern to Africans with a view to coordinating and harmonizing the OAU's general policy and to review the structure, function, and acts of all the organs and any specialized agencies.

The Council of Ministers consists of foreign ministers or such other ministers as are designated by the governments of member states. It meets twice a year. It is entrusted not only with preparing the AHG conferences, but also with implementing decisions taken at such conferences. In effect, the Council of Ministers is the executive organ of the OAU. In this regard it is interesting to note that the secretary-general of the OAU is officially designated "administrative secretary-general" in order to emphasize the position's administrative role as director of the affairs of the Secretariat, as described in Article XVI. In practice, and depending on the personality of the incumbent, the administrative secretary-general has not only wielded considerable influence in all spheres of OAU activities, but has also provided the main focus and direction of intra-African cooperation.

The Commission of Mediation, Conciliation and Arbitration was established as a principal institution of the OAU in order to give practical effect to the principle of peaceful settlement of disputes. Because of its importance, Elias has called the commission Africa's equivalent of the International Court of Justice.[23] Yet, the commission remained virtually a dormant institution until 11 December 1967, when it held its first meeting. Thus the main theaters of the politics and diplomacy of intra-African functionalism were not the sporadic meetings of the commission, but the three other organs, especially the AHG and the Council of Ministers.

The functional commissions

The main functional agencies of the OAU, known as specialized commissions, are, as provided in Article XX: (1) Economic and Social; (2) Educational and Cultural; (3) Health, Sanitation, and Nutrition; (4) Defence; and (5) Scientific, Technical and Research.

The early development of intra-African cooperation within the framework of these commissions was hampered by three initial limitations. First, the commissions were not given the degree of autonomy required for effective operation. One significant feature common to them all is the provision that they will operate in accordance with regulations approved by the Council of Ministers as well as under, and as part of, the General Secretariat. Thus although all five commissions met within the first year after 1963, their operational relations with the Council of Ministers became a source of tension. The main problem was whether the commissions should report directly to the AHG or indirectly, through the Council of Ministers. It was argued that since each commission was composed of the appropriate ministers or plenipotentiaries of the member states, their decisions on issues within their functional areas should not be subject to review by the council.[24]

The second limitation seriously constraining the work of the functional commissions was the lack of technical manpower, money, and an efficient internal organization. This limitation had far-reaching implications because at the time of the formation of the OAU, the United Nations Economic Commission for Africa (ECA), a parallel continentwide functional agency, was already effectively established. Thus, the OAU's specialized commissions, especially the Economic and Social Commission, were ill equipped vis-à-vis the ECA on issues related to Africa's economic and social development. In the six to seven years after 1963, a relationship of mutual cooperation and conflict existed between the OAU and the ECA with respect to inter-African cooperation.[25]

The third bottleneck in the early development of the functional commissions was associated with the confusion and uncertainty arising from an attempt at proliferating the commissions, especially when the necessary political and material support had not been mobilized sufficiently to make the existing ones function effectively. Due to pressure from an interest group of eminent African lawyers, the first ordinary session of the AHG held at Cairo in July 1964 approved the establishment of a Commission of Jurists as one of the specialized commissions. A Transport and

23. Elias, *Africa and the Development of International Law,* chaps. 7 and 9, pp. 121-47, 160-76.

24. Ibid., p. 145.
25. James S. Magee, "ECA and the Paradox of African Cooperation," *International Conciliation,* no. 580 (Nov. 1970).

Communications Commission was also approved, and both became operative after 1964, bringing the total number of specialized commissions to seven.[26] Conferences multiplied, as did the administrative and financial costs of servicing them. Furthermore, the increase in the number of commissions created a great deal of pressure on the General Secretariat, and piled up arrears of work for the administrative secretary-general, inadvertently forcing him to rely more than he could tolerate on the ECA's resources.

FUNCTIONAL COOPERATION AND CONFLICT

Despite limited financial and manpower resources, as well as the newness and scale of problems to be solved, the OAU's functional institutions managed to produce a not too unimpressive range of achievements in its first decade, 1963-73. These achievements, and the setbacks that were encountered, will be discussed under five main headings: economic and social development, education and culture, scientific and technological development, defense, and international economic relations.

Economic and social development

The OAU appeared to recognize at the outset the technical, organizational, and social issues. The first major achievement of the OAU was that it succeeded not only in eliciting the ECA's cooperation during the difficult years of 1963-65, but also in arriving at a mutual working relationship that defined each organization's areas of competence and limitations.

The ECA's warm, sympathetic, and cautious attitude toward the functional aspirations of the OAU favored collaboration. For example, the ECA sent a message of goodwill to the founding conference at Addis Ababa and submitted a paper on approaches to African economic integration. Furthermore, at the first meeting of the Economic and Social Commission at Niamey, Niger, in December 1963 the executive secretary of the ECA, Robert Gardiner of Ghana, sent a note in which he specifically called for OAU-ECA cooperation in mobilizing Africa's human and material resources, for only through joint endeavors "would it be reasonable to envisage at least some parts of Africa achieving present-day levels of European economic development in the next fifty years."[27]

The ECA's gesture was reluctantly reciprocated by the OAU. Paradoxically, this gesture became suspect; and, in defining the spheres of activity of the Economic and Social Commission at the Council of Ministers meeting at Accra in October 1965, the OAU administrative secretary-general, Diallo Telli of Guinea, cautioned against indiscriminate use of the ECA's resources.[28] Although the December 1965 accord between the United Nations and the OAU[29] confined cooperation between the two "within their respective spheres of responsibility," it opened up, rather than buried, the fundamental differences in each side's perception of the path to African integration.

26. Elias, *Africa and the Development of International Law,* p. 144.

27. Quoted in Michael Wolfers, *Politics in the Organization of African Unity* (London: Methuen, 1976), p. 76.

28. Ibid., p. 99.

29. UN Dec. A/6174, 16 Dec. 1965.

The major cause of OAU-ECA rivalry was ideological. Fundamentally, whereas ECA's Gardiner was an international technocrat with a conservative political outlook and a strong belief in the capitalist development model, OAU's Telli was a pan-African socialist technocrat deeply committed to African autonomy and disengagement from the capitalist world system. Gardiner's argument to the effect that it would take half a century of collective action to achieve for "some parts of Africa" a certain level of European development and that even "this would be a bloodless—and perhaps the most peaceful revolution in the history of mankind" appeared to suggest a situation of hopelessness, a call to a gradualist, stage-by-stage approach till the fateful year 2013!

Furthermore, whereas Gardiner's development ideas reflected the classical and neoclassical conception of the separation of politics and economics in socioeconomic transformation and international politics, Telli believed the two were so intertwined that neither politics nor economics could be divorced from issues of Africa's economic and social development.[30] At Kinshasa in 1967, the Council of Ministers endorsed Telli's position in its resolution on intra-African cooperation[31] and urged that as a matter of urgency African states should develop regional economic groupings and establish an African Common Market. Although the ECA recognized the necessity of establishing an African Common Market, it had nevertheless argued that such a common market could not be established until detailed empirical studies had been carried out and arrangements completed regarding customs, different monetary systems, finance, transport, and necessary legislation.[32]

Functional cooperation in Africa received one of its deadliest blows from the OAU-ECA rivalry. First, the rivalry drastically slowed down the OAU's activities until 1969, when, at its ninth session the ECA "affirmed the political and policy-making supremacy of the OAU."[33] Second, the rivalry undermined the spirit of intra-African cooperation built up laboriously by ECA technical expertise during the quinquennium prior to the OAU's founding—1958-63—and presented in 1963 for translation into concrete action.[34] As a consequence, most of the OAU's regulations on economic and social problems in the 1960s—issues relating to industrialization, intra-African cooperation, African regional groupings, African civil aviation, telecommunications, road and maritime transport, and, above all, an African Common Market—came to naught. Third, the "political and policy-making supremacy of the OAU" over the ECA, achieved in 1969, was more qualitative than quantitative in nature. Telli's diplomatic ingenuity and material resources in no way matched Gardiner's tested technical and administrative expertise, to say nothing of the enormous range of available resources at Gardiner's disposal. At the end of 1971, the economic and social affairs department of the OAU's General Secretariat had only ten senior staff and three secretaries.

Education and culture

Interest in educational development and cultural revival was so great that the first session of the Educational and

30. CM/Res. 148 (IX), 1967.
31. CM/Res. 123(IX), 1967.

32. E/CN. 14/Res. 86 (VI), 1963.
33. E/CN. 14/Res. 19 (IX), 11 Feb. 1969.
34. E/CN. 14/239, Part B, 13 Jan. 1964.

Cultural Commission held at Leopold-ville—now Kinshasa—in January 1964 was attended by as many as 29 African states. But this initial interest was not matched by a determined commitment to implement proposed projects, especially the establishment of a Pan-African News Agency, a Pan-African University, and a Plan for Educational Development of Africa.

With the exception of the news agency, none of these projects has materialized to date. Apart from the lack of intra-African support, the decision to rely on extra-African agencies, such as the United Nations Educational, Scientific, and Cultural Organization in this case, though convenient in the short run, obviously slowed down their realization. That decision also inhibited measures for breaking down language barriers, coordinating secondary and university education, accelerating development of scientific and technological education, and, of course, promoting intra-African cultural and literary activities in areas such as music, drama, and art.

Scientific and
technological development

When, in May 1964, the Scientific, Technical and Research Commission took over the assets and liabilities of the former colonial Commission for Technical Co-operation in Africa South of the Sahara, the change was expected to accelerate the pace of intra-Africa cooperation in this sphere. The first setback resulted from the 1967 decision to incorporate the original commissions dealing with education, health, and science into a new and greatly enlarged Educational, Scientific, Cultural and Health Commission in the name of streamlining institutional agencies for cooperation and of minimizing duplication of effort. The price that Africa had to pay for these reorganizations was an unwieldy and cumbersome commission, lacking the manpower and resources to carry out even the job of regularly collecting, collating, and publishing reasonably reliable data for use in the planning process.

Defense

Cooperation in defense was considered vital to the end goal of African unity and independence partly to satisfy those who pressed for political union and partly to reassure the mostly smaller states in the UAM of Africa's preparedness to rally behind them in the event of threats to their sovereignty and territorial integrity. In translating this function into concrete arrangements for action, however, the OAU was again divided along the pre-1963 lines.

The controversy centered around the proposal put forward by Ghana at both the first meeting of the Defence Commission, in Accra, October-November 1963, and the second summit of the AHG, in Cairo, July 1964, for the establishment of an African High Command. The command's functions would be to protect African states from external aggression and to give assistance to African freedom fighters to liberate their countries from foreign domination. The command was not intended for use in the maintenance of internal law and order in any member state without the express request by the duly constituted government, deemed to be acting on behalf of the majority of its people.[35]

The proposal was rejected. Led by Liberia and Cameroon, protagonists of

35. Doc. AHG/3, 13 July 1964.

functional cooperation attacked it as premature and inconsistent with the Addis Ababa compromise, which merely called for the need to "co-ordinate and harmonise" general policies on defense and security. They also disagreed with the suggestion that the immediate threat to the territorial integrity and independence of Africa was not external aggression, but, as Ahmadu Ahidjo of Cameroon put it, "subsidized subversion teleguided from other African States."[36]

Events in Africa in the late 1960s and early 1970s proved the need for the rejected African High Command. With Portugal's attempted invasion of Guinea in November 1970, the Defence Commission, which had become moribund since its last meeting in Freetown, Sierra Leone, in February 1965, quickly convened in Lagos in December 1970. A study of "the ways and means of establishing an adequate and speedy defence of African States" was commissioned. The report from the study was discussed at a subsequent meeting in Addis Ababa in December 1971. It was agreed that a regional defense system to combat external aggression and to coordinate national armed forces units be established.[37] This proposal was presented to the AHG in Rabat, Morocco, in July 1972, but, like the African High Command project of the mid-1960s, it received a cold and unenthusiastic response.

International economic relations

While it could be argued that the OAU-ECA rivalry derived from complex personality and ideological differences between the two administrative and executive secretaries, it was nevertheless

indisputable that the two functional organs collaborated effectively in the critical area of international economic relations. Two outstanding arenas where functional cooperation was remarkably manifest and successful were the United Nations Conference on Trade and Development (UNCTAD) and Africa's relations with the EEC.

As regards UNCTAD, African states collectively under the OAU and in association with the ECA have attempted to coordinate Africa's positions prior to each round of conferences.[38] In preparation for UNCTAD I, held in Geneva, 23 March-16 June 1964, the OAU Council of Ministers met in Lagos, 24-29 February, and recommended the formation of a working party of African states. The ECA, at the end of its meeting on 28 February 1964, set up a coordinating committee for UNCTAD, which included the OAU.

One of the most significant efforts at cooperation was the OAU-sponsored Algiers Conference of 7-15 October 1967. Attended by 31 African states, the conference adopted a document known as the African Declaration of Algiers,[39] which was also endorsed by the non-aligned countries and submitted as a working paper for UNCTAD II, held in New Delhi, 1 February-28 March 1968. More important, the African Declaration of Algiers became substantially the basis of a joint OAU-ECA blueprint for Africa's development in the 1970s,[40] which was formally launched at

36. Doc. AHG/PV 7, 13 July 1964.
37. DEF/Res. 4 (IV), 1971.

38. See G. Aforka Nweke, *Harmonization of African Foreign Policies, 1955-1975: The Political Economy of African Diplomacy* (Boston: Boston University, African Studies Center, 1980), chaps. 7 and 8, pp. 125-79.
39. E/CN. 14/UNCTAD II/PM.2/Res. 2.
40. Organization of African Unity and Economic Commission for Africa, *Africa's Strategy for Development in the 1970s* (Addis Ababa:

the first meeting of the Conference of Ministers of the ECA in Tunis in February 1971. The blueprint not only emphasized the development of agro-based programs, export promotion, and intra-African trade, but also placed on its priority list the promotion of labor-intensive industries relying on local raw materials as well as industrial and agricultural research. The underlying principle was self-reliance.

The OAU and the ECA also played a vital role in generating an African common front in the negotiations prior to the Lomé I Convention between the EEC and the African, Caribbean and Pacific states (ACP). They not only arranged contact points, but also provided the organizational frameworks and the technical expertise for the construction of a common position package prior to negotiations with the EEC. Thus a series of meetings under the aegis of the OAU and the ECA was held between February and July 1973, which culminated in an eight-point platform of Africa's collective position vis-à-vis the EEC.[41]

FUNCTIONALISM AND AFRICAN SELF-RELIANCE

The African common front against the West at UNCTAD and against the EEC at the Lomé Convention negotiations must be seen against the background of the OAU's failure to translate into concrete action its numerous resolutions on functional cooperation within the African continent. The hope lay not in the present, but in the future;[42] and in African initiative and self-confidence, not in the emergence of the so-called New International Economic Order or in Western largess. The Lagos Plan of Action,[43] adopted at the Lagos AHG meeting in April 1980, is both a solemn reminder of past failures and an attempt at readaptation, redefinition, and rededication to the end goal of intra-African cooperation.

The plan defines the functionalist strategy for 1980 and beyond as that of "collective self-reliant and endogenous economic, social and cultural development of the African continent" and distinguishes between "action for food" and "action for energy." The two proposed actions are ingenuously linked to the ultimate aspect of the plan, which calls for the establishment of an African Common Market by the year 2000. The agenda for action also includes establishment of functional institutions for research and development in the nuclear and agro-industrial fields; the progressive integration of African economies in the 1990s, with emphasis on harmonization of national economic policies and development plans; and effective programs of social welfare and community development, social security, and the mobilization of the masses for the development of public works and community services.

Specifically for food security, it was agreed that "urgent steps should be taken by every African country to adopt a coherent national food security policy." They should set up national strategic food reserves on the order of 10 percent of total food production, as well as

Economic Commission for Africa, 1973).

41. *West Africa,* no. 2928, p. 992 (23 July 1973).

42. John Ravenhill, "The Future of Regionalism in Africa," in *The Future of Regionalism in Africa* ed. Ralph I. Onwuka and Amadu Sesay (London: Macmillan, 1985), chap. 12, pp. 205-24.

43. OAU Doc. ECM/ECO. 8 (SIV) Rev. 2, Add. 1.

promote adequate and realistic agrarian reform programs consistent with the political and social conditions prevailing in respective countries. In addition, the action calls for the strengthening of national and intercountry cooperative research programs "to support the objectives of food self-sufficiency."

Throughout the proposals for food security, the doctrine of self-reliance is proclaimed. It is stated, for instance, that "the need for collective self-reliance will require subregional food security arrangements"; hence the endorsement of the Regional Food Plan for Africa, approved by the ministers of agriculture in Arusha, Tanzania, in 1978, and of the master plans for the establishment of model farms in the Sahel region.

The second component of the Lagos plan concerns action with respect to energy security. Two main features of this component are the timing and the significance of substantive proposals. The former is divided into short-term, medium-term, and long-term measures. The latter is aimed at increasing national and pan-African capabilities ranging from the development of hydro power resources to the construction of nuclear power plants and the conservation of locally produced uranium to meet the requirements of the nuclear option.[44]

As in the case of ensuring food security, proposals to meet the demands of energy security are rationalized as deriving from the dictates of African solidarity. It is argued, for instance, that "to ensure stable and guaranteed supplies of oil to African countries" in the short term, "various ways of integrating the impact of oil prices, particularly on the balance of payments" and of assisting African

non-oil-producing countries "in the training of cadres and technical staff and in prospecting for and exploiting of oil deposits" must be seen as a deliberate policy "to demonstrate African solidarity."

Such strategies for development have been proposed before. What is significant about the Lagos plan is that it reflects on the one hand an open disenchantment with the un-African strategies of the First and Second United Nations Development Decades and their woefully disappointing results, and on the other an endeavor through collective action to break away from those externally guided models. At the Monrovia colloquium of 12-15 February 1979, African scholars called for a specifically African strategy of growth and development based on "the region's own resources and innate capabilities consistent with its own cultural values, social systems and its dignity" and recommended the establishment of an African Economic Community as an instrument for autonomous change.[45]

CONCLUSION

From this discussion, we observe that almost without exception African countries are theoretically committed to one kind of intra-African cooperation or unity, which is a reflection both of their colonial backgrounds and of problems of development and welfare after attainment of political independence. To regain control over the economic base, the lifeline of any sociopsychological community, a self-reliant development model for survival has been put forward

44. See G. Aforka Nweke, *African Security in the Nuclear Age* (Enugu: Fourth Dimension, 1985), chaps. 6 and 7, pp. 69-103.

45. *What Kind of Africa by the Year 2000? Final Report of the Monrovia Symposium on the Future Development Prospects of Africa towards the Year 2000* (Addis Ababa: Organization of African Unity, 1979).

and collectively endorsed by African states. It is more pertinent to ask what kind of self-reliance is envisaged by the Lagos Plan of Action than to investigate how much progress has been made to actualize its goals.

By "collective self-reliance" African states certainly do not mean autarky. They probably envisage at least four interrelated behavioral postures: (1) the severance of dependency links operated through the world capitalist system; (2) radical restructing of the national economy and external economic relations to promote national security, meet the basic social needs of the people, and eliminate socioeconomic inequality; (3) full mobilization of domestic capabilities and resources, relying largely on themselves; and (4) fostering and strengthening cooperation, alliances, and collective action in the underdeveloped South, including harmonization of foreign economic and political policies. In fact, intra-African functionalism has failed because African states have not addressed themselves to these four basic problems.

Collective self-reliance rejects the present atomization of Africa into a multiplicity of sovereign, weak states, with dependent and disarticulated national economies. It also rejects development models that are not people oriented, that cater to the privileged class of property owners. Julius Nyerere of Tanzania has stated that it is the people of Africa who must fight the poverty of Africa. At the same time, he maintains that national development is not enough, but must form part of a wider African experience. The strategy is that of evolving one continental political and economic community, which will define its priorities and the ideology for mobilizing the people. So far, the OAU has not evolved such a strategy and is not likely to evolve one unless African political economies are transformed along those lines.

ANNALS, *AAPSS,* **489,** January 1987

Between Scylla and Charybdis: The Foreign Economic Relations of Sub-Saharan African States

By THOMAS M. CALLAGHY

ABSTRACT: Over the last decade the foreign economic relations of sub-Saharan African states have focused increasingly on their severe debt and economic crises. These relations have involved wrestling with debt service burdens and the rigors of rescheduling with the Paris and London Clubs; conducting difficult negotiations with bilateral and private creditors; bargaining over conditionality packages with the International Monetary Fund and the World Bank or fending them off; distributing the painful costs of adjustment; coping with import strangulation; and devising new development policies and strategies. The sub-Saharan states were already highly dependent on the outside world; the intensity, stakes, and levels of conditionality of these states' foreign economic relations have increased substantially since the middle of the 1970s. They are certainly political, as they impinge on very central issues—sovereignty, political order, development, and mass welfare. In this sense, they are foreign economic relations with very powerful domestic roots and consequences. African states and external actors are going to have to work together to ameliorate Africa's crises.

Thomas M. Callaghy is assistant professor of political science and associate director of the Research Institute on International Change at Columbia University. He earned his doctorate from the University of California, Berkeley. He is author of The State-Society Struggle: Zaire in Comparative Perspective, *editor of* South Africa in Southern Africa: The Intensifying Vortex of Violence, *and coeditor of* Socialism in Sub-Saharan Africa: A New Assessment.

What all this [International Monetary Fund activity] amounts to is an increasing tendency towards a kind of international authoritarianism. Economic power is used as a substitute for gun-boats . . . in enforcing the unilateral will of the powerful. The sovereign equality of all nations is ignored, as is the future stability of the world.

—Julius Nyerere

Nigeria . . . has already fallen into "debt trap peonage." . . . And like the heroin addict, we are craving these loans, not for sound purposes, but simply to finance our spendthrift consumer habits and our ambitious maldevelopment plans. . . . Economic history shows that development happens to be one of those journeys . . . for which there are no easy paths, only more or less difficult ones.

—Chinweizu

Within the cluster of internal causes of Africa's external indebtedness, the following can be identified: . . . a policy of excessive dependence on external resources for financing development . . . poor economic management coupled with misuse of resources and wastage of public funds . . . the inability to utilise fully external finance to generate enough surpluses to enable them to repay the loans . . . the inadequacy of policies and institutions for monitoring the contracting of external debts, their utilisation and servicing (poor debt management) and . . . lack of trained personnel to administer resource policies.

—Adebayo Adedeji
Executive Secretary
Economic Commission for Africa[1]

Over the last decade the foreign relations of sub-Saharan African states have focused increasingly on their severe

economic and fiscal crises.[2] These foreign economic relations have involved wrestling with the burdens of debt service and the rigors of rescheduling; conducting difficult negotiations with bilateral and private creditors; bargaining over conditionality packages with the International Monetary Fund (IMF) and the World Bank or fending them off; distributing the painful costs of adjustment; coping with import strangulation; and devising new development policies and strategies. Sub-Saharan states were already highly dependent on the outside world; the intensity, stakes, and levels of conditionality of these states' economic relations with external actors have increased substantially since the middle of the 1970s.

Foreign economic relations are in many ways high foreign policy writ large. They are certainly political. There is very little that is neutral about them, impinging as they do on very central issues—sovereignty, political and social order, development, mass welfare, and class formation, consolidation, and conflict. In this sense, they are foreign economic relations with very powerful domestic roots and consequences.

The weak, predominantly primary-product-dependent, highly trade-dependent African economies were hit severely by a rapid sequence of external shocks—the oil shocks of 1973 and 1979; extensive drought; a major recession in the industrialized North, forcing a decline in both demand and price for

---

1. Julius K. Nyerere, "Africa and the Debt Crisis," *African Affairs,* 84(337):494 (Oct. 1985); Chinweizu, "Debt Trap Peonage," *Monthly Review,* 3(6):22, 22, 34 (Nov. 1985); Adebayo Adedeji, "Foreign Debt and Prospects for Growth in Africa during the 1980s," *Journal of Modern African Studies,* 23(1):60-61 (Mar. 1985).

2. This article concerns the 39 countries that the World Bank considers to be in sub-Saharan Africa; it does not include South Africa. Because comprehensive data on Angola and Mozambique are usually not available to the bank, much but not all of the data presented here exclude these two countries. Whenever "Africa" is used in the text, it refers only to sub-Saharan Africa.

their commodity exports not seen since the Great Depression; increasing protectionism by the Organization for Economic Cooperation and Development; generalized inflation in the world economy, which encouraged the accumulation of debt, and then disinflation in the context of relatively high levels of debt at high real interest rates; and, as new credit and direct foreign investment dried up, the tapering off of aid. In the face of these shocks, the already weak states of Africa were confronted with decreasing or negative growth rates, stagnant or falling per capita income figures, and severe balance-of-payments and debt-service problems. These difficulties were often exacerbated by inappropriate policies, unproductive investment, deteriorating infrastructure and productive capacity, lax implementation, limited administrative and technical capabilities, the rise of magendo or parallel economies, and pervasive corruption. Many of these phenomena predated the external shocks and were not caused by them, but they certainly aggravated their effects.

By the 1980s the situation had become catastrophic, for much of the continent output per head was lower than in 1960. Between 1980 and 1984, the gross domestic product of African countries declined an average of 1.4 percent a year; per capita gross national product, an average of 4.4 percent a year; export volume, 7.4 percent a year; and import volume, 5.9 percent per year.[3] There has been

considerable debate about the primary causes of this multifaceted crisis between those who believe that they are predominantly exogenous and those who aver that they are largely internal. Clearly they are both, and counterfactual arguments are important.

If the external variables had been significantly more favorable, would development prospects have been strikingly better? If the internal factors had been much more propitious, would the overall outcome have been dramatically improved? The answer in both cases is probably no. Whatever the importance of the various causes, debt has been a central feature of this pervasive crisis, and, by looking at the debt problems, we can examine the major actors, processes, issues, and policies that have affected Africa's foreign economic relations over the last decade.

SIZE AND NATURE OF THE DEBT

In 1974 the total debt of sub-Saharan Africa was about $14.8 billion, but by

---

3. Since space precludes item-by-item citations for the bulk of the data presented in the text, please note that in addition to the sources cited later, the data are drawn directly from or recalculated from the following: World Bank, *Financing Adjustment with Growth in Sub-Saharan Africa, 1986-90* (Washington, DC: World Bank, 1986); idem, *Development and Debt Service* (Wash-

ington, DC: World Bank, 1986); idem, *World Development Report 1985* (New York: Oxford University Press, 1985); idem, *Toward Sustained Development in Sub-Saharan Africa* (Washington, DC: World Bank, 1984); Chandra Hardy, "Africa's Debt: Structural Adjustment with Stability," in *Strategies for African Development*, ed. Robert J. Berg and Jennifer Seymour Whitaker (Berkeley: University of California Press, 1986), pp. 453-75; Rupert Pennant-Rea, *The African Burden* (New York: Twentieth Century Fund/ Priority Press, 1986); *IMF Survey*, 15(7):106 (31 Mar. 1986); and the following chapters from Carol Lancaster and John Williamson, eds., *African Debt and Financing* (Washington, DC: Institute for International Economics, 1986); Eduard Brau, "African Debt: Facts and Figures on the Current Situation," pp. 11-15, 30-43; John Williamson, "Prospects for the Flow of IMF Finance," pp. 134-41; Edward V. K. Jaycox et al., "The Nature of the Debt Problem in Eastern and Southern Africa," pp. 47-62.

the end of 1984, according to World Bank figures, it had reached about $91 billion. Other estimates put the figure closer to $125 billion. Of the $91 billion, 63.5 percent was public and publicly guaranteed medium- and long-term debt, broken down as follows, as percentages of the total $91 billion: bilateral, 24.3 percent; multilateral, 16.1 percent; suppliers' credits, 2.4 percent; and private bank, 20.7 percent. The remaining 36.5 percent is as follows: private nonguaranteed medium- and long-term debt, 4 percent; short-term, 13.6 percent; IMF, 5.9 percent; and arrears, 13 percent.

By comparison to Latin American debt, which has so riveted world attention, several factors are striking. First, the total amount is not large; it is about 10 percent of total developing-country debt and less than that of either Mexico or Brazil. Second is the very low percentage of private-bank debt, which makes up by far the bulk of Latin American debt. In addition, a large percentage of Africa's private-bank debt is guaranteed by public agencies of countries of the Organization for Economic Cooperation and Development such as the U.S. Export-Import Bank. As a result, this debt is rescheduled by these countries under the auspices of the Paris Club mechanism, rather than by the banks themselves, usually referred to as the London Club. Third is the relatively high percentage of African debt that is owed to the IMF and the World Bank, 5.9 and 5.2 percent, respectively. This type of debt cannot be rescheduled. These facts reflect great differences in the level of development and nature and degree of incorporation into the world capitalist economy of the two regions.

The following countries are sub-Saharan Africa's major debtors; they are listed with their debts, in billions of U.S. dollars, as of the end of 1984: Nigeria, 19.7; Ivory Coast, 7.4; Sudan, 7.2; Zaire, 5.0; Zambia, 4.8; Kenya, 3.8; Tanzania, 3.3; Cameroon, 2.7; Zimbabwe, 2.1; Senegal, 2.0; Ghana, 2.0; Madagascar, 2.0; Congo, 1.6; and Ethiopia, 1.5. Despite the low percentage of debt owed to private creditors, six countries owe more than two-thirds of their 1985-87 debt service to private sources—Benin, Congo, Gabon, Ivory Coast, Zimbabwe, and Nigeria. The figures for debt owed to private creditors for Nigeria and the Ivory Coast are 88.2 and 64.1 percent, respectively.

African debt has grown faster than that of any other region. The annual nominal growth rate between 1970 and 1984 was 20.4 percent, slightly higher than that of Argentina, Brazil, and Mexico; between 1975 and 1980 it was 25.2 percent. Medium- and long-term debt quadrupled between 1975 nad 1983. Until 1981 borrowing from commercial sources increased more rapidly than that from official sources, but then dropped off dramatically. The terms of borrowing also worsened over time. In 1979, 54 percent of debt was on concessional terms; by 1981 it was only 35 percent. For bilateral debt, from 1974 to 1984 average interest rates rose from 3.1 to 4.6 percent, while maturities declined from 22.5 to 19.6 years, grace periods from 7.7 to 5.6 years, and grant elements from 49.2 to 36.3 percent. For commercial borrowing, interest rates went from 8.7 to 10.4 percent, while maturities declined from 9.5 to 8.0 years. In 1983 an average of 15.1 percent of the debt was at floating rates. As a result, the recent drop in interest rates will not help African states as much as others. On the other hand, that same year 47 percent of the Ivory Coast's debt was at floating rates and 62 percent of Nigeria's was. For Nigeria, of course, the dramatic fall in oil prices will greatly overshadow any benefit from falling interest rates.

DEBT MANAGEMENT AND SERVICE

African debt use and management capabilities are on average the worst in the world. Many African countries at first had little idea how much they owed or to whom; debt service was haphazard at best; and borrowed resources were often poorly used or invested. The World Bank states its position bluntly:

A major cause of Africa's precarious situation has been the failure of many countries to invest borrowed resources productively . . . [and] hand-in-hand with economic policy reform, African economies need to strengthen their debt-management capabilities, requiring, in some cases, changes [in] the legislative framework for foreign borrowing as well as improvements in the institutional and administrative procedures used to monitor and process information on external debt.

And, as one seasoned and sympathetic observer has noted, this "institutional infrastructure . . . appears to have deteriorated radically in many sub-Saharan states over the past few years."[4]

In short, state capability is central to much of Africa's difficulties, and, even if all the major external constraints were greatly ameliorated, significant problems would remain. One result has been the frequent use of external financial advisers—individuals, investment bank groups, and legal, public relations, accounting, and consulting firms. For example, Lazard Frères; Lehman Brothers; S. G. Warburg; Morgan Grenfel; Samuel Montague; Arthur D. Little; Elliot Berg Associates; White and Case; Peat, Marwick, Mitchell and Company; and several major money-center banks have all been involved in Africa. As one experienced observer notes, "This can lend a comic-opera character to some of the international squabbling, wherein virtually all of the local memoranda are in fact drafted by foreign advisors." External actors took more extreme action in Zaire, where expatriate teams were placed directly in management positions in the Bank of Zaire, the Office of Debt Management, the finance and planning ministries, and the customs office. The effectiveness of the forward and backward linkages of foreign advisers and such technocratic enclaves is questionable. As Green has stressed, "'Have a headache? Take two expatriates' has at times worked well in a technico-managerial context, but it is neither generally practicable nor desirable even in the short run, and it is inherently dangerously addictive."[5]

The size of a country's debt is not the important issue; it is, rather, the ability to use it productively and to service it. While the size of Africa's debt has increased, the ability to use it productively and service it has declined significantly. As a result, Africa's dependence on the IMF and the World Bank, with all its attendant conditionality and monitoring, has increased dramatically, as has its reliance on rescheduling. This

4. World Bank, *Development and Debt Service*, p. xxvi; Reginald Herbold Green, "Reflections on the State of Knowledge and Ways Forward," in *Crisis and Recovery in Sub-Saharan Africa*, ed. Tore Rose (Paris: Organization for Economic Cooperation and Development, 1985), p. 299.

5. G. K. Helleiner, "The IMF and Africa in the 1980s," *Canadian Journal of African Studies*, 17(1):61 (1983); Green, "Reflections," p. 308; on the case of Zaire, see Thomas M. Callaghy, "The Political Economy of African Debt: The Case of Zaire," in *Africa in Economic Crisis*, ed. John Ravenhill (New York: Columbia University Press, 1986), pp. 307-46.

pattern can affect a country with a large debt, such as Nigeria, or countries with quite small debts, such as Sierra Leone, with a debt of $416 million, and Togo, with a debt of $798 million.

In 1970 Africa paid $449 million in debt service; by 1984 the figure had risen to $7.4 billion—a sixteenfold increase. For most countries there will be no significant decline in debt service before the end of the century. Over the next five years Africa will be required to pay out over $6.8 billion a year in debt service. In the context of extreme foreign exchange scarcity, such burdens pose very stark choices for governments between debt service, upon which their external financial, economic, and political relations depend, and food, fuel, and other imports necessary to protect their peoples and maintain order and existing productive capacity and infrastructure.

Debt service ability is most accurately reflected in scheduled debt service ratios, that is, annual payment of principal and interest as a percentage of exports of goods and services. African states have the highest average scheduled debt service ratios in the world. The average for 1986-87 is 31.1 percent; for 1986-90 it is projected at 38.6 percent, and at 31.5 percent for 1991.[6] For about ten countries the figures are significantly higher. For example, for the Sudan they are 150.9, 128.0, and 88.5 percent, respectively; for Somalia, 97.2, 77.7, and 67.2 percent; for Zambia, 59.0, 71.2, and 71.4 percent; for Tanzania, 50.4, 60.0, and 54.8 percent; for Nigeria, 36.2, 48.6, and 38.9 percent; and for Benin, 34.9, 43.5, and 44.4 percent.

6. It is important to note that these figures are based on World Bank projections of commodity prices, which often prove to be overly optimistic. These figures therefore may prove too low.

These amounts can be lowered by rescheduling, but often the relief simply postpones and even increases eventual burdens. For example, Liberia, Senegal, the Sudan, Zaire, and Zambia have each rescheduled more than once in the 1975-85 period, and their scheduled debt service is more than three times what they paid in 1982-84. The same holds true for countries that have rescheduled only once or not at all during this period, such as Benin, Mali, Somalia, and Tanzania. Only Gabon, Lesotho, and Mauritius have projected debt service less than they paid in 1982-84. These figures include IMF repurchases, and World Bank and African Development Bank debt service, none of which can be rescheduled. When linked to the fact that African states have been drawing increasingly on the resources of these institutions, repayments to them become an increasingly large percentage of debt service. Debt service ratios can grow despite rescheduling and important adjustment progress; Ghana is an important recent example.

Actual debt service is often substantially less than what is scheduled. In 1984, Benin had a scheduled debt service ratio of 38.3 percent; it paid only 16.4 percent. The respective figures for Madagascar were 80.9 and 40.5 percent; for the Sudan, 96.4 and 25.0; for Zambia, 55.2 and 24.5; and for Senegal, 29.0 and 16.9. Arrears thus become an increasingly contentious aspect of Africa's foreign relations. In 1980, 19 countries were in arrears for a total of $4.2 billion. At the end of 1984, there were 22 countries in arrears for 13 percent of the total debt. Of the $12 billion in arrears, 70.6 percent was on short-term debt and 29.4 percent on medium- and long-term. Arrears are particularly significant because they can threaten new loans, disbursements of existing ones, prospects for reschedulings, and assistance from the IMF and World Bank. Arrears to the IMF are projected to be nearly 20 percent of the 1985-90 debt service for the most severely affected countries.

For a couple of countries arrears to the IMF have led to their being declared temporarily ineligible for IMF assistance. This means no rescheduling and probably no private credit either. Short-term trade arrears often lead to the refusal of suppliers to sell or higher import prices as suppliers hedge against payment uncertainty. The issue of arrears leads directly to a discussion of rescheduling.

Both Paris and London Club reschedulings are increasingly important in the foreign relations of African states. Repeat reschedulings are now the norm for Africa, which is by far the most rescheduled region of the world. The low capability of Africa to service its debt is reflected in the number and frequency of the reschedulings. The following data are for Paris and London Club reschedulings for the period 1975-85. Of the 42 countries that rescheduled, 19, or 45.0 percent, were from Africa. Of the 144 reschedulings, 67, or 46.5 percent, were African; 49 of the African reschedulings were with the Paris Club and 18 with the London Club.

This ratio of Paris to London Club reschedulings is not surprising given the composition of Africa's debt discussed earlier. Zaire and Togo have each rescheduled seven times; the Sudan, Senegal, Madagascar, and Liberia, six times; Sierra Leone and Niger, four times; and Zambia, Malawi, the Ivory Coast, and the Central African Republic, three times. By the end of 1984, rescheduled debt constituted three-quarters of the total debt of both Zaire and the Sudan. In 1975 the one Paris Club rescheduling was not African; in 1976 the only one was; in 1977 both of them were; in 1978, 1 of the 2; in 1979 all 3; in 1980 both were; in 1981 all 7; in 1982, 5 of the 6; in 1983, 9 of the 17; in 1984, 9 of the 13; and in 1985, 10 of the 19.

Because of the severity of the African situation, the Paris Club creditor countries have shown some flexibility by quietly bending a number of norms—amounts and types of debt, the period of debt service covered, the length of grace and repayment periods, and the rescheduling of interest and previously rescheduled debt.[7] This is all done, however, at or near commercial rates and on a tight leash. It is not coordinated with Consultative Group aid consortia and is done on a case-by-case basis for fear of losing leverage and setting precedents for Africa or other regions. In addition, these frequent reschedulings generate considerable uncertainty and are very consuming of scarce talent and time, with resulting high opportunity costs. Repeated pleas for multiyear and concessional reschedulings have been ignored. In short, rescheduling has rarely resulted in viable or stable financial conditions. Finally, a few African countries, such as Botswana and Rwanda, have serviced their debt and have not needed rescheduling, or, like Gabon, have rescheduled once and subsequently maintained good debt service.

7. It might be possible to argue that interaction between countries of the Organization for Economic Cooperation and Development on African debt matters in the Paris Club and other fora in the 1970s and early 1980s laid the important case law that greatly facilitated Group of Five cooperation in coping with the Mexican debt crisis in 1982 and other major cases since then. On the international political economy of the post-1982 efforts, see Miles Kahler, "Politics and International Debt: Explaining the Crisis," *International Organization,* 39(3):357-82 (Summer 1985).

ADJUSTMENT: THE IMF
AND CONDITIONALITY

With severe debt service difficulties and limited relief from reschedulings, adjustment became necessary for many African states. Such adjustment, planned or unplanned, imposed or voluntary, is a dramatic, difficult, and unsettling phenomenon. With major foreign exchange scarcity, declining levels of aid, especially bilateral, and increasingly limited access to private capital markets, the dire need for adjustment resources has led to an increasing reliance on the IMF. The fund plays a central linchpin role. Relations with the World Bank, the Paris and London Clubs, private capital markets, and bilateral creditors are usually contingent on a viable relationship with the fund—the IMF's seal of approval. These ties to the fund have usually meant high levels of imposed conditionality, especially as its upper-tranche, or upper-level, resources—stand-by agreements and extended fund facilities (EFFs)—came into increasing use. In addition, the IMF became but the leading edge of greatly increased conditionality that has now spread to almost all forms of external assistance to Africa—multilateral, especially from the World Bank, bilateral, and even private. Over time the initial focus of conditionality on balance-of-payments adjustment to facilitate repayment shifted to a much broader structural adjustment, which entails substantial monitoring of African economies.

Structural adjustment has meant efforts to restructure African political economies in significant ways. It has been based on an increasingly pervasive dual belief that without structural adjustment any new resources would be poured down a voracious sinkhole and that

African leaders will not make appropriate changes unless they are pressured. This position is based on the view that the major causes of the crisis, or at least those that anybody is able or willing to do anything about, are internal to Africa. There is, as the World Bank contends, an increasing consensus between African governments and external actors that a crisis exists and that fundamental changes must take place.

There is much less agreement on the causes of the crisis and on the specific changes, their relevance and effectiveness, and whose interests they serve. Many African rulers would agree with Nyerere when he points to "an increasing determination by donors to use their aid for ideological and foreign policy purposes . . . monies are now set aside to be allocated just to such African countries as accept an untrammelled capitalist economy."[8] Is it "policy dialogue" as the fund and World Bank contend or neo-colonialism as Nyerere asserts? These are clearly two faces, two sides of the same phenomenon.

Helleiner notes that, given this perception,

the stage is set for a decade of battles between African governments and the IMF. There will undoubtedly be mutual exasperation and fatigue—with charges of foreign interference in domestic affairs on the one hand, and countercharges of policy "slippage," "indiscipline," and failure to abide by agreements on the other.

The ultimate outcome of these efforts is clearly open to question. As Green suggests, "Strategies and their articulation can, up to a point, be imposed on desperate countries. But they are unlikely to avoid major technical flaws, to be

8. Nyerere, "Africa and the Debt Crisis," p. 492.

implemented more than grudgingly and partially, or to yield the intended results of their sponsors."[9]

The ability of a state to adjust depends on three major factors: (1) political will; (2) administrative capacity; and (3) economic capacity. African countries are often weak in all three areas, which accounts in large part for the heavy reliance on the IMF. Between 1970 and 1978, African countries accounted for 3 percent of total IMF assistance from stand-bys and EFFs. Their share of the total number of IMF programs for this period was 17 percent; it rose to 55 percent in 1979. These countries have the highest number of repeat programs of any region of the world. In 1978 only two African countries had agreements with the IMF. At the end of February 1986, 15 of the 31 active programs were for Africa—14 stand-bys and 1 EFF. Between 1979 and early 1986, 28 African countries had a total of 95 programs, and 24 of those countries had more than 1 program. Seven countries had 2 programs; 2 had 3 programs; 8 had 4; 3 had 5; 3 had 6; and 1 country, Madagascar, had 7.

Due to this heavy reliance on the IMF, African countries now owe about 6 percent of their total debt to the fund. At the end of 1984, 27 of the 39 sub-Saharan countries owed money to the IMF, ranging from Zambia's $698 million, or 14.6 percent of its total debt, to Guinea's $11 million, or 0.9 percent. Nigeria, the Congo, Gabon, and Botswana did not owe the fund anything. Percentages of debt service owed to the fund are increasing rapidly. For debt service owed during 1986-87, the African average is 11.8 percent, but for low-income countries it is 20.1 percent.

Some countries have significantly higher figures: Ghana, 50.9 percent; Uganda, 44.7 percent; Sierra Leone, 38.7 percent; and Zambia, 32.6 percent. Since these amounts cannot be rescheduled and must be paid on time, arrears become a very contentious issue. In early 1986 eight countries were in arrears to the fund, and the Sudan and Liberia were temporarily declared ineligible for IMF resources due to $280 million in arrears. Given the fund's linchpin role, this is a significant sanction, one that countries will go to interesting lengths to avoid. Zambia had arrears that threatened to impend the flow of fund resources. To pay them off, Zambia borrowed funds from a British bank, which presumably will be repaid with new IMF funds.[10]

The standard IMF conditionality package is heavily weighted toward demand management and includes the following basic elements: budget and money supply contraction, especially to control inflation; reduction or elimination of subsidies, especially for consumer goods and services; changes in exchange rate policy, especially large devaluations; raising nominal interest rates; liberalization of import controls, especially of licensing systems; expansion of primary product exports; reduction and rationalization of the role of the state in the economy, especially in the parastatal sector; and encouragement of the private sector through increased reliance on market and price incentives, especially in agriculture. Disagreement about the appropriateness of this package for African conditions focuses on

9. Helleiner, "IMF and Africa," p. 61; Green, "Reflections," p. 308.

10. Carol Lancaster, "Multilateral Development Banks and Africa" (Paper delivered at the Conference on African Debt and Financing, Institute for International Economics and Georgetown University, Washington, DC, 20-22 Feb. 1986), p. 21.

devaluations, import controls, market and price incentives, the size and role of the state, and reliance on primary product export-led growth.

How effective have the IMF adjustment programs been? There is considerable variance of opinion. Given the unreliable statistical capabilities of African states, it is genuinely difficult to gauge effectiveness. The overall impact, however, appears to be modest. General agreement exists that the fund has had less success in Africa than in other regions. This largely has to do with the nature and level of development and state capabilities. Based on recent fund studies, Helleiner notes that "one may infer that previous IMF proclamations of 'success' have been overstated," and he points to "the extraordinary difficulty of successful adjustment under severe economic and political constraints in a rapidly changing environment."[11]

Most commonly the country formally accepts the conditions and then evades them or waters them down in implementation because they threaten deeply rooted interests or are perceived to be a threat to political order or socioeconomic peace. Even where sufficient will exists, economic inflexibility and limited administrative capability make full implementation difficult. Unsustainability and "slippage," as the IMF refers to it, are major phenomena.

Recently, the IMF and the World Bank have, themselves, been modest in assessment. The latest of the major World Bank reports on Africa, issued in the spring of 1986, notes that while many governments have made some progress, "they still have much to do to correct the accumulated policy distortions of the past."[12] In a study of 1980-81 programs, the IMF asserts that "generally adjustment efforts of African countries remained fairly limited. . . . The implementation of programs showed mixed results. Where data are available, they show that only one fifth of the countries reached the targeted level of economic growth." The major constraint was "slippages in implementation" due primarily to "the emergence of unforseen developments, an inability to mobilize sufficient political support to implement the requisite adjustment measures, limitations in administrative infrastructure, overly optimistic targets, and delays or shortfalls in net inflows of development assistance."[13] Of the 82 programs between 1979 and 1984, 16, or 19.5 percent, were canceled for noncompliance. For the remainder, waivers were used extensively for unmet targets. For the 12- to 18-month stand-bys, which constituted 89 percent of the 82 programs, there was significant rollover of both canceled and noncanceled programs.

One method of coping with the problems generated by the short duration of stand-bys has been to use three-year EFFs instead. There have been nine of them in Africa, all but one since 1980, used by Kenya, the Sudan, Gabon, Senegal, Sierra Leone, the Ivory Coast, Zambia, Zaire, and Malawi. Five EFFs were formally canceled for noncompliance, and one was allowed to lapse. Only two were completed, and the only current one—Malawi's—ended in September 1986. The problems that plagued

11. Gerald K. Helleiner, "The Question of Conditionality," in *African Debt and Financing,* ed. Lancaster and Williamson, p. 70.

12. World Bank, *Financing Adjustment,* p. 1.

13. Justin B. Zulu and Saleh M. Nsouli, "Adjustment Programs in Africa: The Recent Experience," IMF Occasional Paper no. 34 (International Monetary Fund, 1985), pp. 26-27.

the EFFs were essentially the same as for the stand-bys.[14]

In 1982 the IMF decided to rely almost exclusively on stand-bys, but to use a medium-term view of adjustment and a slightly wider set of policies to augment exports and improve monitoring and implementation. While things improved, success remained modest, leading the fund to stress its "catalytic role." Some in the fund have become quite uncomfortable with this record. They advocate pulling back in Africa, arguing that the fund is only meant to be used for situations of short-term adjustment.[15] Pulling back is not likely to occur, however.

An important psychological side effect of these foreign economic relations is that scarce talent is constantly preoccupied by negotiations with external actors about adjustment issues, while attempting to implement previous agreements. When linked to limited results, the impact can be quite damaging. As Green notes,

In political and national terms continued stagnation makes the mobilisation of energy ever harder: confidence in the ability to succeed is increasingly eroded by repeated failures, whatever their cause. Unfortunately, both nationally and internationally there is often an unhappy mix of frenetic, ill thought out attempted action, which proves unsustainable, together with interminable debate and negotiation over secondary issues.[16]

The IMF and the World Bank have several African success stories that they

tout. Amazingly, Zaire is now one of them. A March 1986 IMF article extolled the success of reform efforts since the 1983 stand-by, especially greatly improved debt service, which accounted for 56 percent of Zaire's 1985 budget. It compared the reform efforts to the relatively successful 1967 program. In fact, Zaire has had six programs since 1967—in 1976, 1977, 1979, 1981, 1983, and 1985. The article did not, however, bother to mention the 1976-81 programs, the fact that they were all total failures, that in 1979 the fund took the highly unusual step of placing expatriate teams directly into several important ministries, that the 1981 EFF was canceled for noncompliance, or that it was followed by a year-long shadow program before the 1983 stand-by. In discussing the so-called success of the post-1983 reforms, the article notes that "these measures have considerably improved the image of Zaire abroad, but the economic recovery at home has remained modest so far." About the same time a group of World Bank officials pointed out that "the existing debts, despite rescheduling, are unserviceable, and Zaire has a long way to go before its debt problem is resolved." In a 1985 assessment of the reputed reforms, Crawford Young asserts that, "if Rip Van Winkle fell asleep again for a couple of years, chances are he [would] reawaken to a more familiar set of circumstances, and find the fourth reform cycle in its downward phase."[17]

The underlying fact is that Zaire has not reaped the implicit quid pro quo of

14. See Stephan Haggard, "The Politics of Adjustment: Lessons from the IMF's Extended Fund Facility," *International Organization,* 39(3): 505-34 (Summer 1985).

15. Rattan J. Bhatia, "Adjustment Efforts in Sub-Saharan Africa, 1980-84," *Finance and Development,* 22(3):19-22 (Sept. 1985).

16. Green, "Reflections," p. 293.

17. Louis M. Goreux, "Economic Adjustment Efforts of Zaire Require Support of External Creditors," *IMF Survey,* 15(5):72-75 (Mar. 1986); Jaycox et al., "Nature of the Debt Problem," p. 36; M. Crawford Young, "Optimism on Zaire: Illusion or Reality?" *CSIS Africa Notes,* 50:8 (22 Nov. 1985).

substantially increased donor, creditor, and investor support. As the *Financial Times* points out, "Net capital flows from donors have actually been negative for several years, despite the high donor praise for the country's reform efforts." Thus debt service is up substantially, with serious opportunity costs for imports, rehabilitation, and investment and without any new resources. Clearly the IMF article is a plea for badly needed external support. Such are the politics of so-called success. To encourage support, the World Bank announced that it will lend Zaire an additional $550 million between 1986 and 1988, mostly via the International Development Association and the bank's new Special Facility for Sub-Saharan Africa.[18]

THE IMF AND POLITICAL INSTABILITY

Is IMF conditionality a major cause of political instability in Africa, as is often alleged? The answer depends on how political instability is defined. In fact, there has been surprisingly little major political instability or regime change tied directly to IMF programs. As Bienen and Gersovitz point out, "IMF programs are far more common than instances of serious instability." Clearly "there have been some violent reactions to IMF programs in the short-run, such as strikes and food riots after subsidies have been cut or currencies devalued. Governments usually have either persisted and faced down these reactions or backed off from or only partially implemented the IMF package."[19] This is not at all to deny the

obvious harsh consequences for much of the population. Planned or unplanned, imposed or voluntary, adjustment must eventually come, and it will entail harsh consequences.

Since substantial political instability has always existed in Africa, linking it directly to IMF adjustment is a tricky analytic exercise. Rather than the direct causal factor, IMF adjustment is more frequently a triggering or precipitating factor. The Sudan is one of the most commonly cited cases of instability tied directly to the IMF. But, as Jackson has indicated,

IMF conditionality did not cause the coup; Nimeiri's downfall must ultimately be attributed to numerous political and economic failures that had already thrust the country into chaos and bankruptcy. But, insofar as Nimeiri's move to end subsidies for bread and other basic commodities resulted in sharp price rises, which in turn sparked the riots, the IMF program was clearly a precipitating factor.[20]

For both rulers and opposition groups, it is often useful to attribute unrest to the IMF, even when the cause clearly lies elsewhere—commonly in the political logic of struggle itself.

In fact, actual instability is less important than the fear of it, which leads to partial or slack implementation in order to continue the much-needed relationship with the IMF. Haggard points out that for "weak authoritarian regimes," so common in Africa, "the rationalization associated with adjustment and stabilization is . . . in an immediate sense, politically irrational." Rulers often make preemptive changes in adjustment programs for fear of the

18. *Financial Times*, 11 Apr. 1986.

19. Henry S. Bienen and Mark Gersovitz, "Economic Stabilization, Conditionality, and Political Instability," *International Organization,* 39(4):730, 753 (Autumn 1985).

20. Henry F. Jackson, "The African Crisis: Drought and Debt," *Foreign Affairs*, 63(5):1087 (Summer 1985).

political consequences. The result is not regime change or major instability, but weaker adjustment. As one World Bank official has noted, "We need to avoid proposing prescriptive policy packages which are not politically feasible. We must take into account real political fears and carry out detailed analyses of implementation problems."[21]

Regime legitimacy is crucial to how important the political fallout of adjustment becomes. Jerry Rawlings, for example, has been able to pursue quite orthodox IMF adjustment in Ghana precisely because his regime is perceived to be legitimate. This was not the case in the Sudan. The new Babangida military regime in Nigeria will need all the legitimacy it has acquired from its public dialogue about IMF conditionality and the ultimate rejection of it in applying its homegrown brand of adjustment.

How is it possible to account for so little political instability directly linked to the obvious pernicious effects of even partial adjustment? At least part of the answer is that African populations, unlike most of those in Latin American countries, often have the exit options of withdrawing from the national and world economies and/or of participating in the rapidly expanding magendo or informal economies. Magendo economic

21. Haggard, "Politics of Adjustment," p. 511; Edward V.K. Jaycox, "Africa: Development Challenges and the World Bank's Response," *Finance and Development,* 23(1):22 (Mar. 1986); on the nature of the African state and its political economy, see Thomas M. Callahgy, "The State as Lame Leviathan: The Patrimonial Administrative State in Africa," in *The African State in Transition,* ed. Zaki Ergas (New York: St. Martin's, forthcoming); idem, "The State and the Development of Capitalism in Africa: Theoretical, Historical, and Comparative Reflections," in *The Precarious Balance: State-Society Relations in Africa,* ed. Donald Rothchild and Naomi Chazan (Boulder, CO: Westview Press, forthcoming).

activity may play an important role in reducing the tensions created by recession, austerity measures, infrastructure decline, and domestic political repression.

THE WORLD BANK AND STRUCTURAL ADJUSTMENT

One primary effect of Africa's current crisis, which has been greatly aggravated by the IMF's particular conditionality package, is import strangulation. This short-term adjustment strategy badly threatens medium- and long-term adjustment and growth. It has worsened existing underutilization of productive capacity, led to further infrastructure deterioration, hampered state investment, and discouraged foreign and domestic private investment. Imports per capita have been declining since 1970, and Africa's investment rate is now the lowest of any developing region. A broader and longer-term view of adjustment is needed. The World Bank has been attempting to achieve this by concentrating on structural adjustment.

The World Bank now uses a new lending instrument—the structural adjustment loan—particularly to finance badly needed imports and support policy change. By early 1986, it had nine structural adjustment loans in six African countries, with about nine more lined up. These are definitely high-conditionality facilities, and recipients usually must have a program with the IMF or be in its good graces. The World Bank also now uses sector, rehabilitation, and specific import commodity loans, all with lesser conditionality. About 80 percent of the bank's policy-based lending is now in Africa, having doubled between the late 1970s and 1984. By the end of 1984, the bank accounted for 49 percent of all multilateral lending—

including the IMF—and 12.4 percent of total African debt.

How effective has this new policy-based lending been? Like the IMF, the World Bank has found it difficult to achieve its aims in Africa. Results have been quite mixed. For example, a structural adjustment loan to Senegal was canceled for noncompliance. In its 1986 special report on Africa, the bank noted that many countries are making some progress, "but they still have much to do to correct the accumulated policy distortions of the past." One example will suffice. The bank has put considerable emphasis on scaling down and rationalizing the state, especially the parastatal sector. According to the report, many governments are "trying to reduce the size of the public sector and to improve its management. However, these reforms are still at an early stage."[22] Low-income states have closed down or divested only "about 5 percent of their public enterprises during the 1980s."

Two of the World Bank's key recommendations involve scaling down budgets and levels of employment as rationalization efforts. The report notes, however, that implementation has had the diametically opposite outcome from the one desired and expected:

Budget restraint, reflected in lower public employment, is desirable in much of Africa, but in some cases it has led to excessive cuts in financing for equipment, maintenance, operating costs, and materials. The result has been a steady deterioration in the quality of public services and further declines in the productivity of public employees. . . . This deterioration in public services is especially disruptive for programs designed to deal with the basic constraints on development.[23]

22. World Bank, *Financing Adjustment*, pp. 1, 21-22.

23. Ibid., p. 22.

Clearly, these governments felt it was politically irrational to reform public enterprises by cutting employment. Wishing to appear compliant with the World Bank, they simply cut the budgets in other less politically sensitive areas.

This role has led to the World Bank to increase its data collection, monitoring, and analysis activities about and in Africa significantly. It now has 24 resident representatives, a large increase over previous levels and more than in any other region. The bank has also gone into the development strategy business in a big way, pushing primary product export-led growth and extolling the virtues of the private sector—what Green has called the "Bank's apparent aspiration to become SSA's [sub-Saharan Africa's] . . . planning ministry and Platonic Guardian." Considerable African skepticism remains about relying heavily on a primary product export-led development strategy, but there is also considerable confusion about what else to do. Many observers have noted the fallacy of composition inherent in the bank's development strategy recommendation; that is, if all countries follow the advice, undertake reform, and significantly increase production, they will all be worse off. Those supportive of the bank's position have noted in response that "not all countries will follow counsel to expand primary exports. So those that do will capture the markets of those that do not, regardless of their respective comparative advantages." But the bank itself points out that

because of the region's economic structure, exports will be relatively slow to respond. They are mostly primary commodities, which have limited prospects . . . it will be very hard to achieve a rapid expansion of exports in the near term . . . exports in current prices during 1986-90 could, at best, be about 25 percent higher than in 1980-82. And this assumes substantial export-oriented policy reforms in Africa and no increase in protectionism in the industrial countries.[24]

Skepticism about the private sector also abounds.

CONCLUSION

What does the future hold for African countries and their creditors? Modest expectations are in order on both sides. African states cannot expect any major benefical structural or procedural reforms in the international political economy on the part of their Western creditors. Likewise, the latter cannot expect any significant restructuring of African regimes and economies or substantial improvement in their economic and debt performance. Western actors clearly determine most of the rules of the game, shaping the parameters of action, but African regimes do have some autonomy and room for maneuver.

On the external side, the World Bank notes that

the major structural reform efforts undertaken by many African countries to address their long-term development problems have not received adequate donor support . . . growth and equity enhancing reform programs already underway are foundering because of inadequate donor funding, which is often inappropriate in form and timing.

Despite some projected increases in resource flows from Lomé III, an

enlarged International Development Association, the World Bank's new Special Facility for Sub-Saharan Africa, and the IMF's Trust Fund reflows via the new Structural Adjustment Facility, the report still projects a \$3.5 billion to \$5.5 billion resource gap per year for 1986-90.[25] With little new private-bank lending or direct foreign investment and the ongoing peripheralization of Africa in the world economy, these inadequate resource flows are quite alarming. Given current politics on the part of the Organization for Economic Cooperation and Development, it is not likely that this gap can be closed. For example, while the May 1986 United Nations General Assembly special session on Africa—the first ever on a regional economic problem—drew attention to Africa's plight, it produced no change in creditor-country policies or major pledges of new aid. Finally, the World Bank calls for more coherent, coordinated, and realistic donor practices. Again, it is not clear how much this situation will change.

African governments must do their part via more systematic adjustment and realistic proposals of their own about how to cope with the current crisis, as the Latin Americans have now begun to do in a serious way. Some progress was made at the 1985 Organization of African Unity summit, which focused on the economic crisis. As in the past, the governments placed considerable blame on an "unjust and inequitable" international economic system, but they also acknowledged that their policies had contributed to the crisis and need to be changed. More realistic rhetoric must now be transformed into viable action.

24. Reginald Herbold Green and Caroline Allison, "The World Bank's Agenda for Development: Dialectics, Doubts, and Dialogues," in *Africa in Economic Crisis,* ed. Ravenhill, p. 72; Elliot Berg, "The World Bank's Strategy," in ibid., p. 54; World Bank, *Financing Adjustment,* p. 38; see also the very pessimistic analysis of Peter F. Drucker, "The Changed World Economy," *Foreign Affairs,* 64(4):768-91 (Spring 1986).

25. World Bank, *Financing Adjustment,* "Forward."

If Africa is to avoid both Scylla and Charybdis, its leaders and external actors will have to do their respective parts. According to a leading African official,

a more open and constructive dialogue between Africa and the North must take place. This dialogue should include a better articulation of development strategies and policies by African countries themselves than has been the case in the past. It will also require a commitment by the North to improve its understanding of African problems, and to take the steps necessary to improve development prospects and financial strength in Africa.[26]

26. Philip Ndegwa, governor of the Central Bank of Kenya, quoted in *African Debt and Financing*, ed. Lancaster and Williamson, p. 9.

Important Notice from the President to All Members
Regarding the Annual Meeting

As has happened in the past, the Academy has postponed its 1987 annual meeting. The cost of the meetings has become a substantial drain on the Academy's modest funds. We will be proceeding to a new formulation of the function and location of the meetings and will keep you informed as our plans progress. Meanwhile, *The Annals* will continue its excellent publication performance, and we welcome any suggestions of topics for future publications.

Book Department

INTERNATIONAL RELATIONS AND POLITICS

GLASS, JAMES M. *Delusion: Internal Dimensions of Political Life*. Pp. xxiv, 270. Chicago: University of Chicago Press, 1985. No price.

HERZOG, DON. *Without Foundations: Justification in Political Theory*. Pp. 254. Ithaca, NY: Cornell University Press, 1985. $24.95.

Both these books have a quarrel with the way in which political philosophy is currently studied. Both argue for at least a partial redirection of scholarly efforts. Both are well done.

Herzog has written what he calls a "methodological" analysis of traditional political philosophy. Its basis is the search for the manner by which political theories are justified. What, in other words, does a well-justified political theory look like?

Herzog argues that justification itself is a contestable notion. Does one look for scholarly consensus? The weight of evidence? Rigid internal logic? Connection to unarguable premises?

One approach—foundationalism—establishes axiomatic premises and from them deduces propositions. The premises must be both undeniable and located external to society and politics. Herzog rejects this approach for what are essentially historical reasons: they do not work. Stated this baldly, the rejection is an exercise in question begging. In fact, the book is an effort to demonstrate how foundationalist theories fail and to argue instead for what Herzog terms "contextualist" theories.

The bulk of the book consists of analyses of Hobbes, Locke, Mills, Bentham, J. S. Mill, Sidgwick, Harsanyi, R. M. Hare, R. B. Brandy, Hume, and Adam Smith. All these old wines are poured into a new bottle labeled "justification." Herzog views Hobbes, Locke, and the utilitarians—new and old—as foundationalists who fail adequately to justify their theories precisely because they attempt to found them on unassailable premises deriving from recourse to human nature, to God, or to rationality. Hume and Smith, however, pass Herzog's test because, as contextualists, they base their theories on the messy historical reality of politics and society.

Along the way, Herzog's reinterpretation leads him to new looks at old texts, as well as examinations of texts not often looked at by political scientists. Much of the value of the book lies in these comments, and one may profit from this work without necessarily being persuaded by his introductory and concluding chapters.

Herzog's book is concerned basically with reintroducing the stuff of politics to political theory, and with celebrating induction—contextualism—over deduction—foundationalism. It is an excellent piece of work and nicely written as well.

Glass makes a more radical departure from most work on political philosophy by taking a page from Lasswell's *Psychopathology and Politics*. The heart of his book is a series of interviews with schizophrenic patients in a Maryland hospital. They are fascinating reading, and Glass's interpretations of them—they serve as his text—are sensitive and cautious.

Glass's concern is to infer from his subjects basic insights about alternative states of being that might have relevance to political philosophy. The most basic distinction uncovered is the one between the interior and exterior worlds of the schizophrenic, both of which speak to the nature of human nature.

For Glass, the world of the schizophrenic is a world of the interior, a world analogous to the Platonic cave in which the patient lives in an unhappy, Hobbesian world. Glass is particularly concerned with schizophrenia as a language system, both as a logical structure and as a window through which to view the patient's progress or lack thereof. He argues that "the language of delusion provides empirical evidence for both Rousseau's concept of the languages of the heart . . . and the Hobbesian experience of chaos, violence and imminent annihilation." Most basically, delusional language for Glass represents "precivil" thought. Improvement in the patients' conditions is, for Glass, political: the delusional world is dominated by questions of power, violence, and boundaries. The transition from the nature of the delusional world to the community of the nondelusional is both a therapeutic and a political journey.

As with Herzog's work, one need not necessarily subscribe fully to the guiding purpose of the book in order to profit from it. In both cases, the execution of the analysis justifies the trip.

PHILLIP L. GIANOS
California State University
Fullerton

KALTEFLEITER, WERNER and ROBERT L. PFALTZGRAFF, eds. *The Peace Movements in Europe and the United States.* Pp. 211. New York: St. Martin's Press, 1985. $27.50.

LAQUEUR, WALTER and ROBERT HUNTER, eds. *European Peace Movements and the Future of the Western Alliance.* Pp. xii, 450. New Brunswick, NJ: Transaction Books, 1985. $34.95.

The first of these works contains the papers presented at a conference held in 1984 at the Christain-Albrechts-University in West Germany. The second collects a variety of papers, some of which have been previously published. Although the predominant focus of both is on peace movements, the Laqueur-Hunter volume is much more wide-ranging, examining interstate relations in the North Atlantic Treaty Organization (NATO) and theological questions as well as the peace movements in various Western states. Kaltefleiter and Pfaltzgraff's work presents a series of structured comparisons of movements in Sweden. Norway, the Netherlands, Britain, West Germany, France, Italy, and the United States. Each country study is written by a national of that state.

The Laqueur-Hunter collection also contains four papers—by Americans, including Henry Kissinger—concerning the state of NATO. All point to the increasing distance between Western Europe and the United States, in perceptions, interests, and responses, whether the issues be military, economic, or political, confined to Europe or global. The problems of the alliance are not mere creations of the peace movements, though these may increasingly affect the discussion of NATO policy. They generally suggest the need to rework fundamentally the political and military basis of the alliance, including in this the development of a stronger role for Europe in shaping alliance policy and the devising of a credible defense policy.

Neither work is particularly sympathetic to peace movements; both are sometimes marred by a tendency to denunciation, particularly, but not solely, by the American contributors. Together they point to some significant and persisting aspects of the movements as sociological and psychological, as well as political, phenomena. It seems, for example, that the movements are strongest when they can make connections to established traditions of radical politics or to a wider sense of alienation from the mainstream of a society and its politics. This is not to downplay the seriousness of nuclear weapons issues, but it does point out the important extranuclear background of the peace movements, a background too often overlooked. A recurring theme in both works, and the subject of two papers in the Laqueur-Hunter volume, is the involvement of churches. One author, Edward Norman, suggests that this is a secularization of the church rather than a reassertion of its religious authority.

As general descriptions of the movements in many NATO states, both books are of considerable value. In presenting generally reasoned critiques of these movements, and in noting the broader tensions within the alliance on which these movements have built, the Laqueur-Hunter volume is of additional value. Both are, and ought to be, thought provoking in their implications.

JAMES F. KEELEY

University of Calgary
Alberta
Canada

*AFRICA, ASIA, AND
LATIN AMERICA*

DABAT, ALEJANDRO and LUIS LOREN-ZANO. *Argentina: The Malvinas and the End of Military Rule*. Translated by Ralph Johnstone. Pp. 205. New York: Schocken Books, 1985. $27.50. Paperbound, $9.50.

ROCK, DAVID. *Argentina, 1516-1982: From Spanish Colonization to the Falklands War*. Pp. xxix, 478. Berkeley: University of California Press, 1985. $35.00.

Both these books review Argentine history since the first Spanish invasions, but their basic concerns are very different. Dabat and Lorenzano employ a revolutionary Marxist analysis, with syndicalist origins, to examine critically the meaning of the April-June 1982 Malvinas War. Rock consulted over 600 mostly published sources to write an invaluable teaching and reference manual on political and economic history and also to provide a suggestive answer to the perennial question as to why Argentina did not fulfill its great promise of the late nineteenth century.

Dabat and Lorenzano argue that contemporaries wrongly understood the Malvinas War, like Perón's railroad nationalization in 1947, as a struggle against British imperialism. While recognizing the justice in Argentine territorial claims, Dabat and Lorenzano emphasize that the military junta's reactionary aims were to create political support for the dictatorship and to strengthen civilian allies, whom Dabat and Lorenzano style "national monopoly capital." This relatively new fraction of the bourgeoisie made its money in automobiles, steel, petrochemicals, and armaments, and it has attempted to establish Argentina as an "emergent regional power" through investments and military participation in Southern Cone and Central American politics. The book blames the army and navy's incompetence, corruption, and authoritarianism for Argentina's defeat, but it also criticizes most of the civilian opposition, from the traditional parties and union federation leaders through to the Communist Party, the Montonero guerrillas, and some Trotskyists, all of whom suspended protest against the internal "dirty war" to back the "patriotic war" against Britain. Only the "silent" working class, the "heroic and selfless" Mothers of the Plaza de Mayo, and a few small socialist groups avoided jingoism.

The theoretical sophistication of the Dabat and Lorenzano argument should not distract the reader from its dubious predictive value. The final chapter of the original Spanish text, evidently written soon after the war ended, warned of a "bloodbath they [the junta] are beginning to plan which will make the 'dirty war' seem like a mere skirmish." After Alfonsín's victory in the October 1983 elections, Dabat and Lorenzano wisely added a postscript to the English translation, but they expressly discounted the possibility of the 1985 public trials and economic reforms.

Rock synthesizes traditional and modern scholarship that views Argentine history as a series of political cycles between civilization and barbarism. While he devotes over half of his book to the twentieth century, he insists that colonial structures have long prevailed: heavy imports of manufactures and capital; elite monopolization, successively, of indigenous labor, cattle, and land; a single large commercial city dominating the rest of the country; a comprador bourgeoisie; and an imitative culture. But in such a "classically colonial" society, "complementary external partnerships have always been a necessary condition for progress." When these linkages broke down, through war or change in the international order, as in the seventeenth, early nineteenth, and later twentieth centuries, Argentine society "has invariably failed to revolutionize itself in a self-sustaining independent direction" and instead "turned in on itself in fierce competition to monopolize static diminishing resources," with resulting "severe political stress and . . . breakdown."

Even the "shattering, overwhelming and prolonged external blow" made likely by European immigration and capital migration in the late nineteenth century failed to break the colonial mold. Rock concludes pessimistically. If the repressive military regime endured—his book also predates the Alfonsín government—he foresees "increasingly severe social dislocation." If "the urban

sectors and the populist impulse kindled by Yrigoyen and Perón remained strong . . . an endless repetition of the old economic and political cycles" would ensue. In either case, Argentina would not transcend its colonial past.

Dabat and Lorenzano, on the other hand, preserve hope for a wedding of "Marxist thought and socialist practice [with] . . . the most advanced layers of the Christian, Peronist and Radical movements, and . . . an independent rank-and-file freed of the myths and phantasms of the past." The reader can only regret that most of their provocative book gives little basis for such optimism.

PETER L. EISENBERG
Universidade Estadual de Campinas
São Paulo
Brazil

FRIEDMAN, DOUGLAS. *The State and Underdevelopment in Spanish America: The Political Roots of Dependency in Peru and Argentina.* Pp. xi, 236. Boulder, CO: Westview Press, 1984. Paperbound, $22.50.

NICHOLLS, DAVID. *Haiti in Caribbean Context: Ethnicity, Economy and Revolt.* Pp. x, 282. New York: St. Martin's Press, 1985. $27.50.

The books under review have two things in common: both concern the Western Hemisphere, and both, in their own ways, are contributions to our understanding of Latin America and the Caribbean. Otherwise, they could hardly be more disparate.

The State and Underdevelopment in Spanish America is the more broadly gauged and challenging of the two. By examining the political economy of colonial and nineteenth-century Latin America, and particularly that of Peru and Argentina, the book seeks to challenge the thesis of the *dependentistas* that Latin American politics has from the beginning been conditioned—determined?— by its incorporation into the network of international capitalism. Friedman argues that the emergence of dependent export economies in nineteenth-century Latin America grew out of the needs of the state for revenue in order to control the fundamentally political internecine conflicts of the newly independent Latin American nations. In this view, "though the aims of the Peruvian and Argentine states were political, the effects of their policies tended to steer their countries into economic roles in the international economy that are today associated with dependency." The historical roots of under-development and dependency in Latin America are therefore more internal than they are external, more political than they are economic or cultural.

It is doubtful that *dependentistas* will be convinced, and the book is sure to provoke controversy. Indeed, one does sometimes feel confronted with a chicken-or-the-egg pattern of causation. Yet Friedman's approach is scholarly, and the book deserves to be taken as a serious contribution to the debate on the origins of underdevelopment and dependency.

The second book under review, *Haiti in Caribbean Context*, is a compilation of essays by a British historian that are in turn loosely grouped into sections on ethnicity, the economy, and domination and revolt. Most were apparently written separately for other purposes; they therefore tend to be lumped, rather than knit, together and there is considerable overlap among them.

At the same time, the book is steeped in knowledge of Haiti and the Caribbean. Certain themes recur, particularly that of the complex relationship between race and social class. Nicholls also sheds light on such matters as patterns of landownership, the nature and degree of economic dependence, the significance of historic protest movements, and differences in the social base of the respective regimes of Papa Doc and Baby Doc Duvalier that help to explain the recent collapse of the latter's government.

In sum, both books are to be recommended, albeit for quite different reasons.

ROBERT H. DIX

Rice University
Houston
Texas

GILIOMEE, HERMANN and LAWRENCE SCHLEMMER, eds. *Up against the Fences: Poverty, Passes and Privilege in South Africa.* Pp. x, 365. New York: St. Martin's Press, 1985. $29.95.

MANDY, NIGEL. *A City Divided: Johannesburg and Soweto.* Pp. xxii, 447. New York: St. Martin's Press, 1985. $35.00.

Up against the Fences is a timely publication and essential reading for anyone interested in contemporary South Africa. The volume's editors and contributors, who range from liberal-learning academics to advisers to the Nationalist government to South Africa's most prominent businessmen, uniformly argue that increasing urbanization is inevitable, that legal constraints on the movement of blacks, such as influx control, should be done away with, and that more orderly and less offensive measures should be introduced to regulate the movement of blacks into the cities. Their recommendations are particularly prescient given that President P. W. Botha has announced, within the past few months, his government's abandonment of much of the paraphernalia of influx control, such as pass laws. With the government seemingly following the collective advice of *Up against the Fences'* authors with regard to present controls, what should we expect in the future? The prospects are rather chilling. Giliomee and Schlemmer suggest that businessmen, now that there is a strong black trade union movement in South Africa, would prefer to have large numbers of surplus men available in the cities as strikebreakers, thereby keeping wages low; these new urban dwellers, Giliomee and Schlemmer argue, should be permitted to live on the outskirts of the existing cities and to build shanty housing—of "wattle and daub" with perhaps a tin roof—paying market rates for this housing and for all services. Thereby the cost to the government of such urbanization would be minimized, the prices charged for housing and services would limit the numbers coming into town, and the cities of South Africa would remain practically segregated. Nigel Mandy's *City Divided*, a long-winded and disorganized study, berates the Afrikaans Nationalist governments of the late 1940s on for introducing urban apartheid and calls for an end to legal restrictions on the movement of blacks to the cities. Like Giliomee and Schlemmer, however, Mandy essentially forsees a future in which the manipulation of market forces rather than the enforcement of discriminatory laws will leave South Africa comfortably segregated but no longer the butt of the world's criticism. So much for the liberal vision of South Africa's destiny.

WILLIAM WORGER

University of Michigan
Ann Arbor

MÖRNER, MAGNUS. *The Andean Past: Land, Societies and Conflicts*. Pp. xiv, 300. New York: Columbia University Press. $30.00.

Magnus Mörner's brief survey of Peru, Bolivia, and Ecuador is refreshing proof of the possibility of combining solid scholarship with readability. In clear language, supported by worthwhile tables and charts and picturesque illustrations, Mörner presents an overall view of political, economic, and sociological developments in these three Andean nations from the age of Inca civilization to the present.

Although Mörner's special interest is in the ethnic interplay between natives, Spaniards, mestizos, and blacks of African descent, there is valuable information on mining and mineral resources, raw materials and property structures, foreign trade, and economic limitations. Political history as such is barely sketched, but what is presented is sufficient to give the reader an appetite for further knowledge.

Not least of the amenities included in this volume are the drawings of the seventeenth-century Guamán Poma de Ayala, amusingly subtitled by Mörner. Of greater import is the treatment of changes that have taken place over time in the composition of leading exports from each of the three countries and attempts, especially in recent years, to diversify into nontraditional areas.

Although Mörner takes a nontheoretical approach and includes very few generalizations, several of his comments are worth noting. "Maximum exploitation does not automatically trigger rebellion." "Where nobody is able to *govern*, the throne is occupied by he who, at the least, knows how to *command*." In a brief subheading to one of his chapters he says much: "Elite Pleasures and Popular Misery." This is not a Marxist analysis but a foreigner's observation that would hold true for much of the world beyond the Andes.

The Andean Past should be recommended reading not only for tourists who venture south but for American bankers, businessmen, and government officials whose final destiny is more intimately related to the future development of foreign economies than most of us are willing to recognize.

DAVID M. BILLIKOPF

Santiago
Chile

SCALAPINO, ROBERT A. and GEORGE T. YU. *Modern China and Its Revolutionary Process: Recurrent Challenges to the Traditonal Order 1850-1920*. Pp. xiii, 814. Berkeley: University of California Press, 1985. No price.

This volume, the first of a projected three-part study of China's revolutionary process from the Taiping Rebellion to the present, is not only one of the largest but also one of the most innovative studies of its kind. Although Scalapino and Yu begin their study with the Taiping Rebellion and spend some time on various attempts at reform during the nineteenth century, most of the present volume, pages 109-691, is devoted to the unfolding of the 1911 Revolution and its aftermath up to the founding of the Chinese Communist Party in 1920-21. Because of its size and scope, there is a natural tendency to compare this work to the volumes dealing with modern China in *The Cambridge History of China*. The two works are very different in concept and form, however. *The Cambridge History* is a composite work consisting of separate articles written by various specialists in the field of modern Chinese history. Therefore it tends to be much more topical in content and lacks both the sharpness of focus and broad-sweeping interpretation presented in this work of Scalapino and Yu. Furthermore, Scalapino and Yu are essentially political scientists and much more concerned with theories of revolution and social change than many of the contributors to *The Cambridge History*.

Perhaps the outstanding feature of the present work is the attempt to tie together the complexities of socioeconomic and institutional change; foreign influence; territorial and population factors; time; the all-pervasive weight of tradition, personalities, and factions; and constantly shifting ideological positions. It has been a massive undertaking, and the wealth of well-documented detail to be found in the work is impressive. Scalapino and Yu are also to be complimented on the readability of the text and their efforts to provide extensive bibliographical assistance for further study.

Scalapino and Yu have undoubtedly produced one of the most important works on modern China in years. It is also likely to be one of the more controversial. Their attempt to provide a theoretical framework for China's revolutionary process is bound to raise many questions. I had little problem with their theoretical arguments as such, but I often felt that the distribution of factual material in the narrative portions of the text tended to be at odds with those arguments. For example, in their theoretical discussions Scalapino and Yu stress the importance of socioeconomic factors and the primacy of social revolution: "social revolution is always a process, within which political revolution may or may not be a part." However, it is precisely this aspect of the revolutionary process that receives the weakest coverage in the narrative portions of the text. In fact, it quickly becomes clear that what interests Scalapino and Yu most is the personalities involved, their political struggles, and ideological debates, rather than socioeconomic and institutional change. Sun Yat-sen is given far more prominence than most recent studies of the 1911 Revolution would tend to warrant, so much so, in fact, that the reader is left with the uncomfortable feeling that we are being pushed back somewhat into the traditional Kuomintang-Communist interpretation of his role as the great leader. This is not to say that Sun is glorified in the same way, or that his weaknesses are not mentioned, but his role as the leader is stressed in such a way that it tends to obscure the role of others, the fact that one of the chief weaknesses of the revolutionaries was their lack of coherent leadership, and the fact that whatever success the political revolution enjoyed was due more to the collapse of the old society than to any effort on the part of those who claimed to be its leaders. While these points are clearly made in the theoretical interpretive sections of the text, the narrative sections would seem to belie their significance. Perhaps there would have been more coherence between theory and narrative if in the narrative portion Scalapino and Yu had spent more time considering root causes for the failure of the political revolution, including the role of provincial and local elites. After all, it was they and their military allies, not the revolutionaries and their supporters, who proved to be the source of real political power at the time of the 1911 Revolution and in the years to follow.

The greatest difficulty faced in any cooperative work is the attempt to bring the contributions of its separate authors together in a unified whole. In general Scalapino and Yu have accomplished this task very well, but one is still left with the feeling that the broad theoretical contributions of the work would have been better served if they had been provided with a broader base in the socioeconomic and institutional history of the period.

W. ALLYN RICKETT
University of Pennsylvania
Philadelphia

EUROPE

BERG, MAXINE. *The Age of Manufacturers: Industry, Innovation and Work in Britain 1700-1820.* Pp. 378. Totowa, NJ: Barnes & Noble Books, 1985. $33.75.

The industrial revolution in England has been a major focus of innumerable articles and monographs. Yet, as Maxine Berg reminds us, many scholars have presented an incomplete and ill-developed picture of the period. Her book integrates labor, social, and economic history to refute the spate of conventional explanations that focus on strictly economic issues. Her sharpest targets are growth models and stage theories that dominate interpretations of the period and, as a consequence, narrow and limit the issues examined.

Berg's contribution is to present a wide array of evidence suggesting (1) that industrial growth and technological change occurred throughout the eighteenth century, not just in part of the period, and that the latter involved much more than mechanization—for example, development of hand and intermediate techniques; (2) that industrialization was first and foremost concerned with work organization, that is, the organization of production; and (3) that technical and industrial change did not always lead to economic growth.

Berg argues that changes in work organization can have disastrous as well as beneficial effects for labor. She demonstrates that

regional industrial decline took place at the same time as industrial expansion occurred during the eighteenth century. She emphasizes the important role that cultural, political, and social institutions play in promoting or retarding technological change. This was particularly significant where workers resisted the introduction of textile machinery.

Berg's focus on textiles and metals does not limit the breadth of her analysis. She argues that we must go beyond the idea that textiles only referred to cotton. Further research, she suggests, must pay equal attention to mining, building, food, drink, leather trades, and the division between male and female labor markets.

Berg's book is an excellent reference book for students of the industrial revolution. Yet her analysis encounters some serious problems when she tries to develop a framework for future historians. From her interpretation of the industrial revolution it is not possible to discern a particular framework that other scholars could use to expand and widen her analysis. While criticizing neoclassical economic theory for asking the wrong questions, she fails to formulate an alternative framework.

We will certainly benefit by Berg's attempts to synthesize a large body of information that has previously been presented in disparate places. I have no doubt that many of her conclusions and interpretations will be supported as new and ongoing research is completed. Future researchers, however, need to be as rigorous as their opponents if Berg's and other sympathetic interpretations are to replace conventional explanations.

LOU FERLEGER
University of Massachusetts
Boston

CORRIGAN, PHILIP and DEREK SAYER. *The Great Arch: English State Formation as Cultural Revolution.* Pp. viii, 268. New York: Basil Blackwell, 1985. $34.95. Paperbound, $15.95.

The aim of this book is ambitious and exciting. Taking their cue from an argument developed by E. P. Thompson in a famous essay of 1965 on the particular features of English historical development, where the phrase "the great arch" is used to describe an epochal process of bourgeois revolution between the fifteenth and nineteenth centuries, Corrigan and Sayer seek to develop a novel account of English political development that can serve simultaneously as a new model of historical sociology. They see the "embourgeoisement of England's dominant classes" and concomitant "proletarianization of the ruled" as extending between the eleventh and the nineteenth centuries and occurring within a framework of national state formation, in which processes of "moral regulation" are as important as the more commonly recognized administrative and coercive apparatuses. This is the "cultural revolution" of the title—namely, the effort "to give unitary and unifying expression to what are in reality multifaceted and differential historical experiences of groups within society, denying their particularity" and obscuring the structured inequalities of "class, gender, ethnicity, age, religion, occupation, locality." While working to manufacture one kind of national moral community, state agencies systematically disorganize the basis of oppositional collectivities by individualizing people into the juridical objects of state attentions. Thus the state functions, in a phrase of Durkheim's, as "the organ of moral discipline."

Though they insist on the centrality of conflict and negotiation between dominant and oppositional cultures in this process, Corrigan and Sayer focus primarily on writing a history "from above," by distinguishing a series of "'long waves' of revolution in government." The analysis is divided into six main chapters, dealing respectively with the medieval prelude, Elton's "Tudor revolution in government" during the Reformation of the 1530s, the "Elizabethan Consolidation," the revolution of the seventeenth century, the construction of the Whig oligarchy in the eighteenth century, and finally the

period between the 1830s and 1880s, then the "working class question" came to dominate public discourse. The theoretical perspectives are eclectic, composed of Marx, Weber, and Durkheim, together with a variety of contemporary influences, among whom the late Philip Abrams is particularly prominent. Throughout there is an effort to explore how a "particular notion of the public realm organizes, like a prismatic lens, other 'spheres'—notably those contrasting realms of 'the private': familial, dependent and domestic for most women and children; 'independent' and workplace- or task-related for most men." This is also guided by a salutary but somewhat rhetorical emphasis on the gendered character of state interventions.

Unfortunately, the detail of the analysis is disappointing. The earlier chapters are most successful, providing valuable and well-organized commentaries on the specialized literatures involved. The coherence diminishes as the book proceeds, however, and in the long nineteenth-century chapter—roughly a quarter of the whole—the argument disappears in a mélange of qualification and confusing parenthetical commentary. The analysis also stops short in the 1880s, where most other discussions of the modern state tend to begin, and Corrigan and Sayer never fully justify this decision. There is no developed discussion of bourgeois revolution as a general problem, which is surprising given Corrigan and Sayer's larger polemical agenda and the original inspiration of the book's title. In fact, the overall argument is remarkably historicist for two such self-consciously theoretical sociologists, and the grand sweep of eight centuries necessarily entails an inflated conception of continuity. Moreover, comparative perspectives, even as a general dimension of the argument, are notable for their absence, which is particularly disappointing given the centrality of the British societal model to most developmental theory and the recent salience of peculiarity arguments in other national histories. In these ways the book is far less "the milestone in historical sociology" than the jacket proclaims.

GEOFF ELEY
University of Michigan
Ann Arbor

OVENDALE, RITCHIE. *The English-speaking Alliance: Britain, the United States, the Dominions and the Cold War, 1945-1951.* Pp. x, 309. Winchester, MA: George Allen & Unwin, 1985. $27.00.

On this side of the Atlantic, there has been an understandable tendency to regard the cold war as a predominantly American problem, as something that we have defined and struggled about with the Soviets. Ritchie Ovendale provides a corrective lens to this American myopia. He argues persuasively that the cold war—a phrase coined by British statesmen—was not initially an American affair totally. If anything, the British rode point in the early days; and the cold war was a global issue, not just a European one.

Ovendale focuses his considerable research on Ernest Bevin, foreign secretary in the immediate postwar years, who had served under Churchill in the war coalition government. Bevin continued Churchill's foreign policy in two key respects. He was determined to preserve the eroding British Empire and to continue the English-speaking alliance established by Neville Chamberlain in the late 1930s. Furthermore, like Churchill before him, Bevin regarded the Soviets as the primary postwar threat and believed that Britain could maintain its world-power status.

Bevin's assessment of the immediate postwar situation was that the cold war encompassed the entire globe, that the French were defeatist and of no immediate help, and that there was no other European power for Britain to rely upon. Consequently, Britain had to attempt to maintain the English-speaking alliance, which meant working to modify America's accommodationist tendencies toward the Soviet Union, securing American support for the continuation of Britain's world-power claims, and shoring up the Commonwealth, especially the old dominions. With the exception of South Africa, these were all English speaking. Despite South Africa's reprehensible racial policies, Bevin believed that it had to be included in the alliance for economic and strategic reasons.

Ovendale bases his analysis on research carried out in an impressive number of national and private archives and collections in Australia, Britain, South Africa, and the United States. In my opinion, the portrait of Bevin that emerges is of someone whose policies were shrewd and influential in the short run, but whose policies were narrowly conceived and ultimately shortsighted. His stiff resolve to continue the policies of his immediate predecessors served a useful purpose in that they encouraged America not to drift back into prewar isolation. His determination, however, to preserve Britain's links with the dominions and his anti-European stance retarded Britain's participation in the European Economic Community.

NEAL A. FERGUSON
University of Nevada
Reno

WARK, WESLEY K. *The Ultimate Enemy: British Intelligence and Nazi Germany, 1933-1939.* Pp. 304. Ithaca, NY: Cornell University Press, 1985. $32.50.

Wesley K. Wark, assistant professor of history at the University of Calgary, has written a clear, well-documented, revealing account of British intelligence estimates of Germany on the eve of World War II. His research in the unpublished records—the service departments, cabinet, Foreign Office, Prime Minister's Office, Treasury, and War Office—private papers, published documents, and secondary accounts is extensive. The material is well organized and presented with efficiency and verve. His study will interest both the scholar and the layperson concerned with the interwar period, causes of the war, problems of intelligence, and the interdependence of military and diplomatic policy.

Proceeding chronologically, Wark perceives four phases in British assessments of Germany: German "secrecy" (1933-35), Anglo-German relative openness during a "honeymoon" (1935-36), "blindness" causing British pessimism (1936-38), and revived British confidence during "war scares and war" (1938-39). A number of themes link this evolution. Interservice rivalry had the doubly unfortunate consequence of producing competing, sometimes contradictory pictures and excessively pessimistic evaluations based on cumulative worst-case scenarios. The early perception of Germany as the ultimate enemy, the prediction of possible war in 1939, and the expectation of a German blitzkrieg defeated by Britain in a long war were notably accurate. Confirming and preparing for this eventuality were, however, complicated by the paucity of information and above all the inclination to fit the extant information into preconceptions. Wark's overriding point is the basic unanimity of the intelligence community and the cabinet: "at no stage during the 1930s were there any fundamental contradictions between intelligence reporting and the foreign policy of the government." Why? Because both felt caught in a bind: rearmament seemed to risk economic recovery and resistance to Hitler implied another war, which would not resolve the German problem. Pessimistic perceptions of Germany were reinforced by the prevalent assumption of totalitarian military superiority.

While granting the accuracy of long-range evaluations, Wark severely criticizes widely fluctuating and exaggerated estimates of Germany. "There can be no doubt that Britain suffered through a classic intelligence failure stemming, not from an inability to identify one's enemy, but from an inability to understand the real nature of the threat that enemy posed." The major impact of intelligence was "to confirm the government in its conduct of foreign policy"; since "appease-

ment ultimately failed, . . . the contribution of intelligence, in this sense, was strikingly negative." In short, since appeasement failed, intelligence failed. This conclusion is based on two assumptions: that different intelligence might have produced another policy and that appeasement failed. Given prevailing preconceptions, however, it was doubtful that British intelligence could produce different conclusions and, even then, that they could have imposed them on the government. Appeasement certainly failed to stop Hitler without war or produce a war under more promising circumstances—which is highly arguable; but if Hitler was not deterrable and an earlier war was neither more promising nor acceptable to the British public, then appeasement may be seen as the unfortunate precondition for British public support of war. In this sense, British policy and intelligence served better than has been imagined.

L. L. FARRAR, Jr.

Chestnut Hill
Massachusetts

UNITED STATES

DELLI CARPINI, MICHAEL X. *Stability and Change in American Politics: The Coming of Age of the Generation of the 1960s.* Pp. xxv, 374. New York: New York University Press, 1986. $35.00.

Delli Carpini seeks to understand in what ways, if at all, the generation of the 1960s represents a politically distinct generation, and, if it does, what impact it is having on the political system. His data consist of presidential election-year surveys covering the years 1952 to 1980 conducted by the University of Michigan Inter-University Consortium for Political and Social Research.

Delli Carpini defines the sixties as running from 1963—because it marked a sharp acceleration in civil rights and Vietnam war protests—through 1973, when direct U.S. involvement in Vietnam ended. Members of the sixties' generation are individuals who were aged 1 to 36 during this period. Delli Carpini divides this large group into three subgenerations of equal age spans.

A highly simplified version of Delli Carpini's complex thesis is that the sixties' generation is distinguished by having, to some degree, dropped out of politics. Although there are other measurable differences such as a slight preference for the Democratic Party, these differences are not being translated into political impact because of the generation's relative political inactivity. Furthermore, as this generation grows older, its distinctiveness is eroding as it merges into the rest of the population. Delli Carpini concludes that 1960s' ideas have had little permanent impact on society.

Most of the book is a detailed statistical exploration of the data in a manner familiar to students of election and poll results. The sixties' generation is compared with other segments of the population with regard to diffuse political support, political agendas, political involvement, partisan support, and other standard measures of political behavior. Life cycle, economic, and other variables are considered along with generational factors.

This volume is aimed at a much broader range of readers than is common in the often abstruse survey research literature. Subtle definitional problems, comprehensive literature reviews, statistical techniques, and relationships among masses of intertwined variables are explained with unusual clarity.

When Delli Carpini remains close to his data and methodological concerns he is altogether convincing. Occasionally, he strays far from that firm base into larger realms, and he is ill equipped to do so. He attempts to describe the broad cultural and economic characteristics of the sixties, but he founders on the complexity of the period and the heterogeneity of the American population. His portrait of the 1960s seems drawn primarily from record album covers.

When he argues that the ideas of the sixties have had no significant lasting effects he ignores the civil rights movement—even though it is included in his definition of the

sixties—the women's movement, environmentalism, and consumerism. Happily, neither the radical—or perhaps youthful—perspective that allows Delli Carpini to dismiss such forces nor his weak pop sociology mar an otherwise outstanding piece of scholarship.

CARL GRAFTON

Auburn University
Montgomery
Alabama

DENNY, BREWSTER C. *Seeing American Foreign Policy Whole*. Pp. 200. Urbana: University of Illinois Press, 1985. $19.95.

Numerous works detail American foreign policy since World War II. Brewster C. Denny's approach is refreshing because he employs essentially the essay form. After a satisfying interpretive review of our foreign policy, concluding with the cold war, his major analysis is of present components and organization of that policy.

Denny had impressive credentials and extensive government and academic experience. His style is clear, the text professional, analysis and conclusions reasoned, with some being controversial.

The Constitution frames discussion of national security functions and actors. Federal system checks brought Watergate to heel, a result European parliaments might not guarantee. Policy is traced from America's founding, "through the first try at world order," to isolation again, and to permanent global responsibility. Presidential power with respect to the cold war required organization to be effective. The National Security Council system, the merged Defense Department, combined agencies' intelligence, dimensions of science and security, and intergovernment programs like the United Nations are current legacies.

The Eberstadt Report was publicized as the guide for President Kennedy on strong leadership; on excellent authority he never read it. A crucial change in the National

Security Council was the pioneering appointment of substance-attracted academics to the low-profile staff role of the assistant for national security affairs. This made Kissingers and Brzezinskis inevitable.

Judicious is Denny's appraisal of the cold war:

It is difficult to see how events would have unfolded substantially differently unless the Soviet Union had simply abandoned any interest in international communism and accepted Western guarantees of security in central Europe or unless the United States had simply retreated to a position of isolation or appeasement (p. 81).

One can be critical of the Central Intelligence Agency, its awkward dual role in intelligence analysis and clandestine operations, and the impractical position of its director as de facto head of eight competing intelligence agencies. Nevertheless, Denny describes, with examples, intelligence as a functioning facet of national security.

Congressional activism in the formation of foreign policy has grown with the War Powers Act, oversight subcommittees, and markedly increased staff. Operating methods, limiting the executive, have threatened orderly global developments. Diversity and institutional struggles thus mark our democratic process, perhaps even protecting our liberties.

In concluding, Denny analyzes changes in the multifunctional presidency: technology, prolonged campaigns and America's superpower status. He doubts the secretary of state can be the president's coordinator, adviser, and department manager. With no program funds, however, secretary of state as chairman, contrasting with the Pentagon and intelligence community, is the poor relation at the table. The 10 percent of the department the president and secretary "may need suddenly, . . . long unneeded and unused, is not geared to their concerns." Further, despite the absence of a parochial constituency since Truman, it lacks "a national, multidimensional view." Government size would be countered by a dubious concentration of decision making in a White House staff, Denny contends. These are arguable conclusions.

The book is not long and is more reader retentive than other footnote-laden efforts. Student and scholar will find it a suitable backdrop toward understanding American foreign policy.

ROY M. MELBOURNE

Chapel Hill
North Carolina

GRIFFITH, ELISABETH. *In Her Own Right: The Life of Elizabeth Cady Stanton.* Pp. xx, 268. New York: Oxford University Press, 1984. $17.95.

Elizabeth Cady Stanton stands apart from many, if not all, the other leaders of the nineteenth-century woman's movement because of her understanding that reform must touch all aspects of life. Although she early insisted on the right to vote, her demands, unlike those of Lucy Stone, Lucretia Mott, and even Susan B. Anthony, went far beyond the right to vote. She understood that the revolution she sought must include the right of women to seek divorce, changes in the economic system, and even an attack on the reactionary doctrines of the church. Her determination to speak out on these issues brought her into conflict with many other leaders of the movement who feared that her radicalism would taint the cause of suffrage.

Elisabeth Griffith's biography is notable for its attempt to delineate connections between Stanton's personal life and her activist pursuits. She has used social learning theory to explain how and why "Stanton defined and developed a model of independent behavior, and then achieved it." As a result of this focus on role models, Griffith is particularly successful at explaining the relationship between Stanton and such significant figures in her life as her father, Lucretia Mott, her husband, and Susan B. Anthony. These are the most impressive aspects of the volume. In the end, however, as Griffith herself admits, such techniques may illuminate, but can never thoroughly explain, the development of so extraordinary an individual as Elizabeth Cady Stanton.

The volume has flaws. Among these, and one for which Griffith cannot be held responsible, is the nature of the source material. Stanton's own records are incomplete and her handwriting is difficult to decipher. Moreover much of what she left behind was altered by her children in an attempt to make their mother appear more respectable. It is, consequently, difficult to be certain that a particular document is as it was left by Stanton.

Another problem is that Griffith sometimes confuses the reader by introducing subjects that have not yet been explained. For example, *The Woman's Bible* is repeatedly brought into the discussion before it itself is finally discussed. Similar lapses occasionally leave the reader disoriented. Perhaps less important is the exceptionally poor index that either omits topics altogether or contains only incomplete listings.

All in all, however, this is a worthy piece of work and of use to both the uninformed reader, who will learn a great deal about one of America's foremost feminist leaders, as well as the scholar, who will find the discussion of Stanton's relationship with Anthony particularly illuminating.

DAVID AMMERMAN
Florida State University
Tallahassee

SCHOLTEN, CATHERINE M. *Childbearing in American Society: 1650-1850.* Edited by Lynne Withey. Pp. viii, 143. New York: New York University Press, 1985. $22.50.

This brief book opens up broad overviews of the new worlds of American social history. It begins with colonial women who were pregnant an average of six years of their lives while delivering eight children. Pregnant women might still be referred to as "teeming" or "breeding." Their children were born at home, with the assistance of a midwife, in the company of other women. Babies were then bound in swaddling clothes and frequently given to wet nurses. About one-half of these colonial children did not live beyond the age of ten. The survivors were disciplined strictly at any early age to control their sinful inheritances as children of Adam—"innocent vipers".

Scholten criticizes those historians who believe that colonial women, because of their useful roles in the agricultural economy, had a status higher than that of U.S. women of the 1800s. Rather, she argues that women's status rose after the Revolution, because of such factors as urbanization, changes in popular beliefs, alterations in the economy, medical improvements, and mass education; she notes that one-half of all women in New England during the 1700s could not sign their own names. Women increasingly began to have their children in hospitals, under the control of male doctors; to have fewer children; to emphasize the importance of intelligent and well-educated mothers in raising children; and to praise the intrinsic value of each child rather than considering children primarily as an economic asset. These changes could be conservative, stressing that the woman's place was in the home, or they could expand her personal opportunities for education and her new status as idealistic, sensitive, maternal reformer of society.

Scholten's comments are built upon 26 pages of notes—but no bibliography—ranging through such primary sources as diaries, letters, sermons, and women's magazines, along with a knowledgeable reliance on the basic works of women's history, legal history, and social history. Still, this book will be superseded. Scholten completed only 90 pages of the text—the first four chapters—before her death in 1981. She had intended to write a comprehensive history of childbirth and childbearing in the United States up to the 1930s. The future author who does this will rely partially upon this valuable summary by Catherine Scholten.

DAVID De LEON
Howard University
Washington, D.C.

STEINER, GILBERT Y. *Constitutional Inequality: The Political Fortunes of the Equal Rights Amendment.* Pp. 113. Washington, DC: Brookings Institution, 1985. $22.85. Paperbound. $8.95.

REBELL, MICHAEL A. and ARTHUR R. BLOCK. *Equality and Education: Federal Civil Rights Enforcement in the New York City School System.* Pp. xi, 340. Princeton, NJ: Princeton University Press, 1985. $28.50.

It is a sign of the times that the principal constitutional concept now involved in the processes of legislation, administration, and litigation is the guaranty of the equal protection of the laws, and it is in the arena of public education that the claim to the equal protection of the laws has been most extensively reviewed and evaluated in recent years. These two books make a solid contribution to the understanding of the current debate over these equal-protection issues.

Gilbert Steiner, now a senior fellow in the Governmental Studies program of the Brookings Institution and for many years professor of political science at the University of Illinois, seeks to explain why the Equal Rights Amendment (ERA) failed to achieve verification. In this small, well-written book Steiner has assembled the main facts in the history of the ERA, and suggests a number of reasons that explain the demise of the ERA in the ratification process. One factor was presidential indifference. Presidents Ford and Carter said that they left the issue to the care of their wives; President Reagan openly opposed ratification; only President Nixon actually endorsed ratification.

Steiner also argues that the Supreme Court's construction of the equal-protection clause tended to suggest that perhaps the ERA was not really necessary. In addition, the ERA was deeply involved in the angry controversy over abortion, for it was widely feared that the ERA would tend to strengthen the legitimacy of the Court's decision in *Roe* v. *Wade* [410 U.S. 113 (1973)]. Furthermore, the opposition of Senator Sam Ervin, Jr., of North Carolina, who achieved such national attention in chairing the Watergate hearings and who had a great reputation as an expert in the law of the Constitution, carried great weight. Steiner also believes that the Soviet invasion of Afghanistan reawakened old anxieties regarding the possible role of women in combat, especially after registration for the draft was resumed.

Finally, Steiner thinks that the case for the ERA was weakened by resort to suspect procedures. For example, the resolution that extended the ratification time by 39 months was adopted by Congress by much less than a two-third's vote, whereas both houses of Congress were virtually unanimous when the original vote was taken in 1972. The ERA expired in June 1982, short three state ratifications, and Steiner believes that a new move for an ERA would have a much better chance of success "if the sponsors agreed to almost any proviso limiting access to abortion." All in all, this is a thoughtful and useful book.

Rebell and Block are New York lawyers and part-time law school lecturers—at Yale and Columbia—who have been especially involved in the resolution of educational problems. Their book is very densely written and heavily annotated. In a book of 340 pages, the footnotes, which are inconveniently located in the back, occupy 112 pages. Indeed, most of the discussion of the many court decisions dealing with segregation in the schools is buried in the footnotes.

The Office of Civil Rights, which was then located in the Department of Health, Education and Welfare, undertook in the 1970s to investigate in depth conditions in the school systems of four large cities, Chicago, Los Angeles, Philadelphia, and New York—the Big Cities Reviews. The Rebell-

Block book analyzes in almost overpowering detail the compliance review in the New York City School System. The great issue was whether the touchstone of judgment should be measured by equality of opportunity or by equality of result. The two agreements that emerged from the complex activities in New York, it is concluded, "combined substantial result-oriented institutional reforms with a sensitive maintenance of opportunity-oriented emphases on individual options and meritocratic standards."

Rebell and Block also seek to compare the effectiveness of the administrative approach to the problems of education as compared with that of resort to the courts. They conclude that in the short run, where quick results are sought, the administrative process is better, but that the courts have greater staying power in monitoring the implementation of agreements, over the long run.

This book is extremely complex and couched in overly technical language. Too many events and ideas are crowded into overly dense prose, supported by enormous annotations, and too many individuals are identified and worked into the text. It is not an easy read, but it is a valuable contribution to our understanding of how some very complex problems are handled by the various branches of government.

DAVID FELLMAN

University of Wisconsin
Madison

SUNDQUIST, JAMES L. *Constitutional Reform and Effective Government.* Pp. x, 262. Washington, DC: Brookings Institution, 1986. No price.

The election of Ronald Reagan in 1980 has brought forth serious consideration of the issue of reconstructing the U.S. political system. This is an issue that attracts the interest of many political theorists, some politicians, journalists, and some ordinary citizens. *Constitutional Reform and Effective Government* considers the topic.

The division of policymaking authority among three branches of government—the legislative, executive, and judicial—has been the tradition, and it provides a safeguard against hasty and ill-considered action, as the framers intended—a point that Sundquist concedes. The structure does, however, lead to stalemate, deadlock, and conflict. This book and those who advocate change in the name of reform point to the latter issues as the most pressing need for change.

The intent and rationale of the Constitution's framers in creating the U.S. system are examined only in scant detail, with some of the major developments since the adoption of the Constitution being left out or conveniently selected to apply to circumstances of the argument.

The real purpose of this book is to call for a strong office of the presidency, unhampered by the legislative process or by the judiciary. While there are pressing needs for reform in the system, Sundquist and his contributors are not concerned merely with that issue. A clue to the the matter is the overt treatment of the so-called legislative veto. Growing concern over the "imperial presidency" caused Congress to pass a law in the early 1970s that allowed the Congress to override a presidential veto. The U.S. Justice Department, on behalf of the executive branch, challenged the law in the Supreme Court, and the Court overruled the legislative veto by a 6-to-3 vote. Although pleased with the ruling, Sundquist was dissatisfied with the opinion of Chief Justice Burger. The chief justice wrote for the majority because his argument was that arbitrary acts should not be permitted and that independence of the three branches of government was the law.

It is not surprising that this book deals very little with what role the judiciary will play. Its role is thereby left open to question and suspicion.

The parliamentary system of government is presented in summary form—as a possible incrementalism—and is then rejected: "Parliamentary democracy is not a model to be adopted in its entirety, supplanting the entire U.S. Constitutional structure with something new and alien."

Structural reforms can and should be made in the system. But even in this area, Sundquist clouds the issue by using some rather obscure past proposals as possible answers. A case in point is the proposal during the Civil War era of Representative George H. Pendleton, later a U.S. senator and famous for the Pendleton Act, creating the Civil Service System. His proposal called for members of the president's cabinet also to have unelected seats in Congress.

While there is a true need for reform, the specter of a strong executive should raise for consideration the question of how such a system would have served the people if Franklin D. Roosevelt was president? Or to be more contemporary, what would be the fate of the people if Ed Meese, with his views on the Constitution, served under an executive with unlimited and almost absolute powers?

FREDERICK M. FINNEY
Economic Research Center
Dayton
Ohio

VATTER, HAROLD G. *The U.S. Economy in World War I.* Pp. x, 198. New York: Columbia University Press, 1985. $25.00.

FOOT, ROSEMARY. *The Wrong War: American Policy and the Dimensions of the Korean Conflict, 1950-1953.* Pp. 290. Ithaca, NY: Cornell University Press, 1985. $29.95.

Although there are shortcomings in each, scholars and students will find these books useful.

In the first, the data are so voluminous that they cannot be summarized. There are tables and charts, figures and statistics, and footnotes that document everything, even items not in the text. There are citations to

statutes and officials, and there is a sequel that takes us to 1960.

There is, however, no good writing. I would guess that the book was originally written at 400 pages, but that someone decided that only 160 pages could be allowed. Vatter, a professor at Portland State University, then had to cut to meet that limit. No other reason suggests itself for the run-on sentences with widely disparate ideas that leave the reader looking for relief. Nor is there any other plausible explanation for Vatter's promise that the work will be an "interpretive presentation," when one reads many pages without a single interpretation, and other stretches of only unsupported assertions. Many readers will find the book valuable, but no one will likely enjoy it.

The second volume is very well written. It minutely details American attitudes about the People's Republic of China from October 1949 through July 1953. According to Foot, a professor at the University of Sussex in England, materials she turned up under the Freedom of Information Act show that U.S. contingency planning throughout the period called for extending the war into Manchuria and other parts of China proper unless the Chinese did this or that, depending on the time. No one familiar with I. F. Stone's history will be surprised by American pugnacity. But reading the words in the mouths of policymakers who often took different public positions is eye opening. And after what we have learned about the wrong premises that led Washington into Vietnam and kept it there, the erroneous judgments made about so-called monolithic Communism in Korea mark even earlier American shortsightedness.

The Foot book, however, becomes tiring. Not much new occurs over the 200 pages of the history, and the reader wearies of the same old tale. There is a useful chronology of the military and political actions that accompanies what the text focuses on, but the map strangely does not locate some important places. The chapter of conclusions, the bibliography, the documentation, and the index are all excellent.

The two books, then, will more likely serve as references than as solid reading. They will do well in that role.

W. T. GENEROUS, Jr.
Choate Rosemary Hall
Wallingford
Connecticut

WHITE, GRAHAM and JOHN MAZE. *Harold Ickes of the New Deal: His Private Life and Public Career.* Pp. 263. Cambridge, MA: Harvard University Press, 1985. $20.00.

LEFF, MARK. *The Limits of Symbolic Reform: The New Deal and Taxation, 1933-1939.* Pp. ix, 308. New York: Cambridge University Press, 1985. $32.50.

As evidenced by the recent publication of these two works, scholars continue to be drawn to the Great Depression and the New Deal. Harold Ickes, Franklin Roosevelt's head of the Public Works Administration and secretary of the interior, is the subject of a collaborative biography by historian Graham White and psychologist John Maze. Their book focuses on the impact of Ickes's personal life upon his public career. They depict Ickes as a man overwhelmed by anxieties and incapable of understanding the motivations of himself and others. Readers will find this view of Ickes consistent with that revealed in his published three-volume *Secret Diary.*

White's historical analysis is this book's greatest strength. Relying largely upon the unpublished Ickes papers and autobiographical materials in the Library of Congress, he carefully traces Ickes's evolution as a reformer—his brief journalistic stint with the *Chicago Record*, his legal training and law practice, and his involvement in Republican politics in Illinois. White clearly shows how Ickes's early concern for the underdog logically formed the basis for his later defense of oppressed Indians, blacks, women, and other minorities. Similarly, Ickes's fight against exploitation of natural resources as interior secretary was reminiscent of Progressive era reformers' conservation crusades. White skillfully weaves these themes throughout his study of Ickes's careers, thereby lending direction and coherence to portions of this book.

Unfortunately, Maze's exessive use of Freudian analyses detracts from his colleague's efforts. Maze alleges that Ickes suffered from "castration anxiety" and a "mother-fixation." As proof of this latter abnormality, Maze cites Ickes's "serious concern with cooking," his "obsessive minute supervision" of the construction of his home, his unpaid legal defense of women industrial workers, his crusades for minority rights, and "the moral masochism that prevented his escaping from the almost endless misery of his first marriage." Maze interprets Ickes's love of nature as evidence of anxiety over his masculinity:

landscapes often function as symbols for the female body; . . . forest giants . . . are classic phallic symbols, and we have seen how concerned Ickes was with protecting his own genitality. Combining the body of mother earth and the towering forest rising from it we have the image of the phallic mother. Roosevelt had made Ickes the "mother" of PWA, with vast funds to nourish his country.

Ickes also evinced a "feminine attachment" for Roosevelt, Maze argues, because the president "elicited and provided scope for the strong moral convictions Ickes had acquired from his mother" and then "delegated to Ickes an administrative version of the maternal functions he had always wanted to perform."

Maze's ludicrous flights into the realm of "psychoanalytical interpretation"—his term—ruin an otherwise interesting biography. Although psychohistory at its best can be enlightening and fascinating, because of Maze's heavy-handed approach, this work is seriously flawed.

Fortunately, for readers and reviewers alike, Mark Leff's incisive study of New Deal taxation delivers all that it promises. Largely due to Leff's command of his sources and his forceful writing style, this book should interest all serious students of the New Deal. Leff asserts that taxation policy was "a symbolic reform . . . , the lightning rod of the New Deal, neutralizing threats from conservatives and radicals alike." He posits this thesis by contrasting Roosevelt's rhetoric on taxation with tax measures that were proposed and, in some cases, implemented.

During the 1930s, the income tax never applied, Leff urges, to more than 5 percent of Americans, and only a small minority of those shouldered much of the tax burden. Roosevelt extended the regressive excises of the Hoover era and added taxes on liquor, agricultural commodities, and wages covered by social security. Also, because of their political influence in all tax debates, members of the middle class were exempt from a fair share of taxes. The result was a tax system that hit lower-income Americans hardest. Leff concludes from these facts that despite Roosevelt's outcry in 1935 against "male-factors of great wealth," the enemies of the "forgotten man," his tax program lacked any progressive reform measures that would benefit citizens at the bottom of the economic pyramid.

In 1935-36, as Roosevelt's reelection campaign intensified, he and his advisers pursued a "politics of ostracism," uniting "ordinary" citizens against their "economic royalist enemies." Roosevelt employed one of his favorite political ploys—he allowed Congress to take the lead and play to the grandstand with demands that the superrich should share more of the tax load. Leff argues, "FDR never publicly opposed such efforts, but rarely did he endorse them." By 1935, the president no longer needed business cooperation for economic recovery; therefore, he was free to castigate corporate giants for tax abuses when it suited his purposes. He effectively squelched demands from the Left for more progressive tax reform by offering a few symbolic gestures. Again, he focused on alleged tax evasion by the wealthy rather than a comprehensive program to redistribute income across the economic and social spectrum. Leff suggests that "taxation and the polarizing atmosphere associated with it served as a New Deal safety valve,"

allowing Roosevelt to undercut political opponents on the Left and Right. In his conclusion, Leff asserts that although Roosevelt's use of tax policy "to crosscut and cement his electoral coalition was primarily symbolic," he also made substantive concessions to this voting bloc—loans and subsidies for farmers, benefits and union rights for workers, old-age pensions for the elderly, and so forth.

Leff's work is a solid contribution to New Deal scholarship. Yet two minor criticisms are worth mentioning. Some of the quotations and explanatory footnotes are rather lengthy, and the exorbitant price may limit this book's marketability.

DAVID E. ALSOBROOK
Carter Presidential Library
Atlanta
Georgia

SOCIOLOGY

BAUNACH, PHYLLIS JO. *Mothers in Prison.* Pp. xii, 147. New Brunswick, NJ: Transaction Books, 1985. $19.95.

The flood of women joining the labor force begun in the late 1960s and the conflicts arising from this change have illuminated the extent to which apparently universalistic social institutions are in reality designed to meet the singular needs for male clients. Prisons are no exception. In *Women in Prison* Baunach joins a tradition of feminist research documenting the differential impact of social organizations on women and men. Implicitly this research is designed to effect changes in social policy by providing data specifying the types of institutional changes required to service new clients—in this case, women.

The central concern in this mongraph is the impact of separation from dependent children on incarcerated women's self-concept and their ability to resume motherhood roles on their release from prison. The issue is critical in that over half of incarcerated women were living with dependent children at the time of arrest and the number of incarcerated women is increasing. Baunach describes the experiences of incarcerated mothers in three prisons in maintaining relationships with their children and the effectiveness of two experimental programs designed to sustain these relationships. Data were collected from prison documents and by means of personal interviews with inmates, prison staff, and foster mothers. Both inmates and foster mothers completed Tennessee Self-concept and Maryland Parent Attitude scales.

The study assumes that, as motherhood is a dominant feminine role, forced separation from children will result in a loss of self-esteem and parenting skills needed to resume child care on leaving prison. The analysis provides information on both the individual level and the organizational level with major implications for policy implementation. First, incarceration has a differential impact on black and white women due to cultural differences. Second, bureaucratic organizations have difficulty accommodating client participation and unplanned events.

On the individual level, as extended families are more common among blacks, black children are more frequently cared for by grandparents and family members than are white children. White women are more likely to have their children reside with strangers and less likely to participate in the selection of foster care for their children. In some cases they do not know where their children are. As a result in black families the feelings of deprivation have a greater tendency to be ameliorated. On the other hand, in one experimental program, where inmates of a rural prison learned parenting skills through working in a day care center established for children of families residing near the prison, black women were not enthusiastic participants, as the suburban children were white.

Throughout the study the continual bureaucratic lack of awareness and accommodation to the demands of motherhood and children is appalling. Beginning at the time of arrest, women are often not allowed to arrange for child care in their absence. In an experimental program designed to maintain relationships between mothers, foster mothers, and children, all parties were disappointed when prison staff failed to notify mothers of illnesses preventing children's visits. On another occasion the staff failed to provide access to foster mothers and children arriving after a long trip only to find that paperwork was incomplete and the visit canceled.

Mothers are authority figures responsible for the socialization of succeeding generations. There is a conflict between the dependence experienced in prison and the responsibility demands inherent in motherhood roles. The two experimental programs were considered successful for parental training by those who participated. However, the bureaucratic demands of the prison regulations on programs, the distance of prisons from children's residences, and the rural location of prisons were barriers to participation and need to be made accommodative in future programs.

This monograph contributes much to our empirical knowledge of the current limitations of prisons in meeting the needs of a new clientele—mothers—and hints at the radical changes in concept and in policy and funding practices required to design an appropriate organizational response to the incarceration of women. The success of future generations may well be governed to a greater extent than we now envision by the success of this endeavor. This volume should be of interest to policymakers and criminal justice administrators. I would also recommend it as supplementary material in university courses illustrating the use of empirical data.

CAROLYN R. DEXTER
Pennsylvania State University
Middletown

BELL, RUDOLPH M. *Holy Anorexia.* Pp. xii, 248. Chicago: University of Chicago Press, 1985. $22.50.

It happens that some 261 females born after 1199 in Italy have been elevated over the centuries to sainthood by the Roman Catholic Church. Using data from the Church's official sourcebook on its saints, the *Bibliotheca Sanctorum*, and from a multitude of Latin and Italian documents and publications, Bell reports in this intriguing book his study of anorexic behavior among these women.

Bell's basic premise is that some women respond to their sex's ages-old condition of subordination and powerlessness by seeking mastery over, at the least, their own bodies. If this takes the form of stubborn insistence on severely restricted intake of food, accompanied by binge eating, self-induced vomiting, amenorrhea, hyperactivity, and other symptoms, the condition of anorexia nervosa is said to exist. While Bell sees women's status as the primary source of energies for anorexia among them, more proximate causes of the disorder differ between saints and modern secular women. The latter, he thinks, may suffer from neurotic feelings of social inadequacy that can be assuaged by reshaping their bodies to the extreme thinness they see as modish. But because the saints sought mastery through pursuit of such Christian values as asceticism, spirituality, and finding unity with God, their anorexia was holy.

To support his basic premise, Bell gives much attention to the often prickly relationships he discerned between his single-minded subjects and the parents, relatives, and Church authorities who took exception for various reasons to the women's spiritual quests. Writing with a grace and power uncommon among scholars, Bell takes us with immediacy into home, cloister, and cell, where we witness the torments and ecstacies of his subjects. To one not familiar with the lives of saints, the unremitting perseverance (instransigence?), self-imposed regimens of extraordinary harshness (masochism?), and religious fervor (madness?) of these unusual women is astonishing.

Among the 261 saints, Bell identified 102 as anorexic. For 25 of these, he presents more or less detailed histories that describe anorexic behavior so extreme—even bizarre—as permanently to undermine health and, in a few cases, to produce death by starvation. Unfortunately, because characteristics of the remaining 77 anorexics and of the non-anorexic majority are merely summarized, the reader can neither evaluate the overall adequacy of Bell's data nor assess the validity and reliability of his diagnoses. These serious weaknesses aside, *Holy Anorexia* is a suggestive and fascinating study of women for whom religion was a particularly compelling force.

R. W. ENGLAND, Jr.
University of Rhode Island
Kingston

GARDNER, HOWARD. *The Mind's New Science: A History of the Cognitive Revolution.* Pp. xv, 423. New York: Basic Books, 1985. $22.50.

At the strictly professional level, Howard Gardner has made significant contributions to cognitive psychology. He also, however, has a metaprofessional life: presenting books about his intellectual interests to broad public audiences.

In his newest attempt, *The Mind's New Science*, Gardner traces the origins of cognitive science—the amalgam of philosophy, psychology, artificial intelligence, linguistics, anthropology, and neuroscience that deals with issues of what the mind is and how it works. After a brief introductory section, he looks at each of these six cognitive sciences in turn, summing up past achievements—from Plato to the present—and judging the likely success of current research areas. In a final section, he argues that contemporary research can best be considered, not as interdisciplinary problems among the cognitive sciences, but as central problems to a new cognitive science.

This is classic whig history—a scan of earlier disciplines to spot the origins of current intellectual issues. History, of course, is not that simple. Although Gardner does recognize, to a limited degree, social context, available resources, and dead ends now considered incorrect or unproductive, the book is fundamentally a current practitioner's explanation of how we got to where we are now.

Given the book's limits as history, what is its value? Like other works published by Basic Books, Gardner's is proselytizing to a broader audience. He is arguing for a particular view of how knowledge and investigation should be organized.

Gardner is at home in this larger world. He is a cultivated scientist explaining research to a cultivated audience. He fits into the tradition of nineteenth-century man-of-science popularizers like Thomas Huxley, a tradition that continues in the writings of Lewis Thomas and Stephen Jay Gould. These writers do not just make science understandable. They present distinct intellectual programs for public approbation.

The work of these men of science serves a fundamentally different purpose from that of more contemporary styles of popular science, such as newspaper science sections or *Discover* and *Science 86* magazines. These more recent forms are dedicated to the ideal that scientific information should be available to any informed reader—without concern for the philosophical or ideological concerns that inspire much scientific achievement.

Gardner, like Huxley or Gould, has an intellectual goal: to argue that contemporary cognitive sciences should yield certain questions to the forms required by a unified cognitive science. If asked whether the public should receive facts or a worldview from science, Gardner would clearly choose the latter.

He carries out his task elegantly. In the end, however, some of his arguments fail, for he convincingly places crucial research programs firmly in both the old cognitive sciences and in his new unified cognitive science. Moreover, despite the attempt to reach a broad audience, some readers will wish for a much less intellectually complex story that gives a more easily comprehensible and digestible survey of the trends he describes.

BRUCE V. LEWENSTEIN
University of Pennsylvania
Philadelphia

LEHMAN, EDWARD C., Jr. *Women Clergy: Breaking through Gender Barriers.* Pp. xiii, 307. New Brunswick, NJ: Transaction Books, 1985. $24.95.

This volume deals with the impact of the feminist movement on churches, church members' receptivity to clergywomen, and the need to accommodate increasing numbers of women seeking a place in the ministry. The ultimate challenge for churches is to facilitate the implementation of verbalized values of equality and justice. Lehman, who served as principal investigator, reports on the results of a national-sample survey of the United Presbyterian Church, USA. This research was sociological in its approach. Survey questions inquired into the structure of attitudes, the importance of clergy support, factors related to attitude differences, churches as organizations, sources of attitudes, the effect of contact on level of receptivity, attitude change as response to information, problems of getting into the ministry system, and some observations of clergywomen themselves. It is of interest that the data collected indicate that "antipathies associated with changing sex roles can be modified by some of the same techniques as those used to reduce hostilities among racial and ethnic groups."

Almost 4000 individuals nationwide from four subgroups within the denomination participated in an ongoing mail survey for a three-year period. Overall response was high. Analysis of data is enhanced in the text with a generous number of accompanying tables, and at the end of each chapter the reader will find helpful bibliographical suggestions for additional reading.

The survey findings produced some new and useful information. Attitudes toward clergywomen among lay church members and clergy are found to be basically positive. The laity, nevertheless, tends to pursue a gender preference for male pastors. Contact with women in the role of pastor, however, actually results in greater acceptance by church members. A major problem area perceived for female clergy has do with role conflicts—with the cross-pressures of job and home. Other concerns reflected fears that women as pastors would feminize the church and adversely affect financial contributions. Although gender barriers are breaking down, it is axiomatic that established organizations strongly strive to maintain their own viability. The church, as an organization, also has developed patterns of behavior that promote organizational maintenance. Clergymen hold positions of power wherein they create and implement policies that can either validate or invalidate clergywomen's interests. Thus clergywomen were eager to cooperate in the study. The information they provided from their personal experiences generally supported the patterns gleaned from the responses of the church members.

Readers interested in the subject area would benefit from reviewing the detailed findings of this national survey, which explored in considerable depth gender barriers facing women clergy. The insights offered provide direction for achieving further breakthroughs.

FLORENCE P. ENGELHARDT
Arizona State University
Tempe

PETERS, EDWARD. *Torture.* Pp. ix, 202. New York: Basil Blackwell, 1985. $24.95. Paperbound, $9.95.

This is not a book about torment or ill-treatment in general. Rather, it seeks to confine itself to the historical and comparative study of "torment inflicted by a public authority for ostensibly public purposes . . . torture stands in the same relation to such private offences as trespass, battery or aggravated assult as a state execution stands in relation to murder."

This restriction arises from one of Peters's central observations, that the term "torture" has been taken from its legal and historical setting, and that its frequently indiscriminate use has eroded its meaning and muffled the impact of its denunciation.

Peters has a happy facility of covering much historical ground while maintaining both accuracy and a respect for the context of institutional developments. At first arising out of Greek and Roman requirements of proof in cases involving the testimony of slaves, torture embedded itself in criminal and civil procedure through the progressive loss of immunities by the higher social orders, and a determination by rulers to pursue treason investigations by any means, irrespective of the social standing of the accused. The megalomania of some of the Julio-Claudian emperors provided a precedent for an expanded use of torture that later rulers and their officials were diligently to follow.

Treason might well be called the cutting edge of judicial torture, and through the temporal aspirations of the Church, treason and heresy for a time became synonymous in parts of Europe. At a later point the broadening of the offense of treason to any threat, conspiracy, or action against the power of the nation-state—as distinct from the earlier requirement that the treasonable act was directed against the person of the ruler—brought a wide range of political criminals within the ambit of the torturer.

For the more serious nonpolitical defendants torture became part of the judicial process because of the stringency of the rules of proof—two eyewitnesses or a confession were needed for a conviction under Roman law codes. Bits of evidence could not be added together to make a proof, and with confession considered as "the queen of proofs" torture was an inevitable tool of the court.

Total national mobilization, totalitarian ideologies, nuclear weapons and the speed of modern warfare, terrorism and counterterrorism, the colonial experience and rapid decolonization have all contributed to a contemporary revival of torture. It has been estimated that one nation in three now engages in the practice, and things may get worse. One plausible implication of Peters's comparative and historical survey is that the nineteenth-century retreat from torture was but a temporary departure from what has been the norm of the judicial practices of a large and civilized section of the world for the last two and a half millennia.

Its range, the great body of scholarship so concisely and clearly presented, the coherence of its analysis, and the contemporary importance of the topic should all ensure a wide readership for this book. Peters is to be congratulated for applying to such great effect the methods of traditional scholarship to a deeply disturbing aspect of our history and contemporary behavior.

SEAN McCONVILLE
University of Illinois
Chicago

SCHUMAN, HOWARD, CHARLOTTE STEEH, and LAWRENCE BOBO. *Racial Attitudes in America: Trends and Interpretations.* Pp. xi, 260, Cambridge, MA: Harvard University Press, 1985. $22.50.

G. E. ZURIFF, *Behaviorism: A Conceptual Reconstruction.* Pp. xiii, 369. New York: Columbia University Press, 1985. $35.00.

By their titles alone, these books would appear to share little substantive or theoretical ground. Schuman, Steeh, and Bobo describe and analyze trends in racial attitudes of both white and black Americans over the past four decades; Zuriff meticulously dissects the conceptual bases of behaviorism as a method of scientific inquiry. At a more general level, however, these two books represent the ongoing debate surrounding the roles of attitudes and behavior in social

science research. They both require that we reflect on what is worth knowing and how it is known.

Racial Attitudes in America is an important book because it simultaneously reexamines the data on racial attitudes used in previous studies and reviews the explanations that have been given for changes in these attitudes. Its thesis is that making generalizations concerning changes in racial attitudes is a hazardous enterprise, prone to misrepresentation and fraught with methodological difficulties. In relying primarily on three sources of longitudinal data—the National Opinion Research Center, Institute for Social Research, and Gallup—Schuman, Steeh, and Bobo cautiously chart the course of public opinion regarding racial attitudes from 1942 to 1983. They show that the conclusions expressed in these studies are often justified in light of trend data available at a given point in time, but that no single study considers the corpus of extant data simultaneously. Based on this review, Schuman and his colleagues insist that trend analyses of racial attitudes must be understood in the context of the historical circumstances surrounding that research.

Longitudinal comparisons are difficult if for no other reason than because the issues believed central to the controversies surrounding black-white relations have varied over time. Thus, for example, Americans polled in 1942 were asked whether they thought "there should be separate sections for Negroes in street cars and buses," but after 1970, that question was not asked again. By contrast, some questions—such as those concerning busing of black and white school children—did not appear on surveys until 1972. That question wording sometimes differs or that the time interval between the asking of questions is irregular further complicates trend analysis.

Despite these obstacles, Schuman, Steeh, and Bobo provide a through and compelling analysis of these complex data. At the risk of simplifying their conclusions, one finding commands unique attention: while favorable attitudes toward principles of integration have increased steadily during the period under study, attitudes regarding implementation of integrationist programs have failed to show similar positive trends. "Whether the implementation is at the federal or local level, whether it is legal or economic, white Americans are much less enthusiastic about modes of implementation than about abstract principles." The future balance between principles and implementation is left to the political arena.

The title of Zuriff's book provides a succinct, yet apt, description of his ambitious task: to organize and to analyze critically the principal concepts of behaviorism as they have been expounded in this century. He identifies four components of this conceptual framework: behaviorism as a philosophy of science that sets parameters governing the questions it explores and the methods it follows; behaviorism as a philosophy of mind making assumptions concerning human nature; behaviorism as a body of empirical assumptions about the relationship of behavior to its environmental context; and behaviorism as an ideology supportive of certain ways of knowing. He explores each of these in considerable detail with the goal of assessing the contributions that behaviorism can make to the study of human behavior. In large measure he succeeds, for the complex picture of behaviorism drawn by Zuriff clearly illustrates that challenges to behaviorism have not been equally threatening to its scientific validity.

As one example of how behaviorists have responded to their critics, Zuriff discusses the challenge that mentalist language—the realm of emotions, ideas, and beliefs—poses to behaviorism. The variation that characterizes behaviorism itself is represented in the responses to this criticism, ranging from denying the legitimacy of mental language altogether to seeking ways of behaviorally operationalizing mental concepts. Zuriff is quick to point out that these responses present philosophical and methodological difficulties to their proponents, but he fails to conclude that behaviorism cannot meaningfully incorporate the analysis of mental

concepts. Rather, here and elsewhere, his goal is to present "an accurate portrait of behaviorism and an honest search for what is still valuable in it."

In addition to the thorough reviews undertaken by the authors of both books, there are many other good things one could say about their work. The accessibility of these books means that one need not be a trained social scientist to appreciate the richness of their arguments. In many ways *Racial Attitudes in America* serves as a model for those wishing to present quantitative data in an interesting way and without jargon. As part of a larger concern with the problems in analyzing trend data, Schuman, Steeh, and Bobo also provide a short course in the effects of question wording on survey outcomes, reminding us that what we know— especially of issues marked by extreme controversy—depends on what is asked and who does the asking.

Similarly, Zuriff's discussion of behaviorism educates as well as analyzes. Summaries appearing at both the beginning and the end of each chapter serve the essential pedagogical function of carving a path through terrain as dense as that addressed here. Adding to this an exhaustive bibliography and a point-counterpoint organizing scheme, the result is a first-rate guide to the literature on behaviorism.

In the end, both of these books demonstrate the need for a disaggregated analysis of complex issues. Whether in the domain of public opinion, philosophical debate, or elsewhere, we would do well to heed their call.

LEE J. CUBA

Wellesley College
Massachusetts

TOLLISON, ROBERT D., ed. *Smoking and Society: Toward a More Balanced Assessment.* Pp. xi, 368. Lexington, MA: D. C. Heath, 1986. No price.

A majority of adult Americans today do not smoke, reflecting a general attitude, common even among smokers, that smoking has been proven to be harmful to health. Many people are urging governing bodies to take stronger measures to discourage the habit and restrict its exercise. Smokers are increasingly on the defensive. The contributors to this volume have joined to defend the smoker and to try to demonstrate that "there is a serious and useful scholarly case to be made that the conventional wisdom about smoking behavior is either wrong, unproven, built upon faulty analysis, or pushed well beyond the point of common sense." Tollison frankly admits that representatives of the tobacco industry supported the effort.

Hans J. Eysenck attempts the most difficult task. His essay on the health issue is the longest in the book, and he asserts that much of the evidence generally cited by the antismokers is biased by design, ignores other possible interpretations of the data, and does not support the principal claims of antismoking adherents. He suggests the "constitutional hypothesis" as an alternative to the "smoking hypothesis." He raises some interesting questions, but his essay seems unlikely to change any minds. In another article Domingo M. Aviado, M.D., examines the literature and denies that it supports the proposition that second-hand smoke is harmful to nonsmokers.

Charles D. Spielberger reviews why people take up the habit and why they continue. For whatever reason they started, most say they continue to smoke because they enjoy it.

The changing social role of smoking is the subject of a short essay by Sherwin J. Feinhandler. Douglas J. Den Uyl discusses the political and philosophical question of how far government ought to go to restrict the rights of smokers in order to protect the rights of nonsmokers. He and William F. Shughart II, Robert D. Tollison, and Peter L. Berger, in other articles, also examine the antismokers. They all find their crusading zeal unappealing, and Berger describes a developing economic class division between smokers and nonsmokers.

H. Peter Gray and Ingo Walter point out the economic contributions of tobacco producers, manufacturers, and consumers. James M. Savarese and Shughart weigh the significance of tobacco taxes. Stephen C. Littlechild and J. J. Boddewyn in separate articles argue that tobacco advertising ought not be severely limited. Advertising may encourage smokers to choose low-tar and low-nicotine products.

James M. Buchanan, Tollison's senior colleague at George Mason University's Center for Study of Public Choice, argues the case for the rights of the smoker against the "meddlesome preferences" of antismokers. Tollison's concluding comments suggest that what is really at issue is not tobacco but individual freedom. Adherents of the conventional wisdom will continue to disagree.

WILLIAM R. SUTTON

San Antonio
Texas

WRIGHT, ERIK OLIN. *Classes*. Pp. 291. London: Verso, 1985. $25.00.

This is a book focused on a formulation of classical Marxist social thought aimed toward a workable middle-range theory tested by empirical data. Primarily, Wright centers his concern on a detailed examination of Marx's concept of class—which was never systematically defined—along with a major reformulation of his earlier view of Marxist class theory.

Potential readers should know at the outset that Wright is a committed Marxist scholar bent on both theoretical and conceptual clarification of the familiar concerns with class, class consciousness, exploitation, socialism, change, and reform. As such, this is not a book dealing with an eclectic interest in social stratification and the multiple variables and constructs that American sociologists broadly associate with this more encompassing perspective.

Wright has three overall analytic concerns: (1) a reconceptualization of class structure from his earlier writing; (2) the empirical fit of this reformulation into contemporary American society; and (3) the role of politics—change, reform—to redress the current injustices.

In his attempt to go considerably beyond his earlier formulations that classes are aggregates in "contradictory locations," Wright now argues that classes are organized around four structural variables: (1) classes are relational; (2) the relations are antagonistic; (3) the antagonisms are based on exploitation; and (4) the exploitation emerges, generates, from the social relations of production.

Following from the theoretical work of John Roemer, exploitation for Wright now becomes a much more powerful factor in the delineation of class. Wright argues that classes in capitalistic societies result from the intersection of three forms of exploitation: the ownership of capital assets; the control of capital assets; and "the possession of skill and credential assets."

Having established his newer concept of class, Wright in subsequent chapters puts his reformulation to the empirical test. In chapter 5, for example, he compares the exploitation-centered concept with two alternative formulations, the manual-labor definition of the working class and the productive-labor definition. Although he finds some "ambiguities" Wright argues that the exploitation-dominated concept tested considerably better. In chapter 6, he examines the relationship between class structure and income inequality and again finds the exploitation-centered concept to have greater explanatory and predictive value. Once more, in chapter 7, focusing on the relationship between class and class consciousness, Wright finds the newer concept superior to the older formulations. Finally, Wright utilizes the exploitation model in the analysis of both American and Swedish class systems and finds that about a quarter of the work force are "exploiters."

The answer to the inequalities of class, as Wright sees it, is the ultimate triumph of socialist society, which would eliminate the massive waste of capitalistic economies in the form of excessive military budgets, advertising, huge corporate executive salaries, waste, and the like. Hence real production of useful consumption would expand so that many persons in formerly "contradictory locations" would be substantially better off. This, in turn, would result in much more free time for the workers, thereby creating "socially necessary labor time" for democratic participation in the collectively shared systems of production. In short, for Wright, the workers, rather than producing slavishly at the wasteful machines of capitalism, could now spend many more creative hours a day in participatory industrial democracy—the factory equivalent of joyful academic faculty meetings.

Wright's *Classes* is a literate, well-organized, systematic, thoughtful book, articulated within the orthodoxy of Marxist social theory. I was not terribly surprised by his reformulation; it sounded like traditional Marxism to me. As a sociologist, Wright has a sophisticated sense of social theory, construct formation, and the bearing of empirical data on concepts and theory. I do not see this book as being very useful to American undergraduate students of class structure because of its complexity and the foreknowledge of Marxist class theory that it assumes. It should, however, find its way into graduate seminars. For American sociologists, with a serious interest in contemporary Marxist theory regarding the nature of class, this book will be read with interest and—I hope Wright will understand the gentle nature of the usage—profit.

WILLIAM M. DOBRINER
Lafayette College
Easton
Pennsylvania

ECONOMICS

DERTHICK, MARTHA and PAUL J. QUIRK. *The Politics of Deregulation.* Pp. xii, 265. Washington, DC: Brookings Institution, 1985. $28.95. Paperbound, $10.95.

It is a good thing that Chuck Colson did not succeed in his plan to firebomb the Brookings Institution. That might have put a damper on the many valuable policy studies that have emanated from that now-venerable but still vital—if currently a bit unfashionable—institution. The work under review here, as befits its subject, is admirably nonpartisan, devoid of special pleading or cynicism, competently written, even witty at moments. Derthick and Quirk take a puzzling and even surprising development—the success of the deregulation of airline, telecommunication, and trucking industries—and shape it into a coherent story that tells the reader much about the extent to which the ethos of American national politics has changed since the fall of Nixon and especially since the rise of Reagan. Indeed, the book even seems to suggest that there is astonishing continuity between Ford, Carter, and Reagan; thus political scientists left holding the predictive bag in 1980 should have seen the Reagan revolution coming across the political horizon long before, but they did not. This is a story that demonstrates that political inertia is often a property of the received wisdom of political academia and the media and not of active politicians who can read the political handwriting on the wall and act accordingly. Gramm-Rudman would not surprise anyone who has read this book.

The "received wisdom of political science," Derthick and Quirk write, "was that in clashes between a diffuse public interest and a tangible, well-organized interest, the former could be expected to finish a poor second." The "iron triangle" of regulatory agencies, their "clients" in the regulated industry, and their allies in Congress were an unbreakable coalition based on cooptation, beyond the reforms of policy experts—liberal or conservative—and incomprehensible to the public. Like the Egyptian priesthood that regulated everything, the regulators of major American industries seemed destined to go on forever. Much to the amazement of those who think politics static and timeless, and to the chagrin of many of those inside the triangle, there was nothing iron about it at

all. The coalition was broken as much from within as without, although the special interests involved fought hard to sustain the way things were. The defection of key figures such as Senator Kennedy and Alfred Kahn of the Civil Aeronautics Board became crucial to the emergence of reform forces that bored from within, and as the folks at AT&T can tell you, the rest is history. A lot of public policy textbooks will have to be rewritten.

Derthick and Quirk recognize, of course, the limits of deregulation. Clearly not everyone within or without the deregulated industries is happy with the new arrangements, and the procompetitive myth of the Bartertown marketplace is already wearing a bit thin. But Derthick and Quirk seem to suggest that we may never go home again, neither to a pre-New Deal environment of regulatory passivity nor to the new industrial state of business regulation of government. They see the political reform of regulatory policy as an outcome of the "politics of ideas," and they see the army of new analysts—think tanks like Brookings and the American Enterprise Institute—as the new philosopherking: "As vividly and impressively as possible, our cases demonstrate the role that disinterested economic analysis can play in the formation of public policy." Such "expert, well-considered analysis" prevents the democratic tendency for "policy to be dominated by narrow perspectives and interests or to reflect ill-considered, superficial opinions or the impulses of the mass public." Before the thanks of a grateful nation is conveyed, we may ask first whether mass attitudes played all that much of a role in what was essentially an elite process, and, second, whether the experts played a starring or a supporting role. Like Frederick the Great, contemporary American politicians may have done what was necessary or even punitive and found plenty of professors to tell them it was the height of public wisdom. We must also remember that the politician who headed the politics of deregulation gained his or her power from "symbolism and mass appeal," and that the "orderly deliberation" of deregulation occurred at a time in which the superficial impulses of the mass public defined a new atmosphere if not a new policy. So the verdict may still be out on Derthick and Quirk's conclusion that the "new American political system is working well," having overcome irrationalities, particularism, and "interest group regimes," and welded a brave new world of the linked forces of "expert analysis and mass opinion as the basis for action." But they rightly sense that something important is indeed different from the situation a decade or so ago, and that history is characterized more by movement than inertia. They should be commended for writing such a good account of how one aspect of an important movement changed a political arrangement that only yesterday had seemed immune from challenge.

JAMES COMBS

Valparaiso University
Indiana

FORM, WILLIAM. *Divided We Stand: Working-Class Stratification in America.* Pp. xviii, 306. Champaign: University of Illinois Press, 1986. $29.95.

BURAWOY, MICHAEL. *The Politics of Production.* Pp. 240. New York: Schocken Books, 1985. $25.00 Paperbound, $7.95.

Thinned by automation and the flight of smokestack industry, factory work still employs millions, while new service tasks are often low-grade manual or do-it-by-numbers white-collar work. Most jobs still remain industrialized in the way they are designed and supervised. As William Form stresses in his new study, the American working class has not gone away, and this recomposition maintains labor's strength in numbers. But will labor ever refuse to foot most of the bill for reorganizing capitalism? Given manufacturing decline and bosses' skill at divide and rule, probably not. In any case, recomposition perpetuates long-standing gaps between blocks of workers that check labor's ability to coalesce as a political force.

The book amply documents the cleavages in American labor. In going on to compare American and French worker groups, however, Form is less convincing. His final verdict that the American working class could become more homogeneous also goes against much of his own evidence. Nevertheless, this is a solid, research-backed study.

Once a factory worker himself, Burawoy explores a paradox—tough factory work can make workers collude with managers as well as fight them. Erudite in the literature on workplace skills, and with ethnographic flair, he describes factory regimes thown up by an interplay of workplace struggles and government policies—the core of his politics of production. Capitalist factories, he predicts, will increasingly favor "hegemonic despotism." While not an "arbitrary tyranny," this regime obliges work forces that formerly gained enviable—and therefore divisive—concessions to hand them back without protest, or even willingly, under the shadow of job losses.

Burawoy overlooks how closely managers' readiness or competence to act as despots is tied to industries or countries. His polemical passages, though avowedly Marxist, mostly exploit Marxist terminology to lambast old Marxist verities. He confesses, in a strange metaphor, "I have left the tracks of history . . . in disarray, and the engine of history [class struggle] spluttering." Nor does his stress on the inventiveness of workers' action make for an unfashionable book—he says it does, but must know better. Certainly it is a very energetic one.

MICHAEL ROSE

Bath University
England

MAKIN, JOHN H. *The Global Debt Crisis: America's Growing Involvement.* Pp. xiv, 281. New York: Basic Books, 1984. $18.95.

This book tells the story of international debt crisis: its genesis, contributing factors, implications, as well as personalities who actively participated in its unfolding. Partly, it is the story of international bankers and their global search for profit run amok, and partly it is the story of the vulnerability of the present international economic framework that led to a world crisis with serious implications for the global financial system.

The story of global debt crisis is told on two levels. The first is the huge expansion of direct lending by banks in industrial countries to governments of developing countries. The second, and more fundamental than the first, is the fear that the industrial countries' economic machine is running out of steam; that the technological and enterpreneurial superiority of the West has already reached its peak and is on a downward course.

The book is divided into four parts. The first part, consisting of the first two chapters, is a brief description of the current crisis in a historical perspective. In chapters 3 and 4, which comprise the second part, Makin surveys industrial countries' fears of worsening shortages of the world's natural resources and developing countries' fears of losing the benefits of their natural endowments. Makin offers such perceptions of interdependence as the basis for the attraction between the international lender and the borrower. Although such fears may be a factor in the development of long-term economic policies in Northern lenders and Southern borrowers, the significant growth of Third World debt in recent years is due more to recent accumulation of dollars of the Organization of Petroleum Exporting Countries in Western banks and the more or less concurrent economic decline in the West than to policies emanating from perceptions of international interdependence. In fact, contrary to the grim predictions of the Club of Rome, the supply of world resources has actually improved in the last decade and this should only brighten the bankers' perceptions of the future of industrial countries.

Part three of the book—chapters 5-7—describes the origin of the debt crisis. Makin finds it in foreign and domestic policies of the United States. American hegemony in the postwar international financial system was characterized by ambivalence and self-doubt, and the United States did not have a clear and well-defined international economic policy in the 1960s. In addition to large military expenditures during the Vietnam war, the U.S. economy underwent significant expansionary socioeconomic policies during the 1960s and 1970s that also contributed to the crisis. According to Makin, "the decision of two U.S. politicians [President Nixon and his treasury secretary, John Connally] in 1971 to finance a long war and buy time for this and other foreign initiatives by going along with a multiplication of social programs without regard to international economic responsibilities did much to enable" Arabs and others to quadruple the price of oil. In general, throughout the 1960s and 1970s the seeds of the debt problem were nurtured by U.S. policymakers through expansionary demand policies without adequate concern for their impact either on inflation or on the international financial system. While the fourth part—chapters 8 and 9—of the book discusses the role of the International Monetary Fund and the Bank for International Settlements, the fifth part—chapters 10-12—describes the unfolding of the crisis and some of its major ramifications.

Makin places the major blame for the debt crisis—rightly, it seems—on the doorsteps of international bankers who, flush with overflowing petrodollars, were willing to make large foreign loans only with casual and perfunctory analysis. However, Makin's account of the crisis is somewhat anecdotal, repetitive, and painted with a broader brush than is customary in economic analysis. Although such a format makes the book less rigorous for serious students of economics, for those unfamiliar with the institutional and personal sides of the debt crisis it offers useful insights.

P. I. MATHEW
U.S. Coast Guard Academy
New London
Connecticut

REICH, LEONARD S. *The Making of American Industrial Research: Science and Business at GE and Bell, 1876-1926*. Pp. xvi, 309. New York: Cambridge University Press, 1985. $24.95.

WISE, GEORGE. *Willis R. Whitney, General Electric, and the Origins of U.S. Industrial Research*. Pp. 375. New York: Columbia University Press, 1985. $29.00.

These two fine books tell much of the story of early industrial research in the United States. The biography of Whitney, the first director of the General Electric (GE) industrial research laboratory, is written with great intelligence and skill by Wise, a historian at the GE Research Center. It approaches industrial research with an emphasis on personalities, while the study by Reich, a historian at Rutgers who also is an editor of the Edison papers, looks at the subject from the viewpoint of two major companies that pioneered it. Both books depend on unpublished corporate archival sources and on a wide range of secondary publications. For both companies the original spur to engage in their own scientific research was defensive, to protect their market leadership from competitive threats. With both, also, the lab had to produce an early success to ensure support from top management, a harder task at GE than at Bell. Wise and Reich emphasize that the attitudes of the heads of the firms were crucial to the founding and early support of these labs, so personalities did count, and for a lot. They also find that the early directors of these labs set a research style that tried to mediate between the corporations' demands for profitable results and the disinterested curiosity of the scientists. Usually the tension between pure research and development that would pay off did not cause large problems, and I suspect such tension was ultimately more fruitful than its absence would have been.

From the Wise book one gets a fascinating picture of the lives of scientists in a research lab in this period; from Reich one learns more about corporate strategy and how the labs fit into it. The biography of Whitney provides a fuller account of GE research on light bulb filaments; Reich has more on early radio and the corporate maneuvering around it. Neither book is defensive about the institutions and people it describes. Wise and Reich are not hesitant to point out errors and misjudgments. The reader not well versed in this subject may prefer to begin with the Wise volume; those with a little more historical and scientific background might choose the Reich. But neither volume depends on a large dose of scientific training. Both the authors and their publishers can be proud of their work, for these books should remain the standard accounts in their fields for many years.

JAMES M. LAUX
University of Cincinnati
Ohio

ROSENBERG, NATHAN and L. E. BIRDZELL, Jr. *How the West Grew Rich: The Economic Transformation of the Industrial World*. Pp. xii, 368. New York: Basic Books, 1986. $19.95.

Western wealth is mainly the result of innovation, both technological and organizational, and the absence of political interference in the economy. According to Rosenberg, an economist, and Birdzell, a lawyer, all other theories about the reasons for the sustained growth of Western nations—which in this study include Japan, Australia, and New Zealand, as well as Western Europe and North America—fail signally to explain the West's success. After brief rebuttals of mostly unattributed theories in an inadequately footnoted introduction, Rosenberg and Birdzell, using secondary sources, develop their historical argument by surveying the decline of feudalism, the growth of trade and commercial institutions, the development of industry, and the modern growth of technology and scientific research.

How the West Grew Rich is written in a very positive and optimistic manner. Rosenberg and Birdzell emphasize the ability Western nations have shown to effect and accept change, while downplaying the negative results of change. Social dislocation and economic disaster seem to matter little since, in the end, everyone in the West is better off.

In the end, however, this book is less a history than a disguised economic policy statement. Resenberg and Birdzell are not searching for clues to Western success that might eventually help solve the problems of the Third World. In fact, the main thrust of their book seems to be a plea for the continuation of Western practices so that the West might become richer. They state that they see "nothing in the underlying sources of Western economic growth to foreclose the prospect of continuing growth." Though it is nowhere specifically said, it seems reasonable to assume that they discount any studies that have suggested that the Earth and its resources may not stand up to limitless growth.

This is a book for those who applaud the present government's policy of retreat from the economic and social spheres. In a peculiar argument, Rosenberg and Birdzell caution their readers about the present-day concern with social justice. They state that "there is a danger that in thus trying to better our own society, we may pursue policies that will reduce the capacity of future generations to achieve still higher standards of material well-being, within a social and political framework more humane and compassionate than our own." Apparently the West is not yet rich enough to concentrate on social justice or humanity. That can wait until later.

MARY BETH EMMERICHS
University of Pennsylvania
Philadelphia

TETREAULT, MARY ANN. *Revolution in the World Petroleum Market*. Pp. xviii, 271. Westport, CT: Quorum Books, 1985. $45.00.

This excellently written book provides a superb history of the world oil industry in recent decades, with particular attention to the "oil revolution," that is, "the shift in control of oil prices and supplies from oil companies to oil-exporting countries." The shift in control was dramatized by the sharp rise in crude oil prices in 1973-74 and again in 1979-80, but the shift had been in process earlier.

The world oil industry is, and has been, complex, as is well known, but this well-researched and well-documented book makes the complexity understandable. The book covers events into 1985 and provides the necessary background for understanding the recent drop in crude oil prices. Tetreault is not burdened with preconceptions, but she is quite willing to make judgments, on the basis of the evidence available and her general knowledge of international relations, concerning the economic, political, and social effects of the dramatic changes that have taken place in this industry.

Specialists on the economic or political aspects of the world oil industry, as well as more general readers, are certain to find this book well worth reading.

JOSEPH D. COPPOCK
Pennsylvania State University
University Park

OTHER BOOKS

ALFORD, JONATHAN, ed. *The Soviet Union: Security Policies and Constraints.* Pp. xii, 180. New York: St. Martin's Press, 1985. $27.50.

Arms Control and the Arms Race: Readings from Scientific American. Pp. viii, 229. New York: W.H. Freeman, 1985. Paperbound, $14.95.

ARONOFF, MYRON J., ed. *The Frailty of Authority.* Pp. 213. New Brunswick, NJ: Transaction Books, 1986. $29.95. Paperbound, $12.95.

ARTSIBASOV, IVAN. *In Disregard of the Law.* Translated by Vadim Kuleshov. Pp. 268. Moscow: Progress, 1982. Distributed by Imported Publications, Chicago. Paperbound, $2.95.

AUSMUS, HARRY J. *Will Herberg: A Bio-bibliography.* Pp. viii, 112. Westport, CT: Greenwood Press, 1986. $35.00.

BAKER, SUSAN STOUT. *Radical Beginnings: Richard Hofstadter and the 1930's.* Pp. xxi, 268. Westport, CT: Greenwood Press, 1985. $35.00.

BAKHASH, SHAUL. *The Reign of the Ayatollahs: Iran and the Islamic Revolution.* Pp. x, 276. New York: Basic Books, 1984. $18.95.

BAKKEN, GORDEN MORRIS. *The Development of Law in Frontier California: Civil Law and Society, 1850-1890.* Pp. 162. Westport, CT: Greenwood Press, 1985. $29.95.

BOYD, STEVEN R., ed. *The Whiskey Rebellion: Past and Present Perspectives.* Pp. xii, 209. Westport, CT: Greenwood Press, 1985. $35.00.

BRAHAM, RANDOLPH L. and BELA VAGO, eds. *The Holocaust in Hungary: Forty Years Later.* Pp. xv, 235. Boulder, CO: East European Monographs, 1986. Distributed by Columbia University Press, New York. $25.00.

BUZUEV, A. B. *Transnational Corporations and Militarism.* Translated by Alexander Khisimindnov. Pp. 256. Moscow: Progress, 1985. Distributed by Imported Publications, Chicago. $7.95.

BYERS, R. B., ed. *Deterrence in the 1980's: Crisis and Dilemma.* Pp. 235. New York: St. Martin's Press, 1985. $29.95.

CAMPBELL, MAGDA, WAYNE H. GREEN, and STEPHEN I. DEUTSCH. *Child and Adolescent Psychopharmecology.* Vol. 2. Pp. 168. Beverly Hills, CA: Sage, 1985. Paperbound, no price.

COATES, DAVID, GORDEN JOHNSTON, and RAY BUSH, eds. *A Socialist Anatomy of Britain.* Pp. 291. New York: Basil Blackwell, 1985. $29.95. Paperbound, $14.95.

COOPER, RICHARD N. *Economic Policy in an Interdependent World: Essays in World Economics.* Pp. xii, 340. Cambridge, MA: MIT Press, 1986. $27.50.

CREWE, IVOR and DAVID DENVER, eds. *Electoral Change in Western Democracies: Patterns and Sources of Electoral Volatility.* Pp. 438. New York: St. Martin's Press, 1985. $29.95.

DIDSBURY, HOWARD F., Jr., ed. *Communications and the Future: Prospects, Promises, and Problems.* Pp. vii, 357. Bethesda, MD: World Future Society, 1982. Distributed by Westview Press, Boulder, CO. Paperbound, $14.50.

DRAUS, FRANCISZEK, ed. *History, Truth, Liberty: Selected Writings of Raymond Aron.* Pp. 384. Chicago: University of Chicago Press, 1986. $27.50.

DULL, JONATHAN R. *A Diplomatic History of the American Revolution.* Pp. xii, 229. New Haven, CT: Yale University Press, 1985. $15.95.

FERRAROTTI, FRANCO. *The Myth of Inevitable Progress.* Pp. viii, 208. Westport, CT: Greenwood Press, 1985. $35.00.

FINK, ARTHUR E., JANE H. PFOUTS, and ANDREW W. DOBELSTEIN. *The Field of Social Work.* 8th ed. Pp. 400. Beverly Hills, CA: Sage, 1985. No price.

FISHKIN, JAMES S. *Beyond Subjective Morality: Ethical Reasoning and Political Philosophy.* Pp. vii, 201. New Haven,

CT: Yale University Press, 1986. Paperbound, $9.95.

FLYNN, GREGORY et al. *Public Images of Western Security.* Pp. 92. Paris: Atlantic Institute for International Affairs, 1985. Paperbound, $7.00.

GATWOOD, LYNN E. *Devi and the Spouse Godess: Women, Sexuality and Marriage in India.* Pp. xiii, 206. Riverdale, MD: Riverdale, 1985. No price.

GAUHAR, ALTAF, ed. *The Rich and the Poor: Development, Negotiations and Cooperation—An Assessment.* Pp. xix, 273. Boulder, CO: Westview Press, 1985. Paperbound, $12.00.

GAUHAR, ALTAF, ed. *Third World Affairs, 1985.* Pp. xxiii, 436. Boulder, CO: Westview Press, 1985. Paperbound, $28.00.

GERSHUNY, JONATHAN. *Social Innovation and the Division of Labor.* Pp. viii, 191. New York: Oxford University Press, 1983. $32.50. Paperbound, $9.95.

GORMAN, ROBERT A., ed. *Biographical Dictionary of Marxism.* Pp. x, 388. Westport, CT: Greenwood Press, 1986. $55.00.

GREENBERG, EDWARD S. *Capitalism and the American Political Ideal.* Pp. 250. Armonk, NY: M. E. Sharpe, 1985. $30.00. Paperbound, $12.95.

GROMYKO, ANDREI. *The Overseas Expansion of Capital.* Translated by H. Campbell Creighton. Pp. 423. Moscow: Progress, 1985. Distributed by Imported Publications, Chicago. $10.95.

GUTKIND, PETER C.W. and IMMANUEL WALLERSTEIN, eds. *Political Economy of Contemporary Africa.* Vol 1. 2nd ed. Pp. 344. Beverly Hills, CA: Sage, 1985. Paperbound, no price.

HARDEN, SHEILA, ed. *Small Is Dangerous: Micro States in a Macro World.* Pp. ix, 212. New York: St. Martin's Press, 1985. $25.00.

HARDIN, RUSSELL et al., eds. *Nuclear Deterrence: Ethics and Strategy.* Pp. vii, 395. Chicago: University of Chicago Press, 1985. $25.00. Paperbound, $10.95.

HARE, A. PAUL. *Social Interaction as Drama: Applications from Conflict Reso-*

lution. Pp. 183. Beverly Hills, CA: Sage, 1985. Paperbound, $14.00.

HAVEMAN, ROBERT H., VICTOR HALBERSTADT, and RICHARD V. BURKHAUSER. *Public Policy toward Disabled Workers: Cross-National Analyses of Economic Impacts.* Pp. xi, 583. Ithaca, NY: Cornell University Press, 1985. $34.95.

International Migration. Vol. 23, no. 3. Pp. 127. Geneva: Intergovernmental Committee for Migration, 1985. Paperbound, no price.

KENNY, ANTHONY. *The Logic of Deterrence.* Pp. x, 104. Chicago: University of Chicago Press, 1985. $20.00. Paperbound, $6.95.

KOZLOV, IGOR. *Socialism and Energy Resources.* Translated by Glenys Ann Kozlov. Pp. 198. Moscow: Progress, 1985. Distributed by Imported Publications, Chicago. Paperbound, $2.95.

KOZYREV, ANDREI. *The Arms Trade: A New Level of Danger.* Translated by Aini Lehto. Pp. 197. Moscow: Progress, 1985. Distributed by Imported Publications, Chicago. Paperbound, $3.95.

KREPON, MICHAEL. *Strategic Stalemate: Nuclear Weapons and Arms Control in American Politics.* Pp. xvi, 191. New York: St. Martin's Press, 1986. Paperbound, $10.95.

KRUSCHKE, EARL R. *The Right to Keep and Bear Arms: A Continuing American Dilemma.* Pp. xii, 195. Springfield, IL: Charles C Thomas, 1985. $24.50.

KYVIG, DAVID E., ed. *Law, Alcohol, and Order: Perspectives on National Prohibition.* Pp. xiii, 215. Westport, CT: Greenwood Press, 1985. $35.00.

LAMB, H. H. *Climatic History and the Future.* Pp. xxxii, 835. Princeton, NJ: Princeton University Press, 1984. Paperbound, $28.50.

LEE, ALFRED McCLUNG. *Sociology for Whom.* 2nd ed. Pp. xiii, 270. Syracuse, NY: Syracuse University Press, 1986. Paperbound, $12.95.

LEKTORSKY, V. A. *Subject, Object, Cognition.* Translated by S. Syrovatkin.

Pp. 280. Moscow: Progress, 1985. Distributed by Imported Publications, Chicago. $7.95.

LIPSET, SEYMOUR MARTIN. *Consensus and Conflict: Essays in Political Sociology*. Pp. viii, 375. New Brunswick, NJ: Transaction Books, 1985. $24.95. Paperbound, $12.95.

LOW, ALFRED D. *The Anschluss, 1931-1938, and the Great Powers*. Pp. xv, 507. Boulder, CO: East European Monographs, 1985. Distributed by Columbia University Press, New York. $40.00.

LUKER, KRISTIN. *Abortion and the Politics of Motherhood*. Pp. xvi, 324. Berkeley: University of California Press, 1984. $14.95.

MARX, KARL and FREDERICK ENGELS. *The Individual and Society*. Pp. 286. Moscow: Progress, 1985. Distributed by Imported Publications, Chicago. $5.95.

McCAULEY, MARTIN and STEPHEN CARTER, eds. *Leadership and Succession in the Soviet Union, Eastern Europe and China*. Pp. xiii, 256. Armonk, NY: M. E. Sharpe, 1986. $35.00. Paperbound, $14.95.

McCURDY, HOWARD E. *Public Administration: A Bibliographic Guide to the Literature*. Pp. ix, 311. New York: Marcel Dekker, 1986. $29.75.

McGAHAN, PETER. *Urban Sociology in Canada*. 2nd ed. Pp. viii, 334. Toronto: Butterworths, 1986. Paperbound, no price.

MILLER, JAMES. *Rousseau: Dreamer of Democracy*. Pp. xii, 272. New Haven, CT: Yale University Press, 1986. Paperbound, $9.95.

MINSON, JEFFREY. *Genealogies of Morals: Nietzche, Foucault, Donzelot and the Eccentricity of Ethics*. Pp. x, 246. New York: St. Martin's Press, 1985. $25.00.

MOWOE, ISAAC JAMES and RICHARD BJORNSON, eds. *Africa and the West: The Legacies of Empire*. Pp. x, 274. Westport, CT: Greenwood Press, 1986. $35.00.

MUKHINA, VALERIYZ. *Growing up Human*. Translated by Peter Greenwood. Pp. 286. Moscow: Progress, 1985. Distributed by Imported Publications, Chicago. Paperbound, $4.95.

MUTTI, JOHN. *U.S. Adjustment Policies in Trade-Impacted Industries*. Pp. ix, 46. Washington, DC: National Planning Association, 1985. Paperbound, $7.00.

MYERS, DAVID G. *Psychology*. Pp. xviii, 696. New York: Worth, 1986. $29.95.

NIBLOCK, TIM and RICHARD LAWLESS, eds. *Prospects for the World Oil Industry*. Pp. 131. Dover, NH: Croom Helm, 1985. No price.

NICHOLS, HERBERT L., Jr. *Science Blundering: An Outsider's View*. Pp. ix, 118. Greenwich, CT: North Castle Books, 1984. $15.00.

NIKITIN, S. M., ed. *Inflation under Capitalism Today*. Translated by Jane Sayer. Pp. 260. Moscow: Progress, 1985. Distributed by Imported Publications, Chicago. $7.95.

O'BRIEN, ROBERT M. *Crime and Victimization Data*. Pp. 127. Beverly Hills, CA: Sage, 1985. $15.00. Paperbound, $7.95.

PAVLOWITCH, STEVAN K., ed. *Unconventional Perceptions of Yugoslavia, 1940-1945*. Pp. xii, 166. Boulder, CO: East European Monographs, 1985. Distributed by Columbia University Press, New York. $25.00.

PELIKAN, JAROSLAV. *Jesus through the Centuries: His Place in the History of Culture*. Pp. xvi, 270. New Haven, CT: Yale University Press, 1985. $22.50.

PETROVSKY, A. V. *Studies in Psychology: The Collective and the Individual*. Translated by Frances Longman. Pp. 254. Moscow: Progress, 1985. Distributed by Imported Publications, Chicago. $7.95.

PHOMVIHANE, KAYSONE et al. *The Third Congress of the Lao Peoples' Revolutionary Party*. Translated by Dmitry Belyavsky and Stephen Coppen. Pp. 177. Moscow: Progress, 1985. Distributed by Imported Publications, Chicago. Paperbound, $2.95.

PONOMAREV, BORIS et al. *The International Working Class Movement.* Vol 4. Translated by Vladimir Yeryamin. Pp. 750. Moscow: Progress, 1984. Distributed by Imported Publications, Chicago. $11.50.

RABINOVICH, ITAMAR. *The War for Lebanon, 1970-1985.* Pp. 262. Ithaca, NY: Cornell University Press, 1985. Paperbound, $9.95.

RADY, MARTYN C. *Medieval Buda: A Study of Municipal Government and Jurisdiction in the Kingdom of Hungary.* Pp. vii, 255. Boulder, CO: East European Monographs, 1985. Distributed by Columbia University Press, New York. $32.00.

REYNOLDS, EDWARD. *Stand the Storm: A History of the Atlantic Slave Trade.* Pp. vii, 192. New York: Allison and Busby, 1985. Distributed by Schocken Books, New York. $14.95. Paperbound, $6.95.

REZNIKOV, ALEXANDER. *The Comintern and the East: Strategy and Tactics.* Translated by James Riordan. Pp. 294. Moscow: Progress, 1985. Distributed by Imported Publications, Chicago. $7.95.

RINGER, BENJAMIN B. *'We the People' and Others: Duality and America's Treatment of Its Racial Minorities.* Pp. xii, 1165. New York: Tavistock, 1983. Paperbound, $25.00.

RISTE, OLAV, ed. *Western Security: The Formative Years.* Pp. 333. New York: Columbia University Press, 1985. $39.00.

ROBINSON, DONALD L., ed. *Reforming American Government: The Bicentennial Papers of the Committee on the Constitutional System.* Pp. xvi, 334. Boulder, CO: Westview Press, 1985. $35.00. Paperbound, $13.85.

RUESCHEMEYER, MARILYN, IGOR GOLOMSHTOK, and JANET KENNEDY. *Soviet Emigre Artists: Life and Work in the USSR and the United States.* Pp. xii, 170. Armonk, NY: M. E. Sharpe, 1985. $25.00.

RUMBLE, GREVILLE. *The Politics of Nuclear Defense: A Comprehensive Intro-*duction. Pp. xi, 285. New York: Basil Blackwell, 1986. $34.95. Paperbound, $14.95.

RUSTIN, MICHAEL. *For a Pluralist Socialism.* Pp. 277. London: Verso, 1985. Distributed by Schocken Books, New York. $28.00. Paperbound, $7.95.

SEDGWICK, JEFFREY LEIGH. *Law Enforcement Planning: The Limits of an Economic Analysis.* Pp. xix, 198. Westport, CT: Greenwood Press, 1984. $29.95.

SEIDER, MAYNARD. *A Year in the Life of a Factory.* Pp. 152. San Pedro, CA: Singlejack Books, 1984. Paperbound, $7.75.

SEVOSTYANOV, PAVEL. *Before the Nazi Invasion.* Translated by David Skvirsky. Pp. 304. Moscow: Progress, 1984. Distributed by Imported Publications, Chicago. $7.95.

SHAFRITZ, JAY M., C. ALBERT HYDE and DAVID H. ROSENBLOOM. *Personal Management in Government: Politics and Process.* 3rd ed. Pp. xvi, 476. New York: Marcel Dekker, 1986. $29.75.

SHINKARUK, V. I., ed. *Man and Man's World: Categories of "Man" and "World" in the System of Scientific World Outlooks.* Translated by Y. V. Sklyar and N. B. Vyatkina. Pp. 287. Moscow: Progress, 1985. Distributed by Imported Publications, Chicago. $10.95.

SIPOLS, VILNIS. *The Road to Great Victory.* Translated by Lev Bobrov. Pp. 324. Moscow: Progress, 1985. Distributed by Imported Publications, Chicago. $8.95.

SKAFTE, DIANNE. *Child Custody Evaluations: A Practical Guide.* Pp. 215. Beverly Hills, CA: Sage, 1985. $25.00. Paperbound, $12.50.

STERN, SELMA. *The Court Jew: A Contribution to the History of Absolutism in Europe.* Pp. xxiii, 312. New Brunswick, NJ: Transaction Books, 1985. $29.95.

STOVER, ERIC and NIGHTINGALE, ELENA O., eds. *The Breaking of Bodies and Minds: Torture, Psychiatric Abuse, and the Health Professions.* Pp. xvi, 319. New York: W.H. Freeman, 1985. $21.95. Paperbound, $11.95.

SWANSON, JAMES M. *Scientific Discoveries and Soviet Law.* Pp. viii, 150. Gainesville: University of Florida Press, 1985. Paperbound, $11.00.

THOMAS, JOHN R. *Natural Resources in Soviet Foreign Policy.* Pp. xi, 55. New York: National Strategy Information Center, 1985. Paperbound, $3.95.

TRUKHANOVSKY, V. G. *Anthony Eden.* Translated by Ruth English. Pp. 350. Moscow: Progress, 1984. Distributed by Imported Publications, Chicago. $8.95.

TURNER, MARGERY AUSTIN and RAYMOND J. STRUYK. *Urban Housing in the 1980's: Markets and Policies.* Pp. xvii, 113. Washington, DC: Urban Institute Press, 1985. $14.95.

VALENTA, JIRI and HERBERT J. ELLISON, eds. *Grenada and Soviet/Cuban Policy: Internal Crisis and U.S./OECS Intervention.* Pp. xxii, 512. Boulder, CO: Westview Press, 1986. $38.50. Paperbound, $20.00.

VANDER ZANDEN, JAMES W. *Sociology: The Core.* Pp. x, 398, xl. New York: Knopf, 1986. Paperbound, no price.

VITIUK, VIKTOR. *Leftist Terrorism.* Translated by Andrei Zur and Galina Glagoleva. Pp. 236. Moscow: Progress, 1985. Distributed by Imported Publications, Chicago. Paperbound, $3.95.

VITTENBERG, E. *The Working Class and the Trade Unions in the USSR: The Period of Developed Socialism.* Translated by Yuri Davydov. Pp. 316. Moscow: Progress, 1985. Distributed by Imported

Publications, Chicago. Paperbound, $3.95.

WIARDA, HOWARD J., ed. *New Directions in Comparative Politics.* Pp. xiv, 239. Boulder, CO: Westview Press, 1985. $35.00. Paperbound, $16.95.

YETMAN, NORMAN R., ed. *Majority and Minority: The Dynamics of Race and Ethnicity in American Life.* 4th ed. Pp. xi, 584. Boston, MA: Allyn & Bacon, 1985. Paperbound, no price.

YURKOVETS, IVAN. *The Philosophy of Dialectical Materialism.* Translated by L. Lezhneva and A. Zur. Pp. 268. Moscow: Progress, 1985. Distributed by Imported Publications, Chicago. $7.95.

ZAMOSHKIN, YURI and E. Y. BALATOV. *Political Consciousness in the USA: Traditions and Evolution.* Pp. 334. Moscow: Progress, 1985. Distributed by Imported Publications, Chicago. $8.95.

ZHUKOV, GEORGI K. *Reminiscences and Reflections.* Vol 1. Translated by Vic Schneirson et al. Pp. 940. Moscow: Progress, 1985. Distributed by Imported Publications, Chicago. 18.95.

ZHUKOV, G. *Reminiscences and Reflections.* Vol. 2. Translated by N. Burova et al. Pp. 486. Moscow: Progress, 1985. Distributed by Imported Publications, Chicago. No price.

ZIVS, SAMUIL. *The Anatomy of Lies.* Translated by Nadezhda Bugrova. Pp. 159. Moscow: Progress, 1985. Distributed by Imported Publications, Chicago. Paperbound, $2.95.

INDEX

Publisher's Note: The following information is printed in accordance with U.S. postal regulations: Statement of Ownership, Management and Circulation (required by 39 U.S.C. 3685). 1A. Title of Publication: THE ANNALS OF THE AMERICAN ACADEMY OF POLITICAL AND SOCIAL SCIENCE. 1B. Publication No.: 026060. 2. Date of Filing: September 30, 1986. 3. Frequency of Issue: Bi-monthly. 3A. No. of Issues Published Annually: 6. 3B. Annual Subscription Price: paper-inst., $52.00, cloth-inst., $68.00; paper-ind., $26.00, cloth-ind., $40.00. 4. Location of Known Office of Publication: 3937 Chestnut Street, Philadelphia, PA 19104. 5. Location of the Headquarters or General Business Offices of the Publishers: 3937 Chestnut Street, Philadelphia, PA 19104. 6. Names and Complete Addresses of Publisher, Editor, and Managing Editor: Publisher: The American Academy of Political and Social Science, 3937 Chestnut Street, Philadelphia, PA 19104; Editor: Richard D. Lambert, 3937 Chestnut Street, Philadelphia, PA 19104. Managing Editor: None. 7. Owner (if owned by a corporation, its name and address must be stated and also immediately thereunder the names and addresses of stockholders owning or holding 1% or more of total amount of stock. If not owned by a corporation, the names and addresses of the individual owners must be given. If owned by a partnership or other unincorporated firm, its name and address, as well as that of each individual must be given.): The American Academy of Political and Social Science, 3937 Chestnut Street, Philadelphia, PA 19104. 8. Known Bondholders, Mortgagees, and Other Security Holders Owning or Holding 1% or More of Total Amount of Bonds, Mortgages or Other Securities: None. 9. For Completion by Nonprofit Organizations Authorized to Mail at Special Rates (Section 423.12, DMM only): Has not changed during preceding 12 months.

	Av. No. Copies Each Issue During Preceding 12 Months	Actual No. of Copies of Single Issue Published Nearest to Filing Date
10. Extent and Nature of Circulation		
A. Total no. copies printed (net press run)	9362	9158
B. Paid circulation:		
1. Sales through dealers and carriers, street vendors and counter sales	589	138
2. Mail subscription	5603	5730
C. Total paid circulation (sum of 10B1 and 10B2)	6192	5868
D. Free distribution by mail, carrier or other means: samples, complimentary, and other free copies...........................	107	112
E. Total distribution (sum of C and D)	6299	5980
F. Copies not distributed:		
1. Office use, left over, unaccounted, spoiled after printing	3063	3178
2. Return from news agents	0	0
G. Total (sum of E, F1 and 2—should equal net press run shown in A)	9362	9158

11. I certify that the statements made by me above are correct and complete. (Signed) Mary E. Harris, Business Manager.

NEW! from Sage

FIELD METHODS IN CROSS-CULTURAL RESEARCH

edited by WALTER J. LONNER,
Western Washington University,
& JOHN W. BERRY, *Queen's University, Canada*

This book is designed to meet the needs of the field-worker faced with a research question and the teacher who is talking about research problems and issues in the classroom. The intent, therefore, is to provide field-workers—both those actually in the field and those preparing to go into the field—with a handy, comprehensive, practical, and up-to-date book containing helpful guidelines, background material, and even some specific "how to's." It is directed to behavioral scientists who are sophisticated in many research areas. To determine the topics to be covered, the editors carried out a survey of over 100 experienced researchers in cross-cultural psychology; the chapters in the book parallel the results of the survey.

The book provides the relatively sophisticated and thoughtful field-worker a reasonably comprehensive statement of epistomological and methodological issues, a review of what has succeeded for many and failed for others, and in general an overview of common concerns and questions that will be asked and that need to be answered during various phases of any cross-cultural research project. The chapters are arranged so that broader, more methodological issues are considered first, including theoretical issues involved in cross-cultural comparison. Following are more concrete methods, including chapters on sampling, carrying out fieldwork, problems of translation, and problems of using observations in the field.

CONTENTS: Introduction / 1. Making Inferences from Cross-Cultural Data Y.H. POORTINGA & R.S. MALPASS / 2. Strategies for Design and Analysis R.S. MALPASS & Y.H. POORTINGA / 3. Sampling and Surveying W.J. LONNER & J.W. BERRY / 4. Fieldwork in Cross-Cultural Psychology R.L. MUNROE & R.H. MUNROE / 5. The Wording and Translation of Research Instruments R.W. BRISLIN / 6. Observational Methods S. BOCHNER / 7. Cross-Cultural Assessment: From Practice to Theory S.H. IRVINE / 8. Assessment of Personality and Psychopathology G.M. GUTHRIE & W.J. LONNER / 9. Assessment of Social Behavior M. SEGALL / 10. Assessment of Acculturation J.W. BERRY, J.E. TRIMBLE, & E.L. OLMEDO / Index

Cross-Cultural Research and Methodology, Volume 8
1986 / 356 pages / $19.95 (flex.)

SAGE PUBLICATIONS, INC.
275 South Beverly Drive,
Beverly Hills, California 90212

SAGE PUBLICATIONS, INC.
2111 West Hillcrest Drive,
Newbury Park, California 91320

SAGE PUBLICATIONS LTD
28 Banner Street,
London EC1Y 8QE, England

SAGE PUBLICATIONS INDIA PVT LTD
M-32 Market, Greater Kailash I,
New Delhi 110 048 India

THE FOUNDER'S CONSTITUTION

5 Volume Set

Edited by **Philip B. Kurland** *and* **Ralph Lerner**

This monumental set is unique among publications appearing coincidental to the bicentennial of the Constitution of the United States. Editors Kurland and Lerner have gathered in one place, for the first time, important documents from the seventeenth, eighteenth, and nineteenth centuries that were critical to the evolution of the Constitution, in its principles and its particulars, from the Preamble through the Twelfth Amendment. The documents span in time the earliest beginnings of self-government in the English colonies, down through the Marshall Court.

"The rare combination of Professor Kurland's mastery of constitutional law and Professor Lerner's command of constitutional politics makes this a unique work. I cannot think of any comparable collection that gathers such a rich variety of materials."—Marvin Meyers, Professor Emeritus of History, Brandeis University

Cloth, 5 volumes   3,520 pages $250.00 until 6/30/87, $300.00 thereafter
January